T0384721

SHAKESPEARE'S WHITE OTHERS

Examining the racially white "others" whom Shakespeare creates in characters like Richard III, Hamlet, and Tamora – figures who are never quite "white enough" – this bold and compelling work emphasizes how such classification perpetuates anti-Blackness and reaffirms white supremacy. David Sterling Brown offers nothing less here than a wholesale deconstruction of whiteness in Shakespeare's plays, arguing that the "white other" was a racialized category already in formation during the Elizabethan era – and also one to which Shakespeare was himself a crucial contributor. In exploring Shakespeare's determinative role – and strategic investment in identity politics (while drawing powerfully on his own life experiences, including adolescence), Brown argues that even as Shakespearean theatrical texts functioned as engines of white identity formation, they expose the illusion of white racial solidarity. This essential contribution to Shakespeare studies, critical whiteness studies, and critical race studies is an authoritative, urgent dismantling of dramatized racial profiling.

David Sterling Brown is Associate Professor of English at Trinity College, Hartford, Connecticut, and a member of the Curatorial Team for The Racial Imaginary Institute, founded by Claudia Rankine. He is the recipient of numerous awards, including a Mellon/ACLS Scholars and Society fellowship and the Shakespeare Association of America's Publics Award. Additionally, he is an Executive Board member of the Race Before Race conference series and he serves as dramaturg for the Untitled Othello Project, an ensemble that is reconceptualizing how theater practitioners engage with Shakespeare's work. His research, teaching, and public speaking interests include African American literature, drama, mental health, gender, performance, sexuality, and the family. www.DavidSterlingBrown.com

"Brown's much needed study powerfully and persuasively demonstrates how the policing of whiteness within Shakespeare's plays recruits and reproduces anti-Blackness at the heart of early modern English culture."
– Patricia Ahkimie, Director, Folger Institute, Folger Shakespeare Library

"*Shakespeare's White Others* is stunning in its readings of plays from *Macbeth* to *The Comedy of Errors* with respect to the 'intraracial color line' and in the connections it makes to the deadly serious issue of racism. After Brown's book, no analysis of *any* of Shakespeare's plays will be able to efface race as a category of analysis."
– Bernadette Andrea, Professor of Literary and Cultural Studies, University of California, Santa Barbara, and 2022–23 President of the Shakespeare Association of America

"David Sterling Brown's precise scholarship is infused with unapologizing emotion – emotion, *and* scholarship, both rooted as they are in his Black humanity. Brown's articulate and adamant voice is the sound of indomitability shouting through the subterfuge."
– Keith Hamilton Cobb, actor and playwright, *American Moor*

"A remarkable work of scholarship by David Sterling Brown, *Shakespeare's White Others* is an in-depth examination of intraracial dynamics in Shakespeare's work that brilliantly articulates – and offers meaningful correctives to – historical practices. Dr. Brown audaciously illuminates the theatrical possibilities that emerge from a nuanced exploration of Shakespeare's infinite variety."
– Simon Godwin, Artistic Director, Shakespeare Theatre Company, Washington, DC

"With *Shakespeare's White Others*, David Sterling Brown engages racial whiteness and provokes interdisciplinary dialogue through his rhetorically accessible 'critical–personal–experiential' style. The book's unexpected final words, documenting Brown's own racial profiling experience, anticipate the depths of this brilliantly bold Shakespearean discourse that seamlessly blends genres while reimagining the scholarly monograph mode."
– Claudia Rankine

"Maintaining that tensions between white characters are themselves racial conflicts, this paradigm-changing book establishes that *all* of Shakespeare's plays are about race. Rather than understand early modern race in binary terms, *Shakespeare's White Others* attends to the intraracial color line to reveal that whiteness is not an inalienable property, but rather an unstable commodity that is policed and confiscated through the deployment of anti-Black racism and white supremacy."
– Melissa E. Sanchez, Donald T. Regan Professor of English and Comparative Literature, University of Pennsylvania

SHAKESPEARE'S WHITE OTHERS

David Sterling Brown

TRINITY COLLEGE, HARTFORD, CONNECTICUT

CAMBRIDGE
UNIVERSITY PRESS

Shaftesbury Road, Cambridge CB2 8EA, United Kingdom

One Liberty Plaza, 20th Floor, New York, NY 10006, USA

477 Williamstown Road, Port Melbourne, VIC 3207, Australia

314–321, 3rd Floor, Plot 3, Splendor Forum, Jasola District Centre, New Delhi – 110025, India

103 Penang Road, #05–06/07, Visioncrest Commercial, Singapore 238467

Cambridge University Press is part of Cambridge University Press & Assessment, a department of the University of Cambridge.

We share the University's mission to contribute to society through the pursuit of education, learning and research at the highest international levels of excellence.

www.cambridge.org
Information on this title: www.cambridge.org/9781009384162

DOI: 10.1017/9781009384155

First published 2023

Printed in the United Kingdom by CPI Group Ltd, Croydon CR0 4YY

A catalogue record for this publication is available from the British Library.

Library of Congress Cataloging-in-Publication Data
NAMES: Brown, David Sterling, author.
TITLE: Shakespeare's white others / David Sterling Brown.
DESCRIPTION: Cambridge, United Kingdom ; New York : Cambridge University Press, 2023. | Includes bibliographical references.
IDENTIFIERS: LCCN 2023005197 (print) | LCCN 2023005198 (ebook) | ISBN 9781009384162 (hardback) | ISBN 9781009384124 (paperback) | ISBN 9781009384155 (epub)
SUBJECTS: LCSH: Shakespeare, William, 1564-1616–Criticism and interpretation. | White people in literature. | Race in literature. | English drama–Early modern and Elizabethan, 1500-1600–History and criticism.
CLASSIFICATION: LCC PR2992.W45 B76 2023 (print) | LCC PR2992.W45 (ebook) | DDC 822.3/ 3–dc23/eng/20230328
LC record available at https://lccn.loc.gov/2023005197
LC ebook record available at https://lccn.loc.gov/2023005198

ISBN 978–1–009–38416–2 Hardback

*For my vulnerable teenage self and for all the Black selves like him —
may you survive, heal, and thrive.*

*For my parents Audreta and Kevin, and for my sister April — and for all
the dead and the living who wrap me in love, support, prayer, and
protection daily.*

*In loving memory of the ancestors: Great-great grandma Viola Tate,
great grandma Essie Jefferies Hollis, great grandma Thelma
"Big Moma" Leach, great grandma Hattie M. Leslie, Grandma
Christine Wright, Aunt Patricia Lynn Wright, Grandaddy Forse Lee
"Joe" Hollis, Uncle Forest Lamar "Slim" Hollis, and all whom I never
got to know . . . I feel y'all around me.*

Contents

Figures

Preface
"U Better Recognize": Othering Whiteness

Within Shakespeare studies and literary studies – and outside of those realms, as in other academic disciplines and within the real world – the white other matters.[1] This figure is a covert tool for maintaining what bell hooks describes in *Black Looks: Race and Representation* as "the dominator imperialist white supremacist capitalist patriarchal culture."[2] Specifically, the white other contrasts with idealized hegemonic whiteness; reinforces popular and evolving stereotypes about racial Blackness;[3] and helps reify the imagined superiority of the whiteness defining what early modern scholar Peter Erickson calls "white self-fashioning."[4] More significantly, the white other indicates how attitudes toward whiteness are mediated through Blackness and black images.[5] Whenever necessary, in order to reinforce the goodness and supremacy of hegemonic whiteness, images of blackness appear as distant or estranged[6] from whiteness through the white other construct. In this book, I argue that such mediation creates racialized boundaries between white people along lines of superiority/inferiority, ingroup/outgroup – familiar social and psychological dichotomies of inclusion and exclusion that generate racialized harm.[7] In so doing, the white other serves as proof that the commodification of Blackness, often exploited as a dehumanized resource, can occur "in a range of everyday locations" and in the subtlest ways.[8]

In *The Origin of Others*, Toni Morrison observes that "one learns Othering not by lecture or instruction but by example."[9] It is that easy. One learns by example. Morrison adds that "racial identification and exclusion did not begin, or end, with black [people]";[10] this reality helps make sense of how and why whiteness is itself a nuanced racial category. As philosopher Michel Foucault suggests in *The History of Sexuality*, the value of racial whiteness was determined, and still is determined, through exclusionary processes of Othering that facilitated the differentiation of people along lines of blood and skin color.[11] By design, this kind of white

xi

estrangement occurs at Black people's expense, historically through violence of some kind.[12] In a way, then, one could say that when "[Blackness or blackness] collapses into privileged whiteness" it presumably reduces the latter and thus produces the image or idea of the white other.[13] If it is true that "control over images is central to the maintenance of any system of racial domination," then one cannot deny that what audiences receive from Shakespearean drama participates in a racist dynamic that privileges whiteness and devalues Blackness.[14]

Although racially white, the white other can at times, or always, seem foreign and strange in comparison to whatever is deemed "normal."[15] In Shakespeare's tragedy *Hamlet*, for instance, the hero's emblematic blackness, signified by his "inky cloak" and accompanying unmanliness, is disturbing, a stark contrast to his deceased father's celebrated valiant whiteness, which I discuss in Chapter 2 (1.2.77). Shakespeare creates distance between those white people who conform to social expectations and norms and those who do not. In other words, there are white people who register as more legitimate than others, a matter Patricia Akhimie addresses in her article "'Fair' Bianca and 'Brown' Kate: Shakespeare and the Mixed-Race Family in José Esquea's *The Taming of the Shrew*."[16] Those people who conform or act as exemplars of hegemonic whiteness are tolerated, and even revered, whereas those who do not conform are shunned, killed, critiqued, expelled, or marginalized. Although quite different than a fictional Black figure like Aaron from *Titus Andronicus*, the white other, who occupies a liminal space between Black and white, helps sustain the racial hierarchy because their whiteness does not conform to the ideal.[17] Furthermore, the white other's role alleviates the need for a significant inclusion of Black characters in Shakespeare's canon since these racially white figures are strategically designed to embody blackness.

Undeniably, whiteness is a dominating force, *the* dominating force, in the racial hierarchy. By aiding the white superiority narrative, the white other enables racial whiteness to become more noticeable, particularly the positive symbolism of whiteness. I say that because Shakespeare offers correctives to the troubled moments where the dominant culture's standards of whiteness are not upheld: for example, the difference between *Titus'* fair-skinned, virtuous Roman Lavinia and fair-skinned, lascivious Goth Tamora, whom we might consider socially dead because of her barbaric, blackened identity; because of Tamora's sexual association with Aaron, a Black Moor; her "defeated enemy" status; and her "alien culture."[18]

Within Shakespearean drama, one can witness white privilege operating among groups of exclusively white people.[19] Produced through a "white

supremacist orientation,"[20] such harder-to-detect operations of white privilege make the white other a powerful mechanism of white racial, and
racist, construction.[21] Occupying a space between whiteness and
Blackness, the white other's presence generates and solidifies anti-Black
sentiments. This figure is a literary, and perhaps real, force that transports
ideas about white racial superiority, and the metaphorical superiority of
whiteness, within a given play's framework. With respect to anti-
Blackness, othering whiteness also exposes what is wrong with promoting
notions of colorblindness.[22] Moreover, othering whiteness complements
discourse suggesting that colorblindness is harmful in social, cultural,
political, pedagogical, and theatrical practice, as Lisa M. Anderson, Ania
Loomba, Ayanna Thompson and other critics stress in *Colorblind
Shakespeare: New Perspectives on Race and Performance.*[23] Shakespeare
repeatedly embeds figurative blackness in his white characters, or places
blackness on their bodies somehow. Other characters then see this blackness and respond to it accordingly, negatively. They do not deny the
presence of blackness because acknowledging it benefits whiteness. The
acknowledgment of the white other's blackness, I posit, induces symptoms
of ontological insecurity because these othered white characters destabilize
white norms and generate racialized anxiety in the dominant culture.[24]
These moments of insecurity call attention to the privileging of whiteness
as a dangerous trope. Moments of white privilege, or what Claudia
Rankine has suggested we call "white dominance," do not always register
as such, since people are not conditioned to consider this phenomenon
from an *intra*racial standpoint.[25] *Shakespeare's White Others* asks you, dear
reader, to do the hard antiracist work.

Regarding racial construction, the white other is generative from a
critical standpoint because this figure's presence challenges the argument
that race, as we understand it, is only a modern phenomenon denoting
Otherness or non-whiteness.[26] Rather, as Ian Smith explains, "Race, as a
worldly thing, not only denotes a complex of institutional, cultural, and
intersubjective processes, but also the collective exchanges and deliberations – the dialogues and conversations pursuant to racial literacy whether
through reading, scholarship, conference deliberations, classroom learning,
or theatrical performance – that envision fully invested participation,
mobilization, and change."[27] By revealing tiers in whiteness, and sometimes through white tears, the white other exposes the intricate workings
of white solidarity and complicates white supremacist ideologies. This
figure reminds us that even in premodernity not all whiteness was acceptable whiteness, as the plays examined in this book illustrate. Additionally,

tiering whiteness erases the need for focusing exclusively or predominantly on Black characters to understand race or racism or even the powerful impact of white centrality.[28] The white other's presence shows that Shakespeare's plays have a vested interest in negatively critiquing a certain kind of whiteness while simultaneously uplifting hegemonic whiteness. The plays police whiteness. And since attitudes toward that racial category are mediated through blackness in the dramatic literature, it goes without saying that these early modern texts add to the historical policing of Blackness. Such policing occurs outside of the texts, and it occurs *because* of these texts, in Black people's lived realities.

The interconnected race relationships among Shakespeare's plays are united through whiteness. There is not one Shakespeare play that excludes white people. The white other emerges as a figure of symbolic racial difference. The white other is not born, only created or imagined and imaged, thus emphasizing the malleability and mutability of racial boundaries and constructions.[29] Moreover, this figure is a social organizing tool that stabilizes established attitudes toward blackness, normalizing color-based racism and, of course, anti-Blackness.[30] Beyond contributing to developing racist discourse, what has perhaps made this figure a challenge for people to identify is its ability to be an absent presence. Although the white other exists in plain sight, scholars have not yet thoroughly reflected on this figure's role. Therefore, there is room to consider how plays that, on the surface, do not appear committed to perpetuating racism and white supremacy silently do similarly racist work as harmful as that which *Othello* does on and in front of its audience.[31] This harm, in the form of anti-Blackness that intersects with issues such as toxic masculinity, misogyny, sexism, and classism, to name a few, necessitates that antiracist readers, teachers, performers, and activists call out the white other's hazardous presence. This harm necessitates that those who support the cause, those who support antiracism, choose to see and read the white other in its image on the page and on the world's stage. This harm necessitates examination because of its dangerous "ideological intent."[32] Without conscientious interrogation, this kind of harm could one day mean, and be, the death of me.[33] Simply put, the white other is a threat to *our* survival.

Notes

1 In rapper Sam Sneed's 1994 single "U Better Recognize," produced by hip-hop icon Dr. Dre, the phrase "think you better recognize" is repeated throughout. And at one point Sneed raps, "Open your eyes, I think you

better recognize." I allude to his lyrics as a way to introduce this book's call to action for its audience: See, feel, hear . . . use whatever senses you have access to in order to recognize the enduring impact that the Shakespearean white other has had locally and globally as a maintenance tool for (anti-Black) racism and white supremacy. For background and information on Sneed's song, see https://en.wikipedia.org/wiki/U_Better_Recognize. The notion of othering whiteness is also addressed in the *Shakespeare Studies* Forum I co-edited with Patricia Akhimie and Arthur L. Little, Jr. See our co-authored Introduction: "Seeking the (In)Visible: Whiteness and Shakespeare Studies," *Shakespeare Studies* Vol. 50 (September 2022), 17–23. "Whiteness is more than skin color," as Ian Smith claims. He adds, "It is an ideology that saturates and an epistemology that creates its own fictions and ways of seeing the world and texts." I expand on this definitional discourse in my Introduction. See Ian Smith, *Black Shakespeare: Reading and Misreading Race* (Cambridge: Cambridge University Press, 2022), 15. Also see Arthur L. Little, Jr., "Is It Possible to Read Shakespeare through Critical White Studies?," in *The Cambridge Companion to Shakespeare and Race*, ed. Ayanna Thompson (Cambridge: Cambridge University Press, 2021), 268–280; 269.

2 bell hooks, *Black Looks: Race and Representation* (New York: Routledge, 2015), ix.

3 My usage of capitalized "Black"/"Blackness" (racial, ethnic, cultural sense) and lowercase "black"/"blackness" (referring to color, specifically) follows AP style. See "Explaining AP Style on Black and white" (July 20, 2020), https://apnews .com/article/9105661462. When referring to white(ness), I will use adjectives to help readers determine when I am referring to race/skin color or using the term figuratively to denote color symbolism.

4 Peter Erickson, "'God for Harry, England, and Saint George': British National Identity and the Emergence of White Self-Fashioning," in *Early Modern Visual Culture: Representation, Race, Empire in Renaissance England*, eds. Peter Erickson and Clark Hulse (Philadelphia: University of Pennsylvania Press, 2000), 322. For an explanation of "self-fashioning" and its "governing conditions" see Stephen Greenblatt, *Renaissance Self-Fashioning: From More to Shakespeare* (Chicago: University of Chicago Press, 1980), 8–9.

5 hooks, *Black Looks*, 1.

6 Paul Gilroy asserts, "Black and White are bonded together by the mechanisms of 'race' that estrange them from each other and amputate their common humanity." See *Against Race: Imagining Political Culture beyond the Color Line* (Cambridge, MA: The Belknap Press of Harvard University Press, 2002), 15.

7 See David Sterling Brown, "'Don't Hurt Yourself': (Anti)Racism and White Self-Harm," *Los Angeles Review of Books* (Anti-racism miniseries) (July 6, 2021), https://lareviewofbooks.org/article/antiracism-in-the-contemporary-uni versity/#_ftn2.

8 hooks, *Black Looks*, 21–23. See Urvashi Chakravarty, *Fictions of Consent: Slavery, Servitude, and Free Service in Early Modern England* (Philadelphia: University of Pennsylvania Press, 2022), 6. As Octave Mannoni argues,

"Exceptional cases of inferiority occurring in a homogenous community have nothing to do with skin colour, but are due to individual feelings of inferiority of various kinds. As with Europeans, any difference can cause a feeling of inferiority, once certain psychological and sociological conditions are fulfilled." *Prospero and Caliban: The Psychology of Colonization* (Ann Arbor: University of Michigan Press, 1990), 39. Frantz Fanon also considers the psychological impact of racism and colonization, asserting, for example, that "all colonized people – in other words, people in whom an inferiority complex has taken root, whose local cultural identity has been committed to the grave – position themselves in relation to the civilizing language. The more the colonized has assimilated the cultural values of the metropolis, the more he will have escaped the bush. The more he rejects his blackness, the whiter he will become." See *White Skin, Black Masks* (New York: Grove Press, 2008), 2–3.

9 Toni Morrison, *The Origin of Others* (Cambridge, MA: Harvard University Press, 2017), 6.

10 Ibid., 21–22; 24.

11 Michel Foucault, *The History of Sexuality, Vol. 1: An Introduction* (New York: Vintage Books, 1978), 147–149.

12 See Angela Y. Davis, *Freedom Is a Constant Struggle: Ferguson, Palestine, and the Foundations of a Movement* (Chicago: Haymarket Books, 2016), 81–82.

13 Bernadette Andrea, "Black Skin, The Queen's Masques: Africanist Ambivalence and Feminine Author(ity) in the Masques of Blackness and Beauty," *English Literary Renaissance* 29.3 (1999), 246–281; 248. Access to the privileges of whiteness can be gained and/or taken away. See Dorothy Roberts, "Race," in *The 1619 Project: A New Origin Story*, eds. Nikole Hannah-Jones, Caitlin Roper, Ilena Silverman, and Jake Silverstein (New York: OneWorld, 2021), 45–61; 48.

14 hooks, *Black Looks*, 2.

15 Morrison, *The Origin*, 29.

16 Patricia Akhimie, "'Fair' Bianca and 'Brown' Kate: Shakespeare and the Mixed-Race Family in José Esquea's The Taming of the Shrew," *Journal of American Studies* 54.1 (2020), 89–96, esp. 93–94.

17 Little, Jr., "Is It Possible to Read Shakespeare through Critical White Studies?," 271.

18 Orlando Patterson, *Slavery and Social Death: A Comparative Study* (Cambridge, MA: Harvard University Press, 2018), 37–38.

19 Alice Mikal Craven, *Visible and Invisible Whiteness: American White Supremacy through the Cinematic Lens* (New York: Palgrave Macmillan, 2018), 2.

20 Claudia Rankine, *Just Us: An American Conversation* (Minneapolis, MN: Graywolf Press, 2020), 327.

21 We see something similar in communities of color with colorism. I suggest that something akin to colorism is going on among the white communities in these plays.

22 See Philip A. Mazzocco, *The Psychology of Racial Colorblindness: A Critical Review* (New York: Palgrave Macmillan, 2017), 23–25.

23 See Ayanna Thompson, ed. *Colorblind Shakespeare: New Perspectives on Race and Performance* (New York: Routledge, 2006), xiv, 1–2, 89–92. Mazzocco argues "that racial colorblindness is on the whole a socially harmful ideology – a claim consistent with a 1997 report of racial colorblindness issued by the American Psychological Association." See also Mazzocco, *The Psychology of Racial Colorblindness*, vii. Neil Gotanda questions the "disturbing implications" of colorblindness in "A Critique of 'Our Constitution Is Color-Blind',," in *Critical Race Theory: The Key Writings that Formed the Movement*, eds. Kimberlé Crenshaw, Neil Gotanda, Gary Peller, and Kendall Thomas (New York: The New Press, 1995), 257–275; 268.

24 See The Racial Imaginary Institute, *On Whiteness* (SPBH Editions, July 2022), 13.

25 See Claudia Rankine, "I Wanted to Know What White Men Thought About Their Privilege. So I Asked," *The New York Times Magazine*, (July 17, 2019), www.nytimes.com/2019/07/17/magazine/white-men-privilege.html. From a sociological perspective, Matthew W. Hughey, to whom I defer for a useful definition of whiteness in the Introduction, has explored intraracial dynamics and the symbolic boundaries that can emerge between white people. See *White Bound: Nationalists, Antiracists* (Stanford: Stanford University Press, 2012), 68–69, 74–75.

26 Smith, *Black Shakespeare*, 3–4.

27 Ibid., 188.

28 Since Valerie Traub observed in 2016 that, "despite [the efforts of early modern scholars], the uptake of criticism on race in the broader field of early modern studies has been slow," significant progress has been made in early modern race studies as scholars tackle whiteness more robustly and regularly in the race conversation. See *The Oxford Handbook of Shakespeare and Embodiment: Gender, Sexuality, and Race* (Oxford: Oxford University Press, 2016), 20. Founded by Ayanna Thompson, and consisting of an Executive Board with leading premodern race studies scholars from different colleges and universities, the Race Before Race conference series and professional network has contributed to the advancement of pre-1800 race studies. For more information, see https://acmrs.asu.edu/RaceB4Race.

29 Patricia Akhimie, *Shakespeare and the Cultivation of Difference: Race and Conduct in the Early Modern World* (New York: Routledge, 2018), 13; Martha R. Mahoney, "The Social Construction of Whiteness," in *Critical White Studies: Looking behind the Mirror*, eds. Richard Delgado and Jean Stefancic (Philadelphia, PA: Temple University Press, 1997), 330–333; 330.

30 Also outside of this project's scope is an exclusive focus on people of color. However, I do want to note that if added into the intraracial color-line paradigm, people of color would further expand that racial hierarchy and further distance Black people from white people.

31 In a 2019 NPR podcast, "All That Glisters Is Not Gold," Ayanna Thompson names *Othello* as one of "three toxic plays that resist being progressive texts" (*The Merchant of Venice* and *The Taming of the Shrew* are the other two): www .npr.org/2019/08/21/752850055/all-that-glisters-is-not-gold.

32 hooks, *Black Looks*, 5.

33 See Kimberly Anne Coles, *Bad Humor: Race and Religious Essentialism in Early Modern England* (Philadelphia: University of Pennsylvania Press, 2022), ix.

Acknowledgments

These acknowledgments start where *Shakespeare's White Others* ends, in South Norwalk, Connecticut. Thus, I begin by offering gratitude to the community that helped shape me. Immense thanks are due to my grandmothers Lenora Hollis and the late Christine Wright, my parents Kevin and Audreta, and my sister April, who poured strength, faith, and love into me so I could finish this book. I appreciate how you lifted me up and held me up when I needed it most.

From my South Norwalk community, I am indebted to Richard Roselle and the late Dr. Ruby Shaw, hardworking and genuine community activists who created free educational youth programs that taught me to be disciplined and inquisitive, to strive to realize my full potential, to know that, despite the odds, a little Black boy from South Norwalk could. Without them and their selflessness early on in my life – and without my parents and my family (myriad cousins, aunts, and uncles) cheering me on in the face of many challenges – this book would not exist. Thanks to Dr. Ruby Shaw, I also extend much gratitude to Jerome Shaw for keeping the support going in his mother's stead.

From adolescence, I remember the many elementary and secondary schoolteachers who had a significant, positive impact on me. Many of them knew back then that I was destined to be a writer, as noted on a couple of the report cards my father still has. I remember my schoolteachers well, from Kindergarten to fifth grade at Silvermine Elementary School: the late Dr. Lucile Layton (the first Black teacher I ever had), Ms. Besso, Mrs. Glick, Ms. Canal, Ms. Drabek, Mrs. Costabile, Ms. Smith, and Ms. Crosby. Like many of the educators I encountered at St. Luke's School – Barbara Whitcomb, Richard Whitcomb, the late James R. Decatur, Stephen Flachsbart, Mark Bisson, Brinley Ehlers, Robin Zwicker, Bob Leinbach, and others – the faculty from Silvermine taught me to love learning and to nourish my gifts and talents. A very special thanks is due to Shannon Early Johnston for always pushing me and for always believing in me, and to my former piano teacher, Betty Jane Belcher, who once said I was destined to write a "great American novel." Well, hopefully I have at least succeeded in writing a book that is novel.

While I did not know how to name it at the time, Shannon Early Johnston offered me true mentorship during my teenage years. She offered the kind of guidance I would become accustomed to receiving and seeking from various faculty at Trinity College during my undergraduate days and beyond. Trinity support, though of a different kind, continues for me now as a faculty member. First and foremost, I must thank Milla Cozart Riggio. Our deep connection goes all the way back to my first Shakespeare course with her in Fall 2004. That Milla is still such a significant part of my life to this day is an enormous blessing – thank you, Milla. My bond with Sheila Fisher, which started during my time as a Trinity senior in 2005, is yet another blessing I am grateful for. Thank you, Sheila (and Sonia Brand-Fisher and Peter Kritikos). I also must thank a combination of former Trinity professors of mine and current colleagues who believed in me as a student and/or now as a scholar: Robert J. Corber, Jennifer B. Steadman, Davarian Baldwin, John Platoff, Robert R. Peltier, Sylvia DeMore, Ellison Banks Findly, the late Margo Perkins, Dan Lloyd, Cheryl Greenberg, the late Mary Beverly Wall, Lucy Ferriss, Paul Lauter, Margaret D. Lindsey, Carol Correa de Best, Anthony Berry, President Joanne Berger-Sweeney, Patricia Ann Maisch, Karla Spurlock-Evans, Cindy L. Butos, Chloe Wheatley, Diana R. Paulin, David Rosen, Christopher Hager, Katherine L. Bergren, Ciaran M. Berry, Dina Anselmi, Barbara M. Benedict, Sarah Bilston, Francisco Goldman, Tennyson L. O'Donnell, Daniel J. Mrozowski, Clare M. Rossini, Hilary E. Wyss, James Prakash Younger, Ann E. Reuman, Jennifer M. Regan-Lefebvre, Sonia Cardenas, Laura J. Holt, Mitch A. Polin, Laura Lockwood, Joe Barber, Donna-Dale Marcano, Takunari Miyazaki, and, of course, James F. Jones. Without Trinity's former Admissions representative Kalia Kellogg, who recruited me (and my 940 combined SAT score) from St. Luke's School, I might not have become a Trinity College student, alumnus, Ann Plato Fellow, or faculty member. I only half-believed I could get into Trinity and succeed in 2001 but Kalia fully believed. Thank you, Kalia (and your parents, Earl and Jan), for changing the course of my life. Without our connection, I might have never met Sharre Brooks, Colin Levy, Charae Warner, and Olubunmi Amakor, to whom I also owe gratitude. Trinity has allowed me over the years to cross paths with many people, a lot of whom are special to me, including staff members who work in the Cave, Bistro, and Mather Dining Hall. Here, I have to shoutout Al, who has always remembered me and cheered me on since I was an undergraduate! Thank you, Al, and all, especially for being the first people to wish me good luck and hug me on the morning of my Trinity campus visit interview day in Fall 2021 – a fond memory that always brings a smile to my face.

On my journey as a scholar, so many colleagues have offered time, mentorship, and wisdom. Since I graduated from NYU, John Michael Archer, my former dissertation advisor, has been a constant thought partner, especially during our get-togethers at La Lanterna, where joy meets enlightenment for me. Thank you, John, for everything. And the thanks do not stop there, as my career and my Shakespeare scholarship have benefited from engagement with so many people who have also motivated me or helped me directly and indirectly in various ways. Thank you Rosario Muralles, Arthur L. Little, Jr., Jean E. Howard, Peggy O'Brien, Shanta Bryant, Joyce MacDonald, Kim F. Hall, Patricia Akhimie, Ayanna Thompson, Kyle Grady, Farah Karim-Cooper, Niamh Wallace, Jessica Henning, Amanda Nikolov, Anthony Gomez, Patricia Parker, Douglas Clark, Peter Erickson, Jennifer Lynn Stoever, Patricia Cahill, Justin Shaw, Sandra Young, Lee Medovoi, Ruben Espinosa, Matthew Abraham, Christine Tardy, Farid Matuk, Aditya Adireja, John J. Melillo, Susan Miller-Cochran, Christina D. Ramírez, Gillian Woods, Lisa Barksdale-Shaw, Liam Semler, Paul Hurh, Ben Crystal, Erin Sullivan, Gemma Allred, Benjamin Broadribb, Ayesha Ramachandran, Natasha Korda, Kyle Louise DiRoberto, Meg Lota Brown, Eleanor Collins (and the Oxford University Press readers), Tukufu Zuberi, William Germano, Sarah Enloe, Sarah R. Gerk, Kathryn Vomero Santos, Geoff Way, Nedda Mehdizadeh, Thomas P. Miller, Kerstin B. Miller, Reverend Bart Smith, Amy Wratchford, Paul Menzer, Jonathan Burton, Fenton Johnson, Kyle Vitale, Bryan Carter, Jennifer Nichols, Frederick P. Keifer, Anthony Sanchez, Scott Selisker, Johanna Skibsrud, Shelley Staples, Anchuli Felicia King, Keith Hamilton Cobb, Jessica Burr, Heather Benton, Robert Manning, Josh Tyson, Welland Scripps, Aaron Zook, Hettie Barnhill, Tina Harper, Terrell Donnell Sledge, Stephanie Hodge, Michael Patrick Sullivan, Francesca Albrezzi, Carl Cofield, Erika T. Lin, Karen Raber, Urvashi Chakravarty, Carol Mejia-LaPerle, Katherine Gillen, Bryan Terzian, Owen Williams, Richard Paul, Ben Lauer, Noelle Cammon, Jim Marino, Maryam Trowell, Leislie Godo-Solo, Vanessa Powell, Detra Hollis, Kathy Mann, Patricia Hollis, Barbara Brown, Doris Reid, Kathleen Lynch, Jeffrey Jerome Cohen, Simón Ventura Trujillo, Bernadette Andrea, Dennis Austin Britton, Birgit Brander Rasmussen, Thomas Glave, Joseph A. Keith, Marilynn Desmond,

Praseeda Gopinath, John O. Havard, Olivia Holmes, Monika Mehta, Alexandra Moore, Manuel Muñoz, Damian Elias, Debarati Roy, Gail Kern Paster, Barbara Bogaev, Eric Rasmussen, Allen Loomis, Jane Todorski, Reverend Bob Story, Lauryn Moore, Garland Scott, Michael Witmore, Annette Joseph-Gabriel, Adela Licona, Melissa E. Sanchez, Jamie A. Lee, Stuart Crabb, Julie Iromuanya, Jeffrey Wilson, Manya Lempert, the late Bat-Ami Bar On, Jonathan Hope, Reginald Wilburn, Maritza E. Cardenas, Christine Hamel Brown, David McKenzie, Greg Prickmann, Susan Briante, Simone Chess, Mario DiGangi, Skyler Cooper, Emma Smith, Jennifer Earl, the late David Bevington, Sonia Massai, Martha Roca, Alfred L. Roca, Lucy Munro, Mary Janell Metzger, Fei Hillman, Naomi Liebler, Kimberly Anne Coles, Cassander Smith, Miles P. Grier, Aubrey Whitlock, Anne G. Morgan, Nicholas R. Jones, Faith S. Harden, and Kaitlin Murphy. Here, I must also thank the anonymous Cambridge University Press readers and the CUP Syndicate for supporting *Shakespeare's White Others* and for believing that I had something novel to offer Shakespeare Studies, critical race studies, critical whiteness studies, and beyond. And of course, I extend much thanks to my editor, Emily Hockley; her assistant, George Paul Laver; my amazing copy-editor, Maartje Scheltens; and every person who played a role in the production of this book at CUP.

As I worked on *Shakespeare's White Others*, several other people and institutions supported my scholarship in various ways. Many, many thanks are due to: The Racial Imaginary Institute (Claudia Rankine, John Lucas, Emily Skillings, Simon Wu, and the entire TRII Curatorial Team); Duke University's Summer Institute on Tenure and Professional Advancement (Melissa Shields Jenkins and Kerry Haynie); Sacred Heart University (Emily Bryan, Peter Sinclair, Charles A. Gillespie, and colleagues); Untitled Othello Project Ensemble; National Endowment for the Humanities; Race Before Race Executive Board; Arizona Center for Medieval and Renaissance Studies staff; Binghamton University (TAE, IASH, Harpur College, and President's Office); University of Arizona; Shakespeare Association of America (SAA); SAA seminar organizers and my fellow seminarians throughout the years; Mellon Foundation; American Council of Learned Societies (John Paul Christy, Desiree Barron-Callaci, Jaelen Floyd, and colleagues); Shakespeare Unlimited and the whole production team; Cooper and Cooper/Cooper Cares (Meron Langsner); Hudson Strode Program in Renaissance Studies, University of Alabama (Michelle M. Dowd); Boston Symphony Orchestra (David C. Howse); Washington Latin Public Charter School Upper School English (Nathaniel Day); Bates College Arts and Activism

MLK, Jr., Day Symposium (Clayton Spencer, Brenda Pelletier, and staff); Bates College New Scholars Symposium (Therí Pickens and colleagues); Modern Language Association; Yale University Schwarzman Center; American Shakespeare Center (Ralph Alan Cohen and the Board of Trustees); Columbia University Shakespeare Seminar (Caralyn Bialo and Lauren Robertson); University at Buffalo (Danielle Rosvally); Liverpool John Moores University (Rachel Willie); Montclair State University (Adam Rzepka); Howard University (Elisa Oh); The East15 Acting School, London (Tom Clegg); "A Call to Act Research Seminar," University of Essex (Eirini Kartsaki); Aoyama Gakuin University and Speaking of Shakespeare (Thomas Dabbs and Thomas Shomaker); University of Neuchâtel, Switzerland (Patrizia Zanela, Sarah Jane Brazil, Emma Lesley Depledge); Missouri Historical Society in collaboration with St. Louis Shakespeare Festival (Tom Ridgely); University of Winnipeg, Canada (Brandon Christopher); Shakespeare Theatre Company, Shakespeare Hour LIVE! (Simon Godwin, Drew Lichtenberg, and Grace Ann Roberts); Birkbeck, University of London (Stephen Clucas and Paul Cutts); University of Maryland (Tita Chico and Amanda Bailey); The Show Must Go Online (Rob Myles); Shakespeare Institute (Wendy Lennon and Michael Dobson); Folger Institute Critical Race Conversations series and all involved; Folger Education and staff; Folger Shakespeare Library and staff; Mount Saint Mary College (Rob Wakeman); University of Oregon (Leah Middlebrook); Lincoln University (Greg Holtmeyer); Lafayette College Keefe Colloquium in the Humanities (Ian Smith, Diane Shaw, and Alison Byerly); Renaissance Society of America; Arizona Senior Academy; Arizona Theatre Company; The Rogue Theatre of Tucson, AZ (Cynthia Meier and staff); Shakespeare Society of Southern Africa (Sandra Young and Chris Thurman); Institute for Recruitment of Teachers; Consortium for Faculty Diversity; Humanities Texas (Eric Lupfer, Kelsi Tyler, and the many teachers, such as Nina I. Otazo); CUNY James Gallery (Katherine Carl); and Brandeis University Mandel Center for the Humanities (Ulka Anjaria).

Additionally, I must thank the graduate and undergraduate students I have encountered over the years at the University of Arizona, NYU, Binghamton University, and Trinity College, as well as the students I have had the privilege to engage at the secondary education level in recent years. The time I have spent with all of them has made me a better thinker, teacher, researcher, and human being. Collectively, they have taught me how to speak to different audiences and to always aim to make my pedagogy and scholarship relevant to their lives and interests. I am eternally grateful for the lessons learned.

As I worked on this book, I had opportunities to write program notes and public-facing essays as well as peer-reviewed articles and book chapters. For including my work in their publication venues, I thank Arden Shakespeare/Bloomsbury (Mark Dudgeon and Margaret Bartley), Radical Teacher, the Globe Theatre (Emma Gosden), The Hare (Amy Kenny), Literature Compass (Dorothy Kim), Palgrave Macmillan, Red Bull Theater (Jesse Berger), Shakespeare Bulletin (Peter Kirwan), Shakespeare Studies (Diana Henderson, James Siemon, and Megan Bowman), The Sundial, Stratford Festival, Public Books (Ben Platt), Los Angeles Review of Books (Anna Shechtman and Cord Brooks), and Reconstruction.US. I also want to thank the contributors to the volumes I co-edited: Shakespeare Bulletin (39.4) and Shakespeare Studies (50).

I cannot end my acknowledgments without offering sincere thanks to all the people who do the kind of work that my father and sister do, bus drivers and schoolteachers, respectively. Without people like them, minds like mine would not have made it to, or through, school. And so, I end here by giving thanks to the thousands of nameless, faceless bus drivers and teachers out there who work hard daily. Without safe rides to school back in the day, and without the engaging school lessons that nourished and nurtured me, *Shakespeare's White Others* would not exist. Thanks, and thanks, and every thanks.

Introduction
Negotiating Whiteness

This is why to stay alive, forget thriving, I need to negotiate whiteness.

– Claudia Rankine, *Help*[1]

Whiteness emerges as a way of seeing and knowing the world that masquerades as universality and remains largely unnamed and unrecognized.

– Veronica T. Watson, *The Souls of White Folk*[2]

If I could resurrect William Shakespeare from the dead and ask him a question that I am dying to pose, it would be this: "How does it feel to be a problem?"[3] If I could be certain that he would not become defensive; that Shakespeare would not irrationally accuse me of "reverse racism," of being racist toward white people, for respectfully naming and recognizing his whiteness; that he would not remain silent but would actually answer my burning question,[4] then I would ask more pointedly, "How does it feel to be a white problem?"[5] In the context of race, "white" changes everything. Here, in fact, "white" refocuses a question W. E. B. Du Bois considered in relationship to Blackness in his early twentieth-century treatise *The Souls of Black Folk*. For me, if it is clear that Blackness, understood more generally as one's race, is a problem, then of course whiteness, too, is a problem. Yet, white people "do not live with constant reminders that [they] are seen as problems due to [their] race."[6] Therefore, white people do not actively or regularly consider the abovementioned inquiries because the idea of being problematic is estranged from their collective racial consciousness. For white people, the problem is always the somatically different Other.[7] That is to say, *I* am the problem. To that I say, "What about *you*?"[8]

I wrote this book to reflect on the "white problem" question, so that we continue integrating critical whiteness studies into early modern studies and Shakespearean discourse as people engage the playwright's work in different ways: critically, pedagogically, and theatrically, for instance.[9]

Long-term, this book is meant to serve as a reminder that racial whiteness – Shakespeare's, the Macbeths', Tamora's, Hamlet's, Antony's, Iago's – is a problem.[10] To achieve these goals, I use Shakespeare's dramatic literature to position him as a theorist of whiteness who illustrated and critiqued *intra*racial, or white-on-white, conflict.[11] In Shakespeare studies and premodern critical race studies, there exists an unarticulated and therefore understudied problem that I refer to as the "intraracial color-line," another key theoretical intervention of *Shakespeare's White Others*.

Building on Du Bois' *inter*racial "color-line" theory,[12] the intraracial color-line delineates distinctions among early modern English white people that rely on the devaluing of somatically similar white folks: the white others, who violate the dominant culture's norms. Through its engagement with, and as a contribution to, early modern literary criticism, *Shakespeare's White Others* reminds readers that persistent anti-Blackness, often revealed through intraracial violations of whiteness, is a constant problem. This problem substantiates the need for antiracist intervention by exposing through the white other the dark side of whiteness. "It is no longer sufficient to be not racist, as we have come to understand, but we must be actively and declaratively antiracist," according to Smith.[13] Scholarship, too, must be active and declarative in its antiracism. Among other things, *Shakespeare's White Others* asks readers to consider how race is crafted through racism, a process Karen E. Fields and Barbara J. Fields term "racecraft" because, similar to witchcraft, it is "imagined, acted upon, and re-imagined."[14] Importantly, they add that "*racecraft* is not a euphemistic substitute for *racism*. It is a kind of fingerprint evidence that *racism* has been on the scene."[15] It is up to us to do the detective work with respect to Shakespearean drama and examine the residue of racism left behind by white others, for it is within whiteness where one can see the unrelenting workings of racecraft.

Shakespeare's White Others builds on the intellectual insights of scholars who have contributed work to premodern critical race studies, whiteness studies, Black studies, Black feminism, sociology, and social psychology in particular. Regarding the white other concept, this study builds on ideas articulated by Morrison in *The Origin of Others*, by Arthur L. Little, Jr. in *Shakespeare Jungle Fever*, and by Lauren S. Cardon in *The "White Other" in American Intermarriage Stories, 1945–2008*[16] in order to expand the understanding of racial "borders of power."[17] Moreover, as citations throughout the book demonstrate, several scholars within early modern English studies have influenced my thinking about race and whiteness.

Specifically, I argue that Shakespeare strategically othered white figures in his dramatic oeuvre to condition dominant English attitudes toward white people, white others, and non-white people, namely Black people.[18] The playtexts position whiteness as a marked racial category that is heterogenous and unstable. The overt investment in intraracial division and related racialized conflict, even among culturally or ethnically similar white people such as the characters in *Hamlet* and *Macbeth*, reflects early modern preoccupations with "'ideal' and 'less-than'" ideal intraracial conduct.[19] Shakespeare's dramatic literature functioned, then, as a textual and theatrical channel that facilitated processes of white identity formation and manufactured the illusion of white racial solidarity.[20] At the same time, those processes worked to encode racialized distinctions created by and validated among white people. These distinctions illuminate intraracial tensions. And they expose the ever-shifting boundaries that denote the white person's or white other's insider/outsider status.[21]

Spiritually, sexually, psychologically, emotionally, morally, and even sartorially, as I will show, Shakespeare's plays mark and marginalize white people in ways that depend on a character's internal rather than epidermal status. The abstract marking signals the failure to meet white hegemony's expectations. In this sense, the white other reflects crises that develop among the plays' white people. Unsurprisingly, these crises, centered on intraracial otherness, often exploit emblematic blackness and/or racialized Blackness to signify racially a person's less-than-ideal status and to reify the perceived superiority of whiteness. My book invests in acknowledging the playwright's unique past and continued influence on white identity formation. This book invests in the processes of inclusion and exclusion among white people that also have an impact on non-white figures like Othello, Cleopatra, and even me. I consider the white other to be a figure like Richard III, Tamora, or Macbeth who is not "white enough" or who registers as less-than-ideal. This figure is useful for highlighting what manifests in the "racial imaginary" as meaningful differences among white people, differences that work to[22] perpetuate anti-blackness and anti-Blackness; expose the façade of white racial cohesion and identity stability; and reaffirm white supremacy, a phrase I deploy in reference to the imagined superiority of whiteness.[23]

As historian Keith Wrightson asserts, "The most fundamental structural characteristic of English society was its high degree of stratification. The reality of inequality was displayed everywhere" with respect to wealth, rank, living standards, and social power.[24] Within England, and even within England's broader relationships with other white Europeans, it was evident that "degrees of people" existed.[25] Between 1590 and 1610, the approximate time period when Shakespeare wrote most of his plays, for example, a range of historical incidents occurred that marked persistent tensions among white English people, and between the English and ethnically different white Europeans:[26] the Anglo-Spanish War (1585–1604); the Irish-English Nine Years' War (1593–1603); Robert Devereux, the second Earl of Essex's attempted rebellion against Queen Elizabeth I (7–8 January 1601);[27] James VI of Scotland's contentious merger of the English and Scottish crowns (24 March 1603); the attempted Gunpowder Plot (5 November 1605); and the Northamptonshire witch trials (22 July 1612). By acknowledging historical moments such as these, one can see how conflicts within whiteness, a racial category that has a "recognizable" two-thousand-year-old history according to historian Nell Irvin Painter, were being negotiated as the English dominant culture defined for its convenience acceptable and unacceptable racial behavior.[28] To the list of characteristics that were used to distinguish white people from one another I would add race, in the intraracial sense. Degrees of whiteness exist.

More than any other early modern dramatist, Shakespeare's white masculine authorial power permeates various facets of modern local and global society such as education, literature, and theater. And more than a symbol with unlimited cultural capital, Shakespeare, I argue, is a chief literary architect of how hegemonic whiteness was (re)produced and negotiated in early modern England. Thus, *Shakespeare's White Others* interrogates how his plays reflect and/or depend on the emerging, and continually developing, construction of whiteness; the embeddedness of racism in literary art, anti-Black racism in particular; and the centering of white-on-white, or intraracial, tensions that too commonly evade critique. *Shakespeare's White Others* reveals – through readings of five core plays, *Titus Andronicus, Hamlet, Antony and Cleopatra, Othello,* and *The Comedy of Errors* – how ideal behavior among white people was, and still can be, significantly influenced by Shakespeare's dramatic literature. The consequences of this reality cannot be overstated. In targeting less-than-ideal white behavior, the dominant culture deploys racist tropes of blackness that have real-life implications for present-day Black people, as I suggest throughout the book and as I stress in Chapter 4 and the Conclusion. Because of the implications for present-day Black people, this book offers a theoretical intervention that challenges the uncritical pedestalization of Shakespeare, his characters, and his plays.[29] This book also challenges the uncritical theatrical production of Shakespearean drama. I introduce my intraracial color-line theory through Shakespeare's work to articulate and hopefully alter the critical, pedagogical, and theatrical possibilities for deploying Shakespearean drama for antiracist purposes. Among other things, *Shakespeare's White Others* urges white people to understand how antiracist action is a responsibility wrapped up in their socio-political power.[30] One of the most influential ways white people wield power is through policing of all kinds, especially the policing of what it means to be white, white other,[31] and Black.

As I close this opening section of the Introduction, I want to turn to *Much Ado About Nothing*, a romantic comedy that is set in Messina and centers racially white figures and their experiences. Hidden within the centering of people who are "fair," a term used over a dozen times in the play, are representations of the Black/African woman; and these cameos expose the malleability of both the white identity and white superiority, in addition to the ever-present tensions within whiteness that often become apparent in relationship to blackness, as Kim F. Hall cogently outlines in *Things of Darkness* – a masterful early modern race study.[32] When Claudio publicly shames Hero, his wife-to-be, and wrongfully accuses her of being an "approved wanton" (4.1.43) who is "most foul, most fair," phrasing that recalls language spoken by Macbeth's Witches (4.1.103), he blackens and then blackballs her for her alleged offense. He initiates her figurative transition from pure, virtuous white woman to lusty, Black strumpet; in so doing, Hero becomes like Cleopatra – discussed in Chapter 5 – whom Antony labels a "foul Egyptian" (4.12.10). Claudio's description indicates he sees Hero's undeniably white skin and the external somatic similarity between them; yet he also claims to see her unverified lascivious deeds, which cause him to reject Hero because he presumes she is tainted inside, both in her moral character and precious chastity. If Claudio's discourse appears to contradict itself, that is because "skin color is significant but only a piece of the early modern racial story," as Little, Jr. argues.[33]

Hero's racialized transition, which marks the introduction of an invisible Black woman, is fully realized when her father Leonato accepts without proof the whore allegations and essentially disowns his daughter, noting:

> Why, she, oh, she is fallen
> Into a pit of ink, that the wide sea
> Hath drops too few to wash her clean again
> And salt too little which she may season give
> To her foul-tainted flesh.
>
> (4.1.139–143)

Resurfacing as the white other from the pit of ink her father figuratively pushes her into with his racist discourse, Hero, now unclean and being studied, is[34] covered in sin and fallen from the privilege of pedestalized whiteness, and physically covered head to toe in blackness (if one were to stage Leonato's language)[35] that now complements and captures the blackness of the character Claudio thinks he sees. To distance themselves from shame and the loss of their masculine holds on the white female body,[36] and to distance themselves from this manufactured image of the sexually unrestrained and monstrous Black woman,[37] these white men conceptualize[38] a Black woman whose allegedly foul body and soul reflect the play's anti-Black sentiments. For example, Leonato's language links Hero's blackened white skin to death and decomposition, matters I explore at length in Chapter 2. As such, he positions blackness, embodied by Hero, as undesirable and in need of salvation. Fully imagined as black, inside and out, racially white Hero disappears from Act 4 once she is thought to be a whore. She returns in the last scene as the possible African "Ethiop" Claudio notes he would marry right before his redeemed wife-to-be enters (5.4.38).[39] He safely makes the Ethiop remark with his masked misogynoir, for the play does not give us any reason to believe a real Black woman can appear out of nowhere, unless she emerges from a pit of ink. With her credibility and the value of her white womanhood restored, Hero is freed from blackness, from being blackballed by Claudio. She is therefore free to enter with him into the institution of marriage, into which the play does not allow the metaphorical Black woman to enter.

Racial matters present themselves as complicated and deep in this play that does not contain somatic Blackness; an actual Black person, or even the representation of a Black person, never appears onstage.[40] Instead, *Much Ado* utilizes somatic similarity to illustrate *diminished* whiteness and the characters' responses to their white identity crisis, responses that notably differ along gender and class lines. Like the other Shakespeare plays critiqued in this book, *Much Ado About Nothing* shows how ideal whiteness is constructed by exclusion. Through Hero's emblematic racial transformation, *Much Ado* suggests white people are willing to accept and disown other white people based on how they adhere to the tenets of ideal(ized) hegemonic whiteness. Furthermore, this comedy implies that not adhering to the tenets of whiteness – due to an association with blackness or due to the performance of behaviors that defy white propriety, for example – puts one at risk for being seen as or somehow becoming less white. In other words, there is what social psychologists would consider a white ingroup and a white outgroup;[41] and it is this latter group that defines what I refer to as the white other. Upon descending into blackness in *Much Ado*, Hero temporarily becomes viewed as something other than her pure racially and morally white self once beloved by white men – her father and Claudio in particular. I contend that she – a white woman – is racially othered despite no somatic difference between her and the other figures in the play. This kind of racial difference is possible because of anti-Black sentiments that produce the intraracial color-line, the unstable boundary between acceptable and unacceptable whiteness.

Hidden in Plain Sight

Shakespeare's White Others aims to reveal how anti-Black racism, anti-Black violence, and general, harmful anti-Black sentiments were and are integral to white identity formation and white ideology construction. This is true even in the absence of somatic Blackness, as my book shows. With Du Bois' *The Souls of Black Folk* in mind, *Shakespeare's White Others* works with and moves beyond the Du Boisian color-line – by relying on the intraracial color-line – because a predominant theoretical emphasis on just the Black/white binary, while incredibly useful, has its limits. For one, the Black/white binary does not always prompt people to apply antiracist theory and interrogate whiteness in ways that hold the mirror up exclusively for white people to see themselves. Consequently, I establish the intraracial color-line as a theoretical tool that allows a principal critique of and focus on whiteness by way of the white other, a racially white figure like Hero who is blackened, and presented as less-than-ideal, for a variety of reasons I introduced in the Preface and will expand on throughout the book.[42] In short, the white other does not allow white people to escape racial examination of themselves, for the intraracial color-line is relevant to all white folk, as the my analysis of *Much Ado* in the previous section indicates.

Regarding the British preoccupation with perpetuating anti-Blackness, which historian Peter Fryer writes about in *Black People in the British Empire: An Introduction* and which the world saw in prevalent twenty-first-century responses to Meghan Markle's Blackness (Duchess of Sussex and wife of Prince Harry),[43] *The Souls of Black Folk* emerges as a powerfully rewritten history. It is one where Du Bois asserts his agency to rebuff the historical rejection of Blackness by situating himself next to Shakespeare as author, as thinker, as artist, as human. Beyond his direct allusion to *Macbeth*,[44] an allusion that incorporates Shakespeare's white authorial and authoritative voice into the text, Du Bois' poetic statement, "I sit with Shakespeare and he winces not," invites his audience to *see* Black and white together. He invites his audience to (re)imagine their co-existing transhistorically and transnationally. He imagines them existing with accord in the face of pervasive anti-Black sentiments expressed in his time, Shakespeare's time, and our own time. Yet, there is something else happening with Du Bois' language relating to his use of iambic pentameter, which I write about in "(Early) Modern Literature: Crossing the Color-Line."[45] The poetic quality intentionally adds rhythm to his bold claim that draws the premodern into his present to further reject ideas about Black inferiority.[46] As the author of *Souls*, Du Bois wields the power to prevent symbolically white-on-Black policing as he crosses the color-line and negotiates whiteness.

Yet, across the *intraracial* color-line, in a gray area where whiteness polices whiteness and negotiates with itself, a race war rages on. The white self – the social, cultural, physical, and psychological white self that is an amalgamation of conveniently shifting ideologies of superiority – is constantly engaged in battle. The mounting casualties are innumerable. The conflict I refer to is not about the centuries-old physical and rhetorical clashes[47] racially white people have had with various "strange" religious and racial Others such as Muslims, Jews, Asians, Native Americans, Africans, and Black people as a result of discrimination, anti-Semitism, and xenophobia.[48] Rather, the white self is literally and symbolically at war with an "ontologically insecure"[49] version of its own self that is preoccupied with preservation[50] because of perceived threats to the white existence.[51] The white self paradoxically needs but cannot stand the ontologically insecure version of itself, which it must constantly acknowledge only to dismiss, discourage, disappoint, disparage, and attempt to destroy. All of this points toward the instability of whiteness, which depends on the white other's presence. And this instability is reflected historically in certain people's acceptance into whiteness over time, that is, Jewish and Irish[52] people, and in specific intraracial conflicts, such as those that I listed in the first part of this Introduction.

The cyclical sadomasochistic dynamic between the white self and the white other is apparent in the world at present, too. This white-on-white dynamic was apparent in the world as it *was* centuries ago in the early modern period, visible in Shakespearean drama and Elizabethan and Jacobean culture, although sometimes obscured by the disruptive presence of somatically different Others, like the Black characters in Shakespeare's more commonly recognized race plays: *Titus Andronicus, Othello, The Merchant of Venice, The Tempest,* and *Antony and Cleopatra.*[53] For some time, then, the white self has battled with a version of itself that has tried to remain hidden in plain sight. In different ways, the intraracial color-line reveals how such anti-Blackness, whether physical, rhetorical, emotional, metaphorical, or psychological, functions as a multifaceted white supremacist tool. This tool simultaneously and paradoxically shapes and harms white identity and white people's "self-concepts"[54] while undoubtedly harming racial Others, particularly Black people. The intraracial color-line explicitly illustrates racial whiteness as an ideology and intentionally unstable identity category that depends parasitically on violence and imbalanced power relations of all kinds. It is an ideology that necessitates antiracist intervention.

By centering white-on-white relations, the intraracial color-line illuminates the prevalence of white-on-white violence in Shakespeare's plays, especially in tragedy, which I recognize as a white genre that depicts racial whiteness as tragic, as a catastrophic construct. Within this one dramatic genre, Shakespeare centers and sensationalizes intraracial conflicts from his first play, *Titus Andronicus* (circa 1590), to his last, *Timon of Athens* (circa 1608). *Shakespeare's White Others* leans on critiques of Shakespearean tragedy, with references here and there to comedy, romance, and the history plays, to suggest that genre and form can be useful for tracing the development of racial constructions and observing the white other's presence. It is my hope that future book-length studies will address genre more comprehensively in relationship to race. While this study is not invested in explicit analyses of the plays' formal and structural features,[55] this study's awareness of genre informs the Shakespearean textual analyses that engage antiracist theory, critical race studies, whiteness studies, Black feminism, social psychology, and sound studies. Finally, in being a genre that scholar Patricia Parker associates with blackness, when observing that "black was the color of tragedy and revenge tragedy in particular":[56] Tragedy is a prime dramatic site for examining whiteness and the white other because it is consumed by representations of blackness. As I note, tragedy is also preoccupied with centering white people.[57] Given the very few cameos of Black characters in Shakespeare's canon, and certainly within his tragedies, which contain only Aaron, Othello, and Cleopatra amid dozens upon dozens of racially white characters, tragedy functions as a useful site for investigating and thinking about whiteness, which has been treated in so many ways – racially, aesthetically, historically, culturally, socio-politically, religiously, and metaphorically, for instance – as Blackness's binary opposite.

"It [Does] Matter if You're Black or White" ... or White Other[58]

What does it mean to be Black, white, or white other?[59] And why does it matter? In 1991, the late global pop superstar Michael Jackson asserted in the chorus to his wildly popular song "Black or White" that it doesn't matter if someone is Black or white.[60] With Black and white being the extreme ends of the racial hierarchy, the added implication, as suggested by the song's music video visuals, was that the racial backgrounds of everyone in between Black and white do not matter either. Jackson's idealistic song followed significant twentieth-century social, political, and cultural moments that exposed the pervasiveness of global white supremacy and/ or responses to it: South African apartheid, the Harlem Renaissance, *Brown v. Board of Education*, the American Civil Rights Movement, the Black Arts Movement, and the Black Power Movement, to name a few. Moreover, Jackson's song emerged around other significant socio-political moments such as the end of Nelson Mandela's lengthy imprisonment, the infamous Rodney King beating and the 1992 LA Riots. Jackson's racial equality anthem, which was created *because of* global and anti-Black racism, today sounds more like confirmation of a hopeful dream deferred, especially in light of the 2012 killing of Trayvon Martin on my birthday, February 26, and the 2013 inception of the Black Lives Matter movement that continues to be relevant and necessary, and will be so indefinitely. Ironically, Jackson's "Black or White" exists precisely because race matters. Everything in between Black and white matters.

Amplifying "colorblind" rather than antiracist or color-conscious ideals when the song's featured rapper L.T.B. declares in his final verse, "I'm not going to spend my life being a color." Jackson's "Black or White," which contains positive if sometimes naïve messages about race and racism, registers like a harmonious fantasy that elides the incredible authority of white patriarchal power and white supremacy (phenomena Jackson's music video calls attention to throughout, though it is unclear if that is all deliberate).[61] On the heels of the song's release, overt anti-Black racism and violence persisted. Such racism is arguably even more visible now in the post-postracial twenty-first-century, in part, because of how easily racist content moves across the internet and the globe.[62] If it was unclear or seemed irrelevant to some people in the late twentieth century when the world first heard "Black or White," it is certainly apparent now that being white matters, as does being Black and all that lies between Black and white in the racial hierarchy. That it matters, and how it matters, is an integral premise of this book, which situates itself among a range of scholarly and non-academic work invested in antiracism and/or undoing the invisibility of racialized whiteness: texts such as Little, Jr.'s *Shakespeare Jungle Fever* and *White People in Shakespeare*, Smith's *Race and Rhetoric in the Renaissance* and *Black Shakespeare*, Crystal M. Fleming's *How to Be Less Stupid about Race*, and even D. L. Hughley's *How Not to Get Shot: And Other Advice from White People.*[63]

Racial Blackness and whiteness are understood today as social constructions, rather than biological realities. Even so, race still matters significantly in virtually all conversations that involve human beings.[64] To understand this reality, one must consider what it means to be Black and what it means to be white, for the white other exists precisely because of those two racial categories. To that end, I offer first a definition of Blackness, since both white and white other depend on the devaluing of it. With Toni Morrison's (*Playing in the Dark*) and Hall's examinations of "blackness" as a guide, I deploy "Black" and "blackness" here with respect to "the denotative and connotative blackness that African peoples have come to signify, as well as the entire range of views, assumptions, readings, and misreadings that accompany Eurocentric learning about these people."[65] How the Black person, and literal and metaphorical blackness, gets written about, and read, informs anti-Black ideas and even the socio-political reception of real Black people. Morrison's attention to what she calls the "carefully invented Africanist presence"[66] in literature resonates with how Hall uses "'blackness' and 'black' to cover both social practices and cultural categories" that then allow her to discuss Black "Africans and African-descended people" across time and space – then and now, here and there.[67] I find Morrison's and Hall's attention to Blackness and blackness to be useful aids for establishing the parameters defining the Black/white binary as I consider what lies in the gray area between those two racialized categories that are treated as racially oppositional.[68] That gray area is where I locate the white other, a figure "marked as 'white,'" much like Hero, who is metaphorically blackened in a pit of ink.

Because Blackness and its meaning constantly gets policed by white hegemony, and because Blackness is thought to reflect whatever whiteness is not or sometimes even to serve as a surrogate for whiteness,[69] whiteness is more challenging to define.[70] Whiteness is afforded the liberty and privilege to mean whatever it needs to mean in any given moment, since white people retain systemic control[71] and since "whiteness is coterminous with domination," as scholar Zeus Leonardo posits.[72] Despite the definitional difficulty, I lean on one understanding of whiteness and acknowledge others to offer deep consideration of this complex, elusive racial

category. Whiteness, and negotiations of it, depend on a dynamic eluci-
dated by sociologist Matthew W. Hughey's definition of whiteness that
explicitly aids our understanding of the white other: Whiteness is "a
configuration of meanings and practices that simultaneously produce and
maintain racial cohesion and difference in two main ways: (1) through
positioning those marked as 'white' as essentially different from and
superior to those marked 'non-white', and (2) through marginalizing
practices of 'being white' that fail to exemplify dominant ideals."[73]
Simply put, *being* white and being *marked as* white do not mean the same
thing, hence the distinction between white and white other.

Beyond Hughey's useful articulation of what racial whiteness is, there
are other ways to think about this racial category, in addition to the
following definition that frames whiteness as a figurative and literal imitation of socio-cultural superiority and moral goodness, broadly speaking. As
a carefully curated imitation of the things it seeks to represent and embody
(whether it be innocence,[74] supremacy, honor, chastity, beauty,[75] and so
on), the white identity exists as a social, political, cultural chameleon
whose ability to morph at a moment's notice enhances whiteness' overall
purpose and power:[76] Morphing is a survival mechanism designed specifically to protect, serve, and preserve the myth of the stable ideal white
self.[77] That the white self can transform is what makes it especially
dangerous; and this danger is, in part, what links the white identity and
whiteness to violence,[78] since there are no conditions under which the
ideal white self will not work to protect itself amid its constant striving for
perfection – what idealized whiteness ultimately, and perhaps frustratingly,
represents for the dominant culture.[79]

The unattainable goal of perfection makes narrowing down a singular
definition of whiteness a difficult, if not impossible, task. Yet, if I had to
create a definition, it would be this: At its core, whiteness is a violent,
incestuous, interdependent power system; within this system, it is essential
that white females birth, nurture, and celebrate the white males who own,
oppress, and "protect" them. The chameleon aspect of the white identity
helps explain why it has been so challenging for scholars, and even white
people themselves, to define whiteness concretely. On the one hand,
locating an exact definition is a futile endeavor, since malleability[80] and
invisibility are core components of whiteness, which will be forever changing. On the other hand, as the meaning of racialized whiteness constantly
changes, it makes sense that various ways of understanding it would
manifest, given that one of the greatest strengths of whiteness and white
supremacy is to generate chaos and confusion – or what Morrison

succinctly describes as "distraction."[81] The ability simultaneously to destroy and re-produce its own meaning, to seem simple but be "a conglomeration of diverse and complex shapes or forms that resist organi-sation,"[82] is what makes whiteness so intriguing, so prevailing.

Power in its many forms is what aligns various theorists' different articulations about racial whiteness, which is "a product of institutionalized power."[83] Beyond the literal authority instilled in white, or fair, skin and bodies,[84] whiteness also possesses metaphorical[85] power that makes its mean-ing boundless. In *The Souls of White Folk*, cited in my Introduction's second epigraph, Watson presents whiteness "as a way of seeing and knowing the world that masquerades as universality and remains largely unnamed and unrecognized." Watson continues, "It is exposed as a mode of social organi-zation that is shaped by skin-color privilege and that is inextricably enmeshed with other vectors of identity such as gender, class, sexual orientation, and the organization of space."[86] Like Leonardo, Watson links domination and violence to the white identity, specifically by reflecting on how whiteness takes up and occupies space.[87] And who gets to exist where, and who gets what, in society is very much determined by the racial hierarchy and white superiority, as legal scholars Richard Delgado and Jean Stefancic assert in their assessment of the "binary thinking" that generally positions white in contrast to Black or non-white.[88] Yet, as *Shakespeare's White Others* argues, white necessarily stands in contrast to white other, a fact that enables the logic that drives my intraracial color-line theory.

Occupying a position of superiority always, whiteness, according to scholar-activist Peggy McIntosh, inherently comes with a set of privileges[89] made possible by the assets that are white skin and the overall symbolic goodness of whiteness, which legal scholar Cheryl I. Harris describes as "simultaneously an aspect of identity and a property interest." Harris adds that whiteness "is something that can both be experienced and deployed as a resource. Whiteness can move from being a passive characteristic as an aspect of identity to an active entity that – like other types of property – is used to fulfill the will and to exercise systemic power."[90] *Shakespeare's White Others* adds to contemporary understandings of the various mean-ings of whiteness[91] by positioning it as a systemic problem, a colossal socio-political, psychological, and intellectual problem that perpetuates violence and destruction. Approaching this matter slightly differently than Judith H. Katz, who defines racism as white people's problem,[92] I use this study and its theoretical interventions to define the various machinations of racial whiteness as the problem. There is not a single Shakespeare play where such figures are not causing racialized problems.

(De)Centering Whiteness

Shakespearean drama is an exceptionally generative site for interrogating the definitional problems of racial whiteness and Blackness, and for understanding whiteness' dependency on Blackness to generate its own racialized meaning and subsequently the meaning of "white other." For instance, in *Romeo and Juliet*'s climax, Shakespeare illustrates how easy it is to valorize whiteness through contrasting, color-coded sentiments that reject blackness and deem it inferior. Fantasizing about her new husband, Juliet passionately says in a soliloquy:

> Come, night. Come, Romeo. Come, thou day in night;
> For thou wilt lie upon the wings of night
> Whiter than snow upon a raven's back.
> Come, gentle night, come, loving, black-browed night,
> Give me my Romeo, and when I shall die
> Take him and cut him out in little stars,
> And he will make the face of heaven so fine
> That all the world will be in love with night
> And pay no worship to the garish sun.
>
> (3.2.17–25)

Throughout this passage,[93] Juliet beckons blackness, which carries whiteness forward, to augment the beautiful vibrancy of Romeo's racial whiteness.[94] With the raven allusion in particular, the anti-blackness of Juliet's metaphorical love language provides an interesting example of white females' complicity in upholding the superiority of whiteness and patriarchal authority and the alleged inferiority of Blackness. Juliet transforms Romeo into the day and instills his whiteness (and hers through the marriage) with supreme power. Exalted, her husband is the brightness in night's darkness, so stellar that he and his whiteness outdo the sun. Juliet even creates an image of hyperwhiteness, a topic I cover in Chapter 1, by making Romeo whiter than snow. She employs blackness to paint this picture. In the form of the tiny stars that are mentioned, Juliet's rhetoric and Romeo's whiteness do racialized work by decentering blackness – the raven, the night – to emphasize the centrality of a particular kind of whiteness, which is here equated with light. Night, or blackness, becomes lovable only once its proximity to whiteness is visible. Dangerous because of its furtive anti-blackness, Juliet's logic is psychologically violent. Furthermore, by positioning the "little stars" in opposition to the sun, her sentiments transform the sun into a light source that is *less than* Romeo, who is the ideal light and thus the ideal white man.

Homing in on the problematic aspect of whiteness specifically linked to the violence and anti-Blackness generated by the intraracial color-line distinguishes this book from past studies that have in some fashion considered whiteness and/or otherness in relationship to religious, skin color, or ethnic difference. Similar to Matthieu Chapman, whose *Anti-Black Racism in Early Modern English Drama: The Other "Other"* insightfully deploys Afro-pessimism and "argues for the divide between black and non-black as the primary determinant of humanity for both those with an English gaze and those recognized as their Other,"[95] I examine a divide between Black and non-Black. However, my pronounced antiracist agenda exclusively others whiteness, recognizing the strangeness of racially white people, the "normative subjects" who are of the same hue, blood, household, gender, religion, social class, culture, and/or ethnicity as one another.[96]

In that respect, my study also differs from Mary Floyd-Wilson's *English Ethnicity and Race in Early Modern Drama*, which relies on "geohumoralism"[97] to propose, among other things, that we "reinterpret the Englishmen's encounters with West Africa with the understanding that their own sense of whiteness and ethnicity was in flux."[98] As I make clear above and throughout this book, the dominant culture's understanding of whiteness will remain in flux so long as white people embrace white supremacy instead of antiracist practices that acknowledge and interrogate the systemically racist underpinnings of society;[99] take seriously "the history, politics, psychology, and sociology of race relations";[100] resist reinforcing white superiority through the devaluation of Blackness;[101] and directly confront the anti-Black racism and systemic oppression that are integral to the white other's existence.[102] Like Jean Feerick – who, in *Strangers in Blood*, employs the "system of race-as-blood"[103] to explain early modern emerging racial discourse and distinctions that make Black Othello racially superior to white Iago in her reading[104] – Floyd-Wilson maintains an investment in discussing race in a way that destabilizes modern notions of racial construction rooted in premodernity. In so doing, Feerick and Floyd-Wilson sidestep the urgent need to confront racism and anti-Blackness in Shakespeare's time and our own. Contrastingly, *Shakespeare's White Others* illustrates how it is in fact whiteness' embodiment and mediation of Blackness and blackness that nuance and reinforce the "white over black" racial hierarchy both Feerick's and Floyd-Wilson's analyses contradict, contradictions that Dennis Austin Britton provides a useful counter to in *Becoming Christian: Race, Reformation, and Early Modern English Romance.*[105]

Patricia Akhimie's *Shakespeare and the Cultivation of Difference* bears close resemblance to *Shakespeare's White Others* due to its engagement with conduct and its concern with cultivating personal behavior. Yet, whereas Akhimie's text reads the body through both Black and white bodies, and "focuse[s] on conduct literature as a potential source for understanding the production of race through the promotion of stigmatized somatic difference and the racialization of class difference," I concentrate on the somatic sameness of white and white other figures to think exclusively about how racial formation necessitates understanding the inner workings of marked whiteness.[106] Building on Leslie A. Fiedler's *The Strangers in Shakespeare* (Stein and Day, 1973), Marianne Novy's *Shakespeare and Outsiders* acknowledges how "many of Shakespeare's characters move between inside and outside," but, unlike *Shakespeare's White Others*, Novy's text is not invested in analyzing the distinction between characters being marked as white and enacting the power of racial whiteness.[107] Novy is not concerned with how the other is always more near than far: As I suggest, when the self "invents an other," the boundaries of power and status are determined in direct relationship to the self.[108]

The intraracial color-line allows for exploration of the racial polarity between Black and white by putting pressure on distinctions within whiteness. While I do not focus comprehensively on religious difference in this text, I would like to call attention here to *Jews in the Early Modern English Imagination*, a study in which Eva Johanna Holmberg acknowledges the instability of Jewish people's designations as Others with respect to their bodily appearance.[109] For early modern English people, it was largely Jewish people's religion that made them different; what we might interpret as Jewish people's seemingly diminished whiteness, associated with what Christians interpreted as their spiritual blackness. Adding to this conversation by using *The Merchant of Venice* as a guide, Lynda E. Boose observes how "Shylock in particular raises special problems. According to the prevailing connection between skin color and race, 'Jewishness' is not a race; nonetheless, it was and still is treated as if it were – as if Jews and Christians were separated by something (beyond white otherness) more incontrovertible than religious differences alone."[110] (While thorough consideration of Jewishness is outside of this project's scope, I want to note that Shylock does fit into the white other category, albeit in a rather complex way.) In agreement with historian Nell Irvin Painter, I am convinced "the meanings of white race reach into concepts of labor, gender, and class and images of personal beauty."[111] This is evident in Shakespeare's drama, for example, through the application of "fair" across religiously and culturally different groups. And this evidence opens up possibilities for extracting meaning from intraracial moments and for learning how they inform our understanding of anti-Blackness and racism, even in the subtlest ways, as I assert in the following analyses of *Titus Andronicus, Hamlet, Antony and Cleopatra, Othello*, and *The Comedy of Errors*.

Seeing Race: "I Sit With Shakespeare and He Winces Not"[112]

As the previous section stresses, the color-line matters. Introduced in Du Bois' *The Souls of Black Folk*, the color-line emerged as a theoretical tool for identifying and explaining the systemic global and domestic interracial, racist dilemmas one can see and assess with the naked eye, even in Shakespeare's oeuvre.[113] The interracial color-line establishes race and racism as ocular phenomena that depend on people *perceiving* differences between Black and white and, of course, assigning seemingly fixed meanings to those differences that are not natural or biologically significant, but socially prescribed and constructed.[114] Despite being discussed at the turn of the twentieth century, the interracial "race feud"[115] Du Bois described in his writing has undoubtedly bled into the twenty-first century globally. Anti-Black racism has been a problem in American society since its inception; and history indicates this is also true in relationship to the development of Britain, as historian Peter Fryer argues.

Considering how British history has been represented, for instance, Fryer succinctly asserts that "the official version of our history labels itself as 'patriotic'. It is more accurately described as conservative, nationalist, and racist."[116] In other words, if one is looking for more racially inclusive depictions of the British past, certain studies that position themselves as capturing that history tell a racially biased version of reality.[117] Other studies overtly omit important historical information about the Black existence.[118] Nikole Hannah-Jones argues in *The 1619 Project* that the same is true for the past telling of American history.[119] Within British Black history, there is evidence that Peter Negro, a Black man, provided service to the state;[120] there were "five Africans [who] arrived to learn English and thereby facilitate trade" in 1555;[121] Black domestic servants and entertainers were brought in by the English courts in the sixteenth-century;[122] John Blanke was "the 'blacke trumpeter'" associated with the courts of Henry VII and Henry VIII;[123] and Iberian Africans resided in the homes of Jewish Conversos.[124] Beyond these smaller examples, Imtiaz Habib declares in *Black Lives in the English Archives* that the "documentary materials" he utilized indicate the "plentifulness of black people in early modern England."[125] Fryer's fierce indictment of British history and historians aligns the past and present by positioning racism as the common ground between then and now. Moreover, his critique of the British past, and how it is discussed in the present, says a lot about the anti-Black white world in which Shakespeare lived, wrote, and produced his art.

The Du Boisian color-line stresses the tensions between Black and white, and so does the intraracial color-line, this book's ideological driving force, which I use to expose the tensions within whiteness. Such tensions often exploit dominant, negative narratives about blackness and Black people. This is why (as noted previously) racial whiteness is at war with itself and, thus, exists as a figurative but also very real phenomenon that must be fought against – from within and from without. *Shakespeare's White Others* concerns itself with reflecting on, observing, and paying attention to the external and the internal, or psychological, conflicts that are a byproduct of both intraracial and interracial tensions. For me, a Black man and Shakespeare scholar, the racial tensions are best exposed by and fought against with theoretical antiracist weaponry like the intraracial color-line and the white other, concepts engineered to explode the race conversation and to shatter harmful white hegemonic views and values that degrade blackness and Black people because of whiteness' crisis of conflict with itself.

Mining Whiteness

Where there are people, there you will find race, because race is always happening.[126] Race always matters and makes meaning, even when racialized whiteness is the only quality on display. While *Shakespeare's White Others* examines one English dramatist's canon to generate a specific critical conversation, this study by no means suggests that Shakespeare is the only early modern author, or dramatist, whose work can aid understanding about whiteness, race, and the intraracial color-line, for other scholars have considered whiteness in drama and elsewhere.[127] Rather, Shakespeare's work is a way to contain this conversation about the white other that I believe extends to his contemporaries, who also produced interracial as well as racially homogenous plays like *Hamlet*, the subject of Chapter 2.[128]

To bolster its arguments, *Shakespeare's White Others* alludes to a range of Shakespeare plays, including *Richard III*, *Romeo and Juliet*, *Much Ado About Nothing*, *Henry V*, *The Merchant of Venice*, *Troilus and Cressida*,

Love's Labour's Lost, As You Like It, The Tempest, The Winter's Tale, Twelfth Night, and *Macbeth.* Additionally, as previously mentioned there are five core plays at the heart of my four chapters and the Conclusion. *Titus Andronicus'* racial triangulation among the Romans, Goths and Moors makes it a fitting play to introduce the intraracial color-line and several of the white other's distinguishing features. *Hamlet,* beyond dramatizing the tensions between white racial identity and masculinity, nuances the race discussion in a play that only features white characters. I find *Antony and Cleopatra* valuable for its illustration of how white(ned) women are used to reaffirm white supremacy and patriarchal power. With Iago's extreme attention to sex and psychological violence, *Othello* brings into view the psychology of white people's racism. And lastly, in the Conclusion, *The Comedy of Errors* reminds us how the profiling and stereotyping of people is dangerous and, depending on what one looks like, even deadly – especially if one is Black.

While critiquing Shakespeare's dramatic literature and interrogating premodern and contemporary issues, *Shakespeare's White Others* simultaneously capitalizes on and overwrites the years of education that brought me to this intellectual point. By that I mean that interrogating and studying whiteness, and critiquing whiteness, was not an extensive part of my educational training. As one can observe in modern debates, such as the widespread opposition to critical race theory in the USA, UK, and beyond,[129] critiquing whiteness and the history of white dominance is not a formal part of most people's education. In 1996, Hall said as much in her pedagogically oriented article "Beauty and the Beast of Whiteness: Teaching Race and Gender."[130] *Shakespeare's White Others,* then, consciously and conscientiously follows a theoretically antiracist program of action to see and center whiteness, so that people can continue to further their understanding of its functions and idiosyncrasies. I intend for this book to show readers how to apply the intraracial color-line in and beyond Shakespearean drama, for the intraracial color-line is also relevant in our modern world. In the following chapter descriptions, I outline how mining whiteness – actively digging into this racial category – yields racial knowledge from Shakespeare's dramatic works.

Chapter 1, "Somatic Similarity: The White Other in *Titus Andronicus,*" primarily critiques Shakespeare's first tragedy to expose the presence of the intraracial color-line. I begin with this tragedy because it is the Shakespeare play that most efficiently showcases the white/white other binary slippage produced by the intraracial color-line, which separates the play's white characters along spiritual and moral lines. I use *Titus* pedagogically to guide the reader's understanding of the intraracial color-line so they can

then apply that concept both in subsequent chapters and outside of the
plays analyzed here. Shakespeare's oeuvre is replete with appearances of the
white other. This gateway chapter challenges the easy assumption that one
needs somatic Blackness in order to discuss race, in order for race to be
happening. I seek to understand: What is *Titus* without Aaron? Building
on Francesca Royster's field-changing work featured in *Shakespeare
Quarterly*, Chapter 1 reveals *Titus*' concerns with examining white-on-
white violence and violations – intrafamilial, intraracial, and intracultural.
This chapter demands that readers put whiteness under the microscope to
see how intraracial otherness works even in unexpected places, such as the
gruesome pasties *Titus* bakes.

As I argued previously in "Code Black: Whiteness and Unmanliness in
Hamlet," Shakespeare nuances intraracial conflict in *Hamlet*, the subject of
Chapter 2: "Engendering the Fall of White Masculinity."[131] Drawing on
race-centered *Hamlet* scholarship by Ian Smith, Patricia Parker, and Peter
Erickson, and alluding to work edited by Scott Newstok and Ayanna
Thompson, this chapter offers a racially focused analysis of this rich text
that centers white people watching other white people. *Hamlet* surveys
deviations from ideal white conduct and reveals how gender expectations
are violated and how white people repeatedly disrespect, only to redefine,
socially constructed racialized boundaries. I offer a critique of *Hamlet* that
directly associates white unmanliness with Denmark's "rotten" state, its
socio-political ruin. Specifically, I read the intraracial discord against the
play's structure as a decomposition process. *Hamlet* depicts uncouth, less-
than-ideal whiteness in relationship to gender expectations: Unmanliness
gets coded as black, so the play can suggest that certain Danish figures do
not epitomize ideal white masculinity. Defining one side of the intraracial
color-line, these characters contrast with the deceased valiant Old Hamlet
as well as Young Fortinbras, the Norwegian savior who closes *Hamlet* by
restoring ideal masculine whiteness and patriarchal hegemonic values after
the predominant white others are purged in Act 5.

Transitioning to *Antony and Cleopatra*, after beginning with brief analyses of white hands in Shakespeare plays such as *The Winter's Tale* and
Henry V, Chapter 3 homes in on the intersection of femininity and race to
put pressure on Antony's curious whitening of the Black Egyptian Queen's
hand in the play's climactic Act. Extending the second chapter's direct
emphasis on gender, "On the Other Hand: The White(ned) Woman in
Antony and Cleopatra" positions Cleopatra as collateral damage, caught in
the play's intraracial crossfire. This chapter depicts the significant dangers
of the whiteness that gets magically mapped onto Cleopatra's Black body

so she can momentarily become a form of what Arthur L. Little, Jr. has described in *Shakespeare Quarterly* as "Shakespearean white property."[132] Through the Black Queen's whitened body and her interracial relationship with Antony (and by extension, the ensuing *intra*racial tensions caused by Antony's movement between Egypt and Rome), I further complicate the white other concept to reflect on integral matters such as white property, white dominance, and white women as props: patriarchal, racial, theatrical, cultural, social, political, economic, domestic props. Chapter 3 closes by scrutinizing how white hands[133] are always implicated in violence and by asserting that white dominance permits white people to play the ultimate race card – the ace of spades in the invisible race card deck.[134]

Chapter 4, "'Hear Me, See Me': Sex, Violence and Silence in *Othello*," reflects on the psychological and physical consequences of sexual violence in and beyond *Othello* – that is to say, in contemporary times. I argue that the white identity formation process, and allegiance to its ideals, inherently impedes racial equality. The process itself works to reify white superiority. This is evident as I apply the intraracial color-line theory mainly to readings of Iago, the play's most visible and vocal white other. In conjunction with readings of *Othello*, I look back at the transatlantic slave trade and examine the trajectory of white violence that has led to Black silence and the de-victimization of Black boys and men; this is one of many reasons psychologists suggest Black males are not always heard, much like Othello, when it comes to their experiences with sexual and non-sexual violence. With some historical examples in mind, I return to Shakespeare's canon to reflect on how early modern texts amplify the "white voice," a concept Jennifer Stoever and I have examined elsewhere.[135] Within this analysis I accentuate the personal-critical-experiential to consider the Black male Shakespearean voice and how it can get silenced by white people. Ultimately, I assert that the intraracial color-line and the real-life existence of the white other are impediments to racial equality.

My *Othello* reading in particular demonstrates the possibilities for postmodern critical, pedagogical, and theatrical application of my book's theoretical concerns. *Shakespeare's White Others'* formal conclusion engages *The Comedy of Errors* to reaffirm how race always matters. I argue that *The Comedy of Errors'* concern with mistaken identity resonates with the modern Black experience. While considering my book's preoccupation with the effects of racism, othering, anti-Blackness and racial profiling, I turn to Akhimie's *Comedy of Errors* literary criticism to consider how one can be "bruised with adversity" not just physically, but also

psychologically.[136] The Conclusion's title plays on the name of
Shakespeare's comedy because, as I see it, anti-blackness and anti-Black
racism position white people, including white others, in opposition to
Black people in what feels like a theatrical comedy of (t)errors: a space that
is a genre of its own and akin to Negro-Sarah's funnyhouse environment in
Adrienne Kennedy's play *Funnyhouse of a Negro.*[137] Racial tribulation is a
life sentence tied to the Black existence. As scholar Troy Duster reminds
us, Black people "have been engaged in white studies, [and the study of
white people], for at least three centuries."[138] With all of that understood,
the very last words of *Shakespeare's White Others* appear in the form of an
artifact, a letter written at the turn of the twenty-first century by a Black
adolescent who was on the verge of adulthood and registering all that the
Black experience of racial profiling entails. This letter documents a real-life
experience of beginning to understand fully the race-based policing of
bodies and the effects of the Du Boisian and Stoeverian color-lines, the
combination of which left this Black adolescent psychologically bruised
with adversity.

Notes

1 From *Help*, a play by Claudia Rankine. © Claudia Rankine 2022. Premiered
   at The Shed, NYC, March 2022. By kind permission of Claudia Rankine.
2 From "Introduction" to *The Souls of White Folk: African American Writers
   Theorize Whiteness* by Veronica T. Watson (Jackson: University Press of
   Mississippi, 2013), 5. © 2013 by University Press of Mississippi.
3 W. E. B. Du Bois, *The Souls of Black Folk* (New York: Tribeca Books,
   2011), 2.
4 Bridget M. Newell, "Being a White Problem and Feeling It," in *White Self-
   Criticality beyond Anti-racism: How Does It Feel to Be a White Problem?*, ed.
   George Yancy (New York: Lexington Books, 2015), 121–140; 121.
5 George Yancy, "Introduction: Un-Sutured," in *White Self-Criticality beyond
   Anti-racism: How Does It Feel to Be a White Problem?* ed. George Yancy (New
   York: Lexington Books, 2015), xii–xiii, xvii.
6 Newell, "Being a White Problem and Feeling It," 121–122.
7 See Little, Jr., "Is It Possible to Read Shakespeare through Critical White
   Studies?," 269, 277.
8 Channeling sentiments from Nikki Giovanni, Dennis Austin Britton recognizes that all "scholarly inquiry is mediated by the social, cultural, and
   economic realities in which we all must live our lives [. . .] Giovanni's essay
   asks us to think critically about the cultural politics of literary studies in
   general, but it expressly challenges the institution of Shakespeare Studies to
   reconsider how it defines what 'matters.'" With *Shakespeare's White Others,*

I especially am interested in helping white Shakespeareans and white people consider the cultural politics of a racial identity that often still gets rendered invisible. See Dennis Austin Britton, "Ain't She a Shakespearean: Truth, Giovanni, and Shakespeare," in *Early Modern Black Diaspora Studies: A Critical Anthology*, eds. Cassander Smith, Nicholas Jones, and Miles P. Grier (New York: Palgrave Macmillan, 2018), 223–228; 226.

9 See Ayanna Thompson, "Did the Concept of Race Exist for Shakespeare and His Contemporaries?," in *The Cambridge Companion to Shakespeare and Race*, ed. Ayanna Thompson (Cambridge: Cambridge University Press, 2021), 1–16; 4; Smith, *Black Shakespeare*, 17.

10 Sara Ahmed has posed fundamentally important questions about whiteness, questions I am also considering in this book: "If whiteness gains currency by being unnoticed, then what does it mean to notice whiteness? What does making the invisible marks of privilege more visible actually do?" "A Phenomenology of Whiteness," *Feminist Theory* 8.2 (2007), 149–168; 149–150.

11 According to Little, Jr., "One of the things the theater did, more than any other medium, including the Church, was to promulgate and solidify an affinity between a miraculous (cosmological) and a normative (cosmetic) whiteness. The theatre can be argued to have repurposed and celebrated the whiteness of divinity by rediscovering and redeploying it in playworlds and on stages that were as physically corporeal as they were secular." "Is It Possible to Read Shakespeare through Critical White Studies?," 273.

12 Defined and highlighted in *Souls of Black Folk* as "the problem of the twentieth century," the Du Boisian color-line denotes a separation between "the darker to the lighter races of men," what emerges more concretely in the text as urgent racial concerns about vocation, education, segregation, inequality, injustice, voting rights, anti-Black racism, sexual violence, domesticity, biased laws, and more. Du Bois, *Souls*, 9.

13 Smith, *Black Shakespeare*, 15.

14 Karen E. Fields and Barbara J. Fields, *Racecraft: The Soul of Inequality in American Life* (London: Verso, 2014), 5, 16, 18–19. Also see Thompson, "Did the Concept of Race Exist?," 8–9.

15 Fields and Fields, *Racecraft*, 19.

16 Lauren S. Cardon, *The "White Other" in American Intermarriage Stories, 1945–2008* (New York: Palgrave Macmillan, 2012). Here, I must acknowledge Arthur L. Little, Jr.'s earlier mention of "white other" in reference to the culturally different white Goths in *Titus* in *Shakespeare Jungle Fever: National-Imperial Re-Visions of Race, Rape, and Sacrifice* (Stanford: Stanford University Press, 2000), 65.

17 Ta-Nehisi Coates, "Foreword," in *The Origin of Others* by Toni Morrison (Cambridge, MA: Harvard University Press, 2017), vii–xvii, vii.

18 Smith, *Black Shakespeare*, 12.

19 Matthew W. Hughey, "Black Guys and White Guise: The Discursive Construction of White Masculinity," *Journal of Contemporary Ethnography* 20.10 (2012), 1–30, 5.

20 I thank John Michael Archer for helping me crystallize this point.

21 See John Michael Archer, *Citizen Shakespeare: Freemen and Aliens in the Language of the Plays* (New York: Palgrave Macmillan, 2005), 1, 5. Also see Laura Hunt Yungblut, *Strangers Settled Here among Us: Policies, Perceptions and the Presence of Aliens in Elizabethan England* (New York: Routledge, 1996); Scott Oldenburg, *Alien Albion: Literature and Immigration in Early Modern England* (Toronto: University of Toronto Press, 2014); and Edward Said, *Orientalism* (New York: Random House, 1979), 71.

22 Claudia Rankine, Beth Loffreda and Max King Cap, *The Racial Imaginary: Writers on Race in the Life of the Mind* (Albany, NY: Fence Books, 2016).

23 References to "white supremacy" refer specifically to the notion that whiteness is the superior race/culture, as is thought by those with racist mindsets and even those who struggle with internalized racism. Like Francis Lee Ansley, I think of white supremacy as a "political, economic, and cultural system in which whites overwhelmingly control power and material resources, conscious and unconscious ideas of white superiority and entitlement are widespread, and relations of white dominance and non-white subordination are daily reenacted across a broad array of institutions and social settings." See "White Supremacy (And What We Should Do about It)," in *Critical White Studies: Looking behind the Mirror*, eds. Richard Delgado and Jean Stefancic (Philadelphia, PA: Temple University Press, 1997), 592.

24 Keith Wrightson, *English Society: 1580–1680* (London: Hutchinson & Co. Ltd, 1982), 17.

25 Ibid., 17–18.

26 For another example of intraracial tensions/English xenophobia, see Geoffrey Elton, *The English* (Oxford: Blackwell Publishers, 1992), 69.

27 Peter Ackroyd, *The History of England from Henry VII to Elizabeth I: Tudors* (New York: Thomas Dunne Books, 2012), 459–461.

28 Nell Irvin Painter, *The History of White People* (New York: W. W. Norton & Company, 2010), x. Also see hooks, *Black Looks*, 27.

29 Exploring words written by Senator Tom Cotton of Arkansas, Brandi K. Adams observes an example of Shakespeare's implication in white supremacist thinking and "casual and systemic racism." See "The King, and not I: Refusing neutrality – ," *The Sundial* (June 2020), https://medium.com/the-sundial-acmrs/the-king-and-not-i-refusing-neutrality-dbab4239e8a9.

30 Miles P. Grier, "The Color of Professionalism: A Response to Dennis Britton," in *Early Modern Black Diaspora Studies: A Critical Anthology*, eds. Cassander Smith, Nicholas Jones, and Miles P. Grier (New York: Palgrave Macmillan, 2018), 229–238; 230.

31 Michael Eric Dyson asserts, "Some of the greatest victims of whiteness are whites themselves, having to bear the burden of a false belief in superiority." *Tears We Cannot Stop: A Sermon to White America* (New York: St. Martin's Press, 2017), 69.

32 When discussing *Much Ado* and race, scholars have typically turned to somatic blackness and Kenneth Branagh's 1993 film adaptation, in which Denzel

Washington, an Oscar award-winning Black actor, plays the role of white Don Pedro in what Ayanna Thompson has referred to as "a good example of [an] approach to colorblind casting." "Practicing a Theory/Theorizing a Practice: An Introduction to Shakespearean Colorblind Casting," in *Colorblind Shakespeare: New Perspectives on Race and Shakespeare*, ed. Ayanna Thompson (New York: Routledge, 2006), 6, 22. Courtney Lehmann also discusses othering, Denzel's blackness and *Much Ado* in "Faux Show: Falling into History in Kenneth Branagh's *Love's Labour's Lost*," in *Colorblind Shakespeare*, 69–88; 69–70; 72, 83. Also see David Sterling Brown's twenty-first century "untimely" review of Kim F. Hall's work in "*Things of Darkness*: 'The Blueprint of a Methodology'," *The Hare* 5.1, Critical Race Studies Special Issue (September 2020).

33 Arthur L. Little, Jr., "Re-Historicizing Race, White Melancholia, and the Shakespearean Property," *Shakespeare Quarterly*, 67.1 (Spring 2016), 84–103; 91.

34 See Miles P. Grier, "Inkface: The Slave Stigma in England's Early Imperial Imagination," in *Scripturing the Human: The Written as Political*, ed. Vincent L. Wimbush (New York: Routledge, 2015), 193–220; 195. Also see Grier's *Inkface: Othello and the Formation of White Interpretive Community, 1604–1855* (Charlottesville: University of Virginia Press, 2023).

35 As Farah Karim-Cooper observes, "Material cosmetics were a part of and crucial to the art and design of early modern theatrical production. Actors painted their faces; the dramatists knew it and pointedly register this in the language and imagery they use to evoke cosmetics." *Cosmetics in Shakespearean and Renaissance Drama* (Edinburgh: Edinburgh University Press, 2019), 137.

36 Within patriarchal English society, women were seen as both subjects and objects of property. See Natasha Korda, *Shakespeare's Domestic Economies: Gender and Property in Early Modern England* (Philadelphia: University of Pennsylvania Press, 2002), 12.

37 Kim F. Hall, "'Troubling Doubles': Apes, Africans, and Blackface in Mr. Moore's *Revels*," in *Race, Ethnicity and Power in the Renaissance*, ed. Joyce Green MacDonald (London: Associated University Presses, 1997), 120–144; 122.

38 Kim F. Hall distinguishes between how Black men and Black women registered in the period; *Things of Darkness: Economies of Race and Gender in Early Modern England* (Ithaca, NY: Cornell University Press, 1995), 346–348.

39 Thompson, "Did the Concept of Race Exist?", 1.

40 In *Much Ado*, Hero is one example of the somatically similar white other; and another example in this play might very well be the bastard villain Don John, whom Shakespeare blackens morally and ethically.

41 Ingroup and outgroup dynamics have a significant impact on how people interact with one another. In an interesting study on face processing, for example, Kevin D. Cassidy, Kimberly A. Quinn, and Glyn W. Humphreys present their findings that suggest "ingroup/outgroup categorization influences the perception of same- and other-race faces presented in an inter-racial

or intra-racial context." "The Influence of Ingroup/Outgroup Categorization on Same- and Other-Race Face Processing: The Moderating Role of Inter-Versus Intra-racial Context," *Journal of Experimental Social Psychology* 47 (2011), 811–817; 811. As I will discuss, Saturninus recognizes something superficial about Tamora, her white hue, that draws him to her and allows her conditional entry into the ingroup.

42 Hughey, "Black Guys," 5.

43 See Mira Assaf Kafantaris, "Meghan Markle, Good English Housewife," *The Rambling*, 3 (January 6, 2019), https://the-rambling.com/2019/01/26/issue3-kafantaris/. In relationship to Prince Harry, the *white other* concept becomes even more fascinating to think about.

44 During his encounter with the Ghost of Banquo, Macbeth exclaims, "Take any shape but that, and my firm nerves / Shall never tremble" (3.4.103–104). Du Bois includes these lines in his chapter, "Of Our Spiritual Strivings," as he discusses racism and its effects, the sins that disrupt America's peace and haunt society (*Souls*, 5). I thank my colleague Jennifer Stoever for reminding me of this allusion.

45 David Sterling Brown, "(Early) Modern Literature: Crossing the Color-Line," *Radical Teacher*, 105 (Summer 2016), 70–71.

46 There is an aural component to Du Bois' language that gestures toward what Jennifer Lynn Stoever identifies specifically as the "sonic color line," a concept I devote attention to in Chapter 4. See *The Sonic Color Line: Race and the Cultural Politics of Listening* (New York: New York University Press, 2016), 7. In Shakespeare and early modern English studies, there has yet to be deep engagement with how race is heard and how the sonic racial hierarchy operates, despite the fact that some early modern scholars have devoted attention to sound and sounds within Shakespeare's canon, which has been positioned critically as a soundscape. See Bruce R. Smith, *The Acoustic Sound of the Early Modern World: Attending to the O-Factor* (Chicago: University of Chicago Press, 1999); George T. Wright, *Hearing the Measures: Shakespearean and Other Inflections* (Madison: University of Wisconsin Press, 2001); Gina Bloom, *Voice in Motion: Staging Gender, Shaping Sound in Early Modern England* (Philadelphia: University of Pennsylvania Press, 2007); and Keith M. Botelho, *Renaissance Earwitnesses: Rumor and Early Modern Masculinity* (New York: Palgrave Macmillan, 2009). Additionally, in 2010, a special issue of *The Upstart Crow* was published, titled "Shakespearean Hearing," which was heavily influenced by Bruce R. Smith's earlier work, as the editors Leslie Dunn and Wes Folkerth note in their Introduction. See *The Upstart Crow* Vol. 29 (2010). This volume features articles by Michael Witmore, Allison Kay Deuternann, Kurt Schreyer, Erin K. Minear, Joseph M. Ortiz, and others on topics such as music, stage noises, and language.

47 According to Stephanie M. Bahr, Tudor law "blurred the very distinctions between words and deeds." Thus, violence could be literal/physical or not. "*Titus Andronicus* and the Interpretive Violence of the Reformation," *Shakespeare Quarterly*, 68.3 (2017), 246.

48 Hall, *Things of Darkness*, 6–7. Eurocentric, anti-Other views, as expressed by Renaissance thinkers like Erasmus, were used to reinforce white superiority. See Geraldine Heng, *The Invention of Race in the European Middle Ages* (Cambridge: Cambridge University Press, 2018), 15. Also see Nathan Ron, *Erasmus, and the 'Other': On Turks, Jews, and Indigenous Peoples* (Cham, Switzerland: Palgrave Macmillan, 2019), 21; and Onyeka Nubia, *England's Other Countrymen: Black Tudor Society* (London: Zed Books, 2019), 13–14.

49 According to R. D. Laing, "*ontologically* secure [people] will encounter all the hazards of life, social, ethical, spiritual, biological, from a centrally firm sense of [their] own and other people's reality and identity." The ontologically insecure, then, struggle with reality and identity and often feel threats to their existence; they cannot maintain a firm sense of identity, a reality that I see as true for racists (explored much further in the Conclusion of this book). *The Divided Self: An Existential Study in Sanity and Madness* (London: Penguin Books, 1965), 39–47.

50 Laing, *The Divided Self*, 42–43.

51 As George Yancy claims, "It is the seemingly unremarkable ways in which whiteness lives its social ontology that is fundamentally problematic. This distinction is important to make lest we only label those acts racist that are enacted by self-ascribed white racist individuals/groups. In short, then, specifically challenging anti-Black white racism vis-à-vis its embodied lived reality for whites is not just a question of getting them to relinquish a false ontology or simply getting them to be more rational agents through deployment of abstract ethical principles. Much more is required at the level of white *everyday practices* and the ways in which those white practices re-center white power or challenge white power." See "Introduction: Un-Sutured," xii.

52 See Karen Brodkin Sacks, "How Did the Jews Become White Folks?", in *Critical White Studies: Looking behind the Mirror*, eds. Richard Delgado and Jean Stefancic (Philadelphia, PA: Temple University Press, 1997), 395–401. Also see Noel Ignatiev, *How the Irish Became White* (New York: Routledge, 1995).

53 *Titus* and *Othello* sensationalize and exploit the figure of the violent Black Moor, while *Antony and Cleopatra* capitalizes on the exoticism and hypersexuality of the Black African Queen.

54 Social psychologist Steven J. Heine posits that "people participating in a collectivistic culture are more likely to attend to interdependent aspects of their self-concepts," what they believe about themselves and how those beliefs influence their perceptions of self. *Cultural Psychology*, 3rd ed. (New York: W. W. Norton & Company, 2016), 212–218.

55 Genre is a complicated subject that might detract from the importance of the race conversation this project centers. For example, Lawrence Danson reminds us that "Shakespeare's plays are so many explorations and experiments in the endlessly revisionary process of genre-reformation." And he adds that "the definition of Shakespeare's tragic canon has never been stable because the definition of tragedy, as a genre, has not been stable."

Shakespeare's Dramatic Genres (Oxford: Oxford University Press, 2000), 7, 114.

56 Patricia Parker, "Black Hamlet: Battening on the Moor," *Shakespeare Studies*, 31 (2003), 127–164; 40. Smith refers to *Hamlet* as a "black play" in *Black Shakespeare*, 146.

57 As Parker explains: "The emphasis on blackness in the early texts of *Hamlet* might also be expected from the association of a personified blackness or of Moors with tragedy, mourning, revenge, and death. The tragic stage was traditionally hung with black (the 'sable garment' of Tourneur's *The Atheist's Tragedy*), assimilating it to the blackness of night described in Marston's *The Insatiate Countess* ('The stage of heaven, is hung with solemn black, / A time best fitting to act tragedies'). 'The stage is hung with black; and I perceive / The auditors prepared for tragedy', intones the Induction to Heywood's *A Warning for Fair Women*. Drayton's *Peirs Gaveston* invokes the 'cole-black darknes' of 'eternall night', and 'black spirits' with 'sable pens of direfull ebonie / To pen the process of my tragedie." "Black Hamlet," 139–140.

58 On November 11, 1991, Michael Jackson released "Black or White," the lead song from his album *Dangerous*. This quotation is taken from the chorus of that song. For more details, see https://en.wikipedia.org/wiki/Black_or_White.

59 As Heng observes, the distinction between black and white mattered even in the medieval period. See *The Invention of Race*, 16.

60 See the lyrics to "Black or White": https://genius.com/Michael-jackson-black-or-white-lyrics.

61 For the music video I reference, see https://youtu.be/F2AitTPI5Uo.

62 Elaborating on post-postracialism, I have noted elsewhere: "We might think of post-postracialism, then, as an extreme form of regression that has not just opened our eyes to the continued presence of racism – which is presently hypervisible, and even blatantly evident from the highest office in America – but also pulled our eyes out of their sockets so that our vision of the past and present, and our vision for the future, is constantly disturbed by the racial pain of our collectively damaged reality." David Sterling Brown, "'Hood Feminism': Whiteness and Segregated (Premodern) Scholarly Discourse in the Post-Postracial Era," *Literature Compass* 18.10 (2020), 1–15. Also see Smith, *Black Shakespeare*, 157.

63 Arthur L. Little, Jr., *Shakespeare Jungle Fever: National-Imperial Re-Visions of Race, Rape, and Sacrifice* (Stanford, CA: Stanford University Press, 2000); Ian Smith, *Race and Rhetoric in the Renaissance: Barbarian Errors* (New York: Palgrave, 2009); Ian Smith, *Black Shakespeare: Reading and Misreading Race* (Cambridge: Cambridge University Press, 2022); Crystal M. Fleming, *How to Be Less Stupid about Race: On Racism, White Supremacy, and the Racial Divide* (Boston, MA: Beacon Press, 2018); D. L. Hughley and Doug Moe, *How Not to Get Shot: And Other Advice from White People* (New York: William Morrow, 2018).

64 According to Birgit Rasmussen et al., "Whiteness does not exist as a credible biological property. But it is a social construction with real effects that has become a powerful organizing principle around the world. It is not always clear what we mean when we refer to race or whiteness because both empirical and theoretical accounts define them inconsistently or not at all." *The Making and Unmaking of Whiteness*, eds. Birgit Brander Rasmussen, Eric Klinenberg, Irene J. Nexica, and Matt Wray (Durham, NC: Duke University Press, 2001), 8. Martha R. Mahoney posits, "Race derives much of its power from seeming to be a natural or biological phenomenon or, at the very least, a coherent social category." "The Social Construction of Whiteness," 330.

65 Toni Morrison, *Playing in the Dark* (Cambridge, MA: Harvard University Press, 1992), 6–7.

66 Ibid., 6.

67 Hall, *Things of Darkness,* 7. Morrison adds: "There also exists, of course, a European Africanism with a counterpart in colonial literature," thus reminding us how darkness and otherness were not limited or unique to America but in fact mattered in an early modern context predating the transatlantic colonial enterprise. *Playing in the Dark*, 38.

68 Hall, *Things of Darkness,* 7.

69 Morrison, *Playing in the Dark*, 13.

70 In a previously published article, I explore various definitions of whiteness in a similar fashion as I do here. See David Sterling Brown, "I Feel Most White When I Am . . . : Foregrounding the 'Sharp White Background' of Anchuli Felicia King's *Keene*," *Shakespeare Bulletin*, 39.4 (2021), 577–593.

71 By retaining systemic control, "whites also define whiteness, albeit in ways that we cannot fully see, and then impose that vision on the world as much as [they] can." Martha R. Mahoney, "Racial Construction and Women as Differentiated Actors," in *Critical White Studies: Looking behind the Mirror*, eds. Richard Delgado and Jean Stefancic (Philadelphia, PA: Temple University Press, 1997), 305–309; 306.

72 Zeus Leonardo, "Tropics of Whiteness: Metaphor and the Literary Turn in White Studies," *Whiteness and Education*, 1.1 (2016), 3–14; 4.

73 Matthew W. Hughey, "The (Dis)similarities of White Racial Identities: The Conceptual Framework of 'Hegemonic Whiteness'," *Ethnic and Racial Studies*, 33.8 (September 2010), 1289–1309; 1290.

74 See Thomas Ross, "White Innocence, Black Abstraction," in *Critical White Studies: Looking behind the Mirror*, eds. Richard Delgado and Jean Stefancic (Philadelphia, PA: Temple University Press, 1997), 263–266.

75 Painter, *The History of White People*, 59–63.

76 Leonardo, "Tropics of Whiteness," 4.

77 Jonathan Burton asserts: "Race scavenges and improvises, calibrating to the moment whatever ideas are available." "Race," in *A Cultural History of Western Empires in the Renaissance (1450–1650)*, vol. III, ed. Ania Loomba (London: Bloomsbury, 2018), 203–224; 220.

78 White ideology is very much linked to a "violent history." See Leonardo, "Tropics of Whiteness," 4, 9.

79 I am indebted to Ben Crystal – actor, producer and author (*Shakespeare on Toast: Getting a Taste for the Bard* and other titles) – for mentioning *perfection* in a conversation about race that helped trigger my thinking about ideal whiteness as being a goal for white people. Interestingly, perfection was also a desired goal within Christian teachings that would have been familiar to Shakespeare's religious early modern audience.

80 Martha R. Mahoney observes that "race is a phenomenon always in formation. Therefore, whiteness, like other racial constructions, is subject to constant change. Whiteness is historically located, malleable, and contingent." "The Social Construction of Whiteness," 330.

81 Morrison once defined "distraction" as the "function" of racism. See: Portland State, "Black Studies Center Public Dialogue, Pt. 2" (May 30, 1975), https://soundcloud.com/portland-state-library/portland-state-black-studies-1.

82 Leonardo, "Tropics of Whiteness," 8.

83 Rasmussen et al. offer a few definitions of whiteness with which the various contributors to their volume engage: "Whiteness is invisible and unmarked"; "whiteness is 'empty' and white identity is established through appropriation"; "whiteness is structural privilege"; "whiteness is violence and terror"; "whiteness is the institutionalization of European colonialism"; and "critical whiteness studies is an antiracist practice." See "Introduction" in *The Making and Unmaking of Whiteness*, 10–14. Notably, "Du Bois was the first sociologist to develop the study of whiteness as lived experience." José Itzigsohn and Karida L. Brown, *The Sociology of W. E. B. Du Bois: Racialized Modernity and the Global Color Line* (New York: New York University Press, 2020), 22.

84 Hall, *Things of Darkness*, 211.

85 Morrison, *Playing in the Dark*, 63.

86 Watson, *The Souls of White Folk*, 5.

87 Ibid., 14.

88 Richard Delgado and Jean Stefancic, *Critical Race Theory: An Introduction* (New York: New York University Press, 2001), 17, 75, 76.

89 Peggy McIntosh, who gets much credit for the phrase "white privilege," outlines several of those privileges in "White Privilege: Unpacking the Invisible Knapsack," *Peace and Freedom* (July/August 1989), https://psychology.umbc.edu/files/2016/10/White-Privilege_McIntosh-1989.pdf.

90 Cheryl I. Harris, "Whiteness as Property," in *Critical Race Theory: The Key Writings that Formed the Movement*, eds. Kimberlé Crenshaw, Neil Gotanda, Gary Peller, and Kendall Thomas (New York: The New Press, 1995), 276–291, 282.

91 Robert Bernasconi claims that "Whiteness is an alliance, but it is not an alliance in which all partners are equal." "Waking Up White and in Memphis," in *White on White / Black on Black*, ed. George Yancy (New York: Rowman & Littlefield Publishers, Inc., 2005), 17–26; 19. Crispin

Startwell, in an analysis of the "wigger," thinks about whiteness in terms of "aesthetics, usually taken as unmarked and normative." "Wigger," in *White on White / Black on Black*, 35–48; 36. Monique Roelofs also explores "racial formations [as] aesthetic phenomena"in her "Racialization as an Aesthetic Production: What Does the Aesthetic Do for Whiteness and Blackness and Vice Versa?," in *White on White / Black on Black*, 83–124; 83, 102. Eduardo Bonilla-Silva compares the operations of whiteness to those of God, noting that "when whiteness becomes normative, it works like God, in mysterious ways." See Bonilla-Silva's opening vignette in "Toward a Definition of White Logic and White Methods," in *White Logic, White Methods: Racism and Methodology*, eds. Tukufu Zuberi and Eduardo Bonilla-Silva (New York: Rowman & Littlefield Publishers, Inc., 2008), 3–30; 13. Moreover, Zuberi and Bonilla-Silva present whiteness as a way of thinking, "the anchor of Western imagination, which grants centrality to the knowledge, history, science, and culture of elite White men and classifies 'others' as people without knowledge history or science, as people with folklore but not culture." They also present whiteness, in relationship to "white logic," as a set of "practices that have been used to produce 'racial knowledge' since the emergence of white supremacy in the fifteenth and sixteenth centuries and the disciplines a few centuries later" (Ibid., 17–18).

92 Judith H. Katz, *White Awareness: Handbook for Anti-Racism Training* (Norman: University of Oklahoma Press, 1978), 7, 10, 15.

93 During the 1964 National Democratic convention, Robert Kennedy spoke about his recently assassinated brother John F. Kennedy and quoted "take him and cut him out in little stars . . . " from *Romeo and Juliet*. As Juliet does with Romeo, Robert Kennedy makes a spectacle of whiteness as he alludes to Romeo via his own brother's twentieth-century death. See https://en.wikipedia.org/wiki/1964_Democratic_National_Convention.

94 Little, Jr., "Is It Possible to Read Shakespeare through Critical White Studies?," 276.

95 Matthieu Chapman, *Anti-Black Racism in Early Modern English Drama: The Other "Other"* (New York: Routledge, 2017), 19–20.

96 Ibid., 4. Smith, *Black Shakespeare*, 8.

97 Mary Floyd-Wilson, *English Ethnicity and Race in Early Modern Drama* (Cambridge: Cambridge University Press, 2003), 2.

98 Ibid., 19.

99 Fleming, *How to Be Less Stupid about Race*, 2.

100 Ibid., 5.

101 Ibid., 11.

102 Ibid., 14.

103 Jean Feerick, *Strangers in Blood: Relocating Race in the Renaissance* (Toronto: University of Toronto Press, 2010), 6.

104 Ibid., 10–12.

105 Floyd-Wilson, *English Ethnicity and Race*, 7.

106 Akhimie, *Shakespeare and the Cultivation of Difference*, 16.

107 Marianne Novy, *Shakespeare and Outsiders* (Oxford: Oxford University Press, 2013), 1.

108 Morrison, *The Origin*, 24.

109 Eva Johanna Holmberg, *Jews in the Early Modern English Imagination: A Scattered Nation* (New York: Routledge, 2016), 9.

110 Lynda E. Boose, "'The Getting of a Lawful Race': Racial Discourse in Early Modern England and the Unpresentable Black Woman," in *Women, Race, and Writing*, eds. Margo Hendricks and Patricia Parker (New York: Routledge, 1994), 35–54; 39–40. Also see M. Lindsay Kaplan, "Jessica's Mother: Medieval Constructions of Jewish Race and Gender in 'The Merchant of Venice,'" *Shakespeare Quarterly*, 58.1 (Spring 2007), 1–30.

111 Painter, *The History of White People*, xi.

112 Du Bois, *Souls*, 60.

113 As Itzigsohn and Brown note, "For Du Bois, the color-line affected all people of color and all colonized people around the world." *The Sociology of W. E. B. Du Bois*, 3. Also see Nikhil Pal Singh, *Black Is a Country: Race and the Unfinished Struggle for Democracy* (Cambridge, MA: Harvard University Press, 2005), 156–157. My intraracial color-line concept is invested in highlighting the adverse effects of racial division for all, especially white people.

114 Mahoney, "The Social Construction of Whiteness," 330.

115 Du Bois, *Souls*, 22.

116 Peter Fryer, *Black People in the British Empire: An Introduction* (London: Pluto Press, 1988), xii.

117 According to Fryer, "During the period of empire, racism permeated every field of intellectual life in Britain. In no field was its influence more pervasive, or more pernicious, then historiography. Children and young people were taught a version of history which idealized and glamorized Britain, and portrayed black people as inferior. Most of the respected names in British nineteenth-century historiography were racists, and most of them reflected in their writings one or other central tenets of racist ideology." *Black People*, 73. Also see Brown, "'Hood Feminism,'" 5–8.

118 See Helen Berry and Elizabeth Foyster, *The Family in Early Modern England* (Cambridge: Cambridge University Press, 2011), 3, 12, 13, 17; Linda Pollock, *Forgotten Children: Parent-Child Relations from 1500 to 1900* (Cambridge: Cambridge University Press, 1984), 6; Paul Griffiths, *Youth and Authority: Formative Experiences in England, 1560–1640* (New York: Oxford University Press, 1996) 2, 10; Peter Laslett, *Family Life and Illicit Love in Earlier Generations: Essays in Historical Sociology* (New York: Cambridge University Press, 1977), 38; David Cressy, *Birth, Marriage and Death: Ritual, Religion and the Life-Cycle in Tudor and Stuart England* (Oxford: Oxford University Press, 1999), 8; Alan MacFarlane, *Marriage and Love in England: Modes of Reproduction 1300–1840* (New York: Blackwell, 1987), 48; Alan MacFarlane, *The Family Life of Ralph Josselin, a Seventeenth-Century Clergyman* (New York: W. W. Norton and Company,

Inc., 1977), 4; Antony Buxton, *Domestic Culture in Early Modern England* (Woodbridge: Boydell Press, 2015), 1, 17; Richard Helgerson, *Adulterous Alliances: Home, State, and History in Early Modern European Drama and Painting* (Chicago: University of Chicago Press, 2000), 4; Bernard Clapp, *When Gossips Meet: Women, Family, and Neighbourhood in Early Modern England* (Oxford: Oxford University Press, 2003), v, 1; Anthony Fletcher, *Gender, Sex and Subordination in England, 1500–1800* (New Haven, CT: Yale University Press, 1999), xxi; Susan D. Amussen, *An Ordered Society: Gender and Class in Early Modern England* (New York: Columbia University Press, 1988), 38; Miriam Slater, *Family Life in the Seventeenth Century: The Verneys of Claydon House* (London: Routledge, 1984), 1; Ilana Krausman Ben-Amos, *Adolescence and Youth in Early Modern England* (New Haven, CT: Yale University Press, 1994), 9, 205; Don Herzog, *Household Politics: Conflict in Early Modern England* (New Haven, CT: Yale University Press, 2013), xi, 28, 150; and Wrightson, *English* Society, 9, 11.

119 Nikole Hannah-Jones, "Preface," in *The 1619 Project: A New Origin Story*, eds. Nikole Hannah-Jones, Caitlin Roper, Ilena Silverman, and Jake Silverstein (New York: OneWorld, 2021), xvii–xix, xxv, xxx.

120 On Peter Negro, Imtiaz Habib writes: "For his obvious exemplary valor he was knighted in Roxburgh [in 1547] and granted a princely pension of £100 for life. That Negro had by then a distinguished record of service with the Tudor government is evident in the repeated payments made to him in numerous years in the *Acts of the Privy Council* records cited earlier (*Acts of Privy Council of England*, II: 275, 279, 419, 427–428). Negro died in London in 1551, and his burial followed a public funeral procession that, according to one eyewitness, a Tudor London undertaker, had great pomp and ceremony," See "*Othello*, Sir Peter Negro, and Blacks of Early Modern England: Colonial Inscription and Postcolonial Excavation," *Literature Interpretation Theory*, 9.1 (2008), 15–30; 17.

121 Gretchen Gerzina, *Black England: Life before Emancipation* (London: John Murray Publishers Ltd., 1995), 3–4.

122 Ibid., 15.

123 Onyeka Nubia, *Blackamoores: Africans in Tudor England, Their Presence, Status, and Origins* (London, England: Narrative Eye Ltd., 2013), 120.

124 Ibid., 126–127.

125 Imtiaz Habib, *Black Lives in the English Archives, 1500–1677: Imprints of the Invisible* (New York: Routledge, 2008), 4.

126 In preparation for a Folger Institute Critical Race Conversation that we co-led, Jennifer Lynn Stoever remarked that "race happens." I use that phrase here because it denotes how race is an always activated, and therefore active, social phenomenon. A recording of our Folger conversation is available here: https://youtu.be/iBGSh4h-74U.

127 While Shakespeare's "Dark Lady" sonnets contain racialized discourse, so, too, do works by other early modern authors like John Donne ("The Flea," for example) and Edmund Spenser (*Amoretti*). Hall studied the "language of

fairness" in non-Shakespearean texts, for instance. See *Things of Darkness*, 177–210.

128 For example, gender, class, and race intersect in John Webster's *The Duchess of Malfi* (circa 1613) and generate ideas about the politics of white femininity in an oppressive white patriarchal society that is heavily influenced by the Duchess' brothers, Duke Ferdinand and the Cardinal. In *Edward II* (circa 1593), Christopher Marlowe's exclusively white play raises questions about Edward's and Gaveston's sexuality, in addition to concerns about parentage, homosocial bonds, and white women's inconstancy. Furthermore, Philip Massinger's *A New Way to Pay Old Debts* (circa 1625), which includes a strong surrogate white mother figure, Lady Allworth, offers insight into how whiteness demands alternative processes of endogamous familial (parent-child) construction in the absence of maternal and paternal blood bonds. John Lyly's *Gallathea* (circa 1583) promotes a patriarchal narrative about protecting white female beauty and chastity, whereas Thomas Kyd's *The Spanish Tragedy* (circa late 1580s) attends to the white woman's madness, among other racialized matters such as white-on-white violence and self-harm. And with respect to race and dramatic form, Thomas Middleton and Thomas Dekker's *The Roaring Girl* (circa 1610) and Thomas Dekker's *A Chaste Maid in Cheapside* (circa 1613) – two city comedies – reveal how whiteness can define the racial dynamics of an entire subgenre, a reality that is also true for the homogenous subgenre of early modern domestic tragedy in which some scholars situate *Othello* (1603) alongside plays like Thomas Heywood's *A Woman Killed with Kindness* (1603). Sean Benson pushes one of Shakespeare's more recognizable "race plays" into a dramatic category that appears to be all about whiteness, as I argue in "'Hood Feminism.'" According to Benson, "While *Othello* is a tragedy in broad terms, it fits more accurately within the specialized subgenre of domestic tragedy, and this has yet to be fully acknowledged – more often, in fact, the association is explicitly denied." *Shakespeare, Othello and Domestic Tragedy* (London: Bloomsbury, 2007), 3. Emma Whipday expands the *Othello*/domestic trag-edy conversation in *Shakespeare's Domestic Tragedies: Violence in the Early Modern Home* (Cambridge: Cambridge University Press, 2019). There are endless ways to explore race in Shakespearean and non-Shakespearean drama because race – especially whiteness – is always in the spotlight. Whiteness is always performing and being performed, as Margo Hendricks suggests in "Gestures of Performance: Rethinking Race in Contemporary Shakespeare," in *Colorblind Shakespeare: New Perspectives on Race and Performance*, ed. Ayanna Thompson (New York: Routledge, 2006), 187–203; 188.

129 For instance, see Daniel Trilling, "Why Is the UK Government Suddenly Targeting 'Critical Race Theory'?" *The Guardian* (October 23, 2020), https://www.theguardian.com/commentisfree/2020/oct/23/uk-critical-race-theory-trump-conservatives-structural-inequality.

130 Kim F. Hall, "Beauty and the Beast of Whiteness: Teaching Race and Shakespeare," *Shakespeare Quarterly*, 47.4 (Winter, 1996), 461–475.

131 David Sterling Brown, "Code Black: Whiteness and Unmanliness in *Hamlet*," in *Hamlet: The State of Play*, eds. Sonia Massai and Lucy Munro (London: The Arden Shakespeare, 2021), 101–127.

132 Also see Little, Jr., "Re-Historicizing Race," 88.

133 In the podcast "Speaking of Shakespeare," episode #27, Thomas Dabbs speaks with David Sterling Brown and leads into a conversation about white hands that draws an interesting commonality between Black and white hands. https://youtu.be/UJnSVBz9ujg.

134 In his poem, "Race Cards," Neal Hall suggests that the race card is not limited to Black people and that white people hold nearly all of the cards in the deck. In the last stanza, he writes: "You, that calls me, accuses me / of playing the race card / pulled from a deck of 51 / white playing cards bearing alone, / your palm's print." See *The Trembling Tiber: A Black Poet's Musings on Shakespeare's Julius Caesar* (Stockholm: l'Aleph, 2020), 75.

135 David Sterling Brown and Jennifer Lynn Stoever, "'Blanched with Fear': Reading the Racialized Soundscape in Macbeth," *Shakespeare Studies*, 50 (2022), 33–43.

136 In *The Comedy of Errors*, Adriana says to Luciana: "A wretched soul, bruised with adversity, / We bid be quiet when we hear it cry" (2.1.34–35).

137 Adrienne Kennedy, "Funnyhouse of a Negro," in *The Adrienne Kennedy Reader* (Minneapolis: University of Minnesota Press, 2001), 11–26.

138 Troy Duster, "The 'Morphing' Properties of Whiteness," in Rasmussen et al., *The Making and Unmaking of Whiteness*, 132.

CHAPTER I

Somatic Similarity
The White Other and Titus Andronicus

> Given that the concept of racial hierarchy is a strategy employed to make visible what has been intentionally represented as inevitable, whiteness is an important aspect of any conversation about race.
>
>   – The Racial Imaginary Institute Curatorial Team[1]

> Realize one might also make strange what seems obvious, nearby, close.
>
>   – Beth Loffreda and Claudia Rankine, *The Racial Imaginary*[2]

Even when racial similarity exists in the form of skin color, one can still find in early modern discourse racialized difference that affirms the reality of the racial hierarchy while hinting at its instability.[3] Thus, I begin this chapter on *Titus Andronicus* in an unlikely place:[4] with Shakespeare's *Macbeth*, a tragedy that is set in Scotland and centers white people and their experiences. I want to highlight briefly how *Macbeth* exemplifies several of this book's concerns in relation to gender, genre, domesticity, mental well-being, anti-Blackness, power, violence, and, of course, intraracial tension. Through the application of my intraracial color-line theory and the white other concept, I discovered *Macbeth* has an interracial couple (beyond what Amy Scott-Douglass refers to),[5] a pairing that always signals racialized conflict in Shakespeare.[6] In this dramatic work, there is "fair and noble hostess" Lady Macbeth (1.6.24),[7] who embodies masculine qualities, and "black Macbeth" (4.3.53), who fails to embody strong white patriarchal masculinity, as his wife complains (1.7.48–62).[8] The dark, less-than-ideal Macbeths are obvious white others, along with the play's several murderers and Macdonwald, a Scottish rebel who is killed by Macbeth and does not appear in the play. What these different figures have in common, beyond revealing themselves as uncivilized, violent white people, a woman and men, are their sinful violations of whiteness: the Macbeths execute the killing of their esteemed domestic guest, King Duncan, and violate hospitality code; Macdonwald, similar to the previously mentioned Robert

Figure 1.1   Macbeth, Act 3, Scene 4 by Tobias Bauer (nineteenth century printmaker). Image 29151, used by permission of the Folger Shakespeare Library.

Devereux, organizes a rebellion against Scotland; and the murderer characters noted in the dramatis personae are responsible for the deaths of Banquo and of Macduff's family. For their betrayals of whiteness, one can in a sense consider them all "race traitors," a topic I touch on in the Conclusion, as these characters do not adhere to contemporary standards and expectations of white hegemony. Moreover, they engage in white-on-white violence. These are a couple of the reasons they appear darker in Figure 1.1, separated from the whiter-looking background figures and blending in, color-wise, with the slaughtered beast on the banquet table that separates the Macbeths from their peers.

With respect to understanding the intraracial color-line and the white other, *Macbeth*'s Three Witches – the "black and midnight hags" – articulate what I read as a useful theory that underscores the potential for less-than-ideal, uncouth whiteness to exist (4.1.48). At the play's onset, in unison, they declare: "Fair is foul, and foul is fair" (1.1.11). The integration of foulness and fairness, read respectively as synonymous with blackness and whiteness (synonyms I explore in Chapters 2 and 3), illuminate a gray area where whiteness polices blackness to negotiate its own meaning in the absence of Black people. Like Richard III, who finds himself "so far in blood that sin will pluck on sin" (4.2.64), Macbeth finds himself "in blood / Stepped in so far" by the play's climax, reminding us on which side of the intraracial color-line to situate him at that point (3.4.137–138). While I will not analyze here everything that makes *Macbeth* a suitable text to (re)read through the critical lens that defines *Shakespeare's White Others*, I must emphasize a key observation: Macbeth's conflicts make him a fascinating case study because he crosses the intraracial color-line and is, like the Romans and Goths in *Titus*, a convertible white figure. In his case, he begins the play on the right side of the intraracial color-line, so to speak, policing villainous whiteness as a respected member of the dominant culture. Eventually, he becomes one who has "black and deep desires," thus representing the kind of whiteness that needs eradicating, a blackened whiteness that Macduff eventually does destroy (1.4.51). Unlike Malcolm, whose retained white goodness enables him to erase the "black scruples" from his "soul" (4.3.116–117),[9] Macbeth can do no such thing after killing his King and Macduff's family because he permanently mars his once presumably good white soul – "what's done cannot be undone" (5.1.68). As *Macbeth* and *Titus* demonstrate, through imagination, and through images, the white other *becomes*. Through their diminished racial whiteness, the white other becomes metaphorically blackened. As a result, they may even become blackballed or blacklisted . . . black somehow, somehow black . . . in ways that perpetuate the casualness of anti-Black racism and that sustain the centuries-old myth of white superiority.

"Into a Pit of Ink": The Emerging White Other

As *Titus* dramatizes with transparency, racial whiteness is a tiresomely high-maintenance enterprise. It is important to note that the premodern white other was created *only* in, and as far as scholars know, for the white mind.[10] So, we can also think of this figure as a psychological phenomenon, a kind of literal manifestation of a fragmented, split white self that underscores and actualizes what is unhealthy about racism because it generates white identity incongruity. Distinguished from hegemonic whiteness, and also a rejected figure, the white other stabilizes the inferior position of Black people at the bottom of the racial hierarchy. This is relatively unsurprising since we know the early modern English relied on blackness, physical and symbolic, to conceptualize their own sense of self.[11] The incessant reliance on blackness is what makes the white identity itself an unstable one;[12] and the incessant influence of anti-Blackness makes the Black identity difficult to keep stable as well. Nobody wins. Yet, the white other's presence implies stability is the goal. This is particularly evident given white hegemony's constant striving to protect its racial ideals as it reproduces itself and its racist ideologies to ensure the sustainability of white dominance. Shifting the optic slightly, one can also imagine the white other as an (in)visible bulwark against "white racial grief," what Michael Eric Dyson considers a defense mechanism that protects and insulates white people from losing their pure social, political, and cultural meaning, and most importantly from losing their superiority.[13]

The white other is a figure whose internally diminished whiteness contrasts with ideal hegemonic whiteness, however the dominant culture defines it. And sometimes, the definition fluctuates on a whim, as *Titus* suggests. In other words, the white other is the dominant culture's ready-made foil designed to fortify social expectations for fully acceptable white racial identity and conduct. I borrow, and refashion for the early modern context, the concept of the "white other" from Lauren S. Cardon's study, *The "White Other" in American Intermarriage Stories, 1945–2008*, which examines fictional intermarriage narratives to explore how ethnic/racial groups are differentiated and how American identity is constructed within "contemporary politics or [in association with] social norms."[14] Cardon studies popular film and literary examples, such as Disney's *Pocahontas* (1995),[15] that illustrate dynamics where the white person (settler John Smith in Disney's film), rather than the racial/ethnic Other (the Indigenous peoples, that is, Pocahontas and the Powhatan People),[16] is positioned as Other because they are a minority representation of whiteness in a larger group that is culturally, ethnically, or somatically different.

Contrastingly, my white other concept diverges from Cardon's in that I am interested in analyzing how abstract spiritual, ethical, or moral distinctions among white people – the kind evident in humanist Renaissance scholar and philosopher Desiderius Erasmus' *Weltbild* and Christian eurocentrism[17] – can create the appearance of otherness (in relationship to blackness or sin), even in moments where everyone shares the same racial/ethnic makeup, as I reinforce in this book. The primary function of my white other concept is to establish a way to other whiteness, for instance, beyond the kinds of cultural differences depicted in a film like *My Big Fat Greek Wedding*, where a waspy white guy, Ian Miller, "is othered by Toula's Greek family," a family that would be considered racially white by today's standards.[18]

As outlined in the Preface, the white other is critically useful because this figure enhances contemporary understandings of the Black/white racial binary when we interpret it as a system containing white,[19] white other, and Black,[20] a racial system that offers, to quote scholar Francesca T. Royster, "a more complex construction of whiteness that is forever patrolling and disciplining the variations within it [and] help[ing] us to better understand the costs of white supremacy."[21] The white other exposes the confusion that racism generates[22] as well as the one-sidedness of criticism that makes race and racialization solely about non-whiteness without recognizing that whiteness, too, matters.[23] For instance, in *Barbarous Play: Race on the Renaissance Stage*, Lara Bovilsky comments that "racialization of a character is often accompanied by derogatory rhetoric";[24] however, with respect to white hegemony, and the racialization of white people, Bovilsky's claim does not quite hold. *Titus* is a key Shakespeare play to explore how the white other concept works, because the drama contains three distinct groups and attempts, but fails, to solidify a clear boundary between them: the Romans (white), the Goths (white other), and the Moors (Black). The Du Boisian color-line, separating white and white other from Black in my reading, and the intraracial color-line, separating white from white other and Black, are visible in Shakespeare's first tragedy. Hierarchical distinctions are apparent among the three groups in relation to who is more superior to whom, with Aaron and his Black son positioned as most abject, despite the Black baby having matrilineal "royal" white blood (5.1.49). Additionally, hierarchical distinctions are made within the play between the Romans and Goths, albeit with blurry boundaries.

Violence, No Moor: Titus *without Aaron*

In Act 1 of *Titus*, the present absence of Aaron, a Black Moor, is impossible to miss: He enters with the Goth prisoners but never speaks, as critics have noted.[25] He is, as I assert in my essay "Remixing the Family: Blackness and Domesticity in Shakespeare's *Titus Andronicus*," a silent observer in the role of racial/cultural assessor.[26] If one puts oneself in Aaron's shoes in Act 1, then one, too, can become a racial/cultural assessor of the play's intraracial conflicts, which are complicated later by Aaron's deliberately distracting interventions. Beyond seeing Aaron as silent observer, there are other ways to view his purpose, especially considering that Shakespeare's plays were written to be performed. Although hard to miss because of his Blackness, Aaron is not the focal point; the Du Boisian and intraracial color-lines keep him at the bottom of the racial hierarchy – in his prescribed Black place, marginalized and silent.

Without a voice in Act 1, Aaron has no choice, like us, but to listen to and hear, or read, whiteness; and the experience for us all is quite useful for affirming what Shakespeare centers in this play's opening. Whiteness is the *only* thing we hear. Thus, our "listening ears,"[27] guided by the racially white characters' thoughts and subsequent actions, are exclusively tuned into their interpersonal problems before Shakespeare complicates things in Act 2 when he formally introduces Aaron. This Black character adds another dimension to the play's interracial and intraracial dynamics through his relationship with Tamora and through the later introduction of their somatically Black child. But what is *Titus* without Aaron and his baby? What is *Titus* without giving the audience or the characters the opportunity to focus on racial difference or to be overtly racist?[28] Alluding to Toni Morrison, I ask, what happens when we "take [Aaron] out of it?"[29] This is the serious question I seek to answer in this chapter as I engage with what Morrison refers to as white people's "very, very serious problem," racism. It is a problem that "*they* should start thinking about what *they* can do about it."[30]

When used purposefully, *Titus* can function as an integral antiracist tool, as I and other scholars have argued in different ways. It is a generative text for aiding that "thinking" that white people need to do, because it isolates white people's conduct and also exploits what Anthony Gerard Barthelemy calls "the allegorical possibilities of blackness."[31] It is essential to reflect on Aaron's preliminary absence, since doing so permits the concentration on the white other. The play's first lines, spoken by Roman Saturninus, are a call for intraracial and, perhaps, even intrafamilial violence. In a quarrel with his younger brother, Bassianus, over the royal succession, Saturninus urges his followers to "defend the justice of my cause with arms; / And, countrymen, my loving followers, / Plead my successive titles with your swords" (1.1.24).[32] This defense of primogeniture emphasizes the play's preliminary divisions that evolve into bigger conflicts between intraracial "factions" in this opening Act (1.1.18). Saturninus' address to his "countrymen" is intraracially suggestive in light of Aaron's later use of the term "countryman" (4.2.154), said in reference to Black Muly. The white Romans who follow Saturninus believe in a cause that contrasts with the support Bassianus' followers show him (1.1.9). The opposing value systems here symbolically reflect the dynamic between white hegemony, which champions cultural standards and tradition, and the white other figure, which contradicts dominant social norms.

On a micro level, on one side of the intraracial color-line, Shakespeare showcases brothers fighting brothers, Romans fighting Romans, a dynamic that is echoed in later quarrels in this scene when Titus' son Mutius gets in his way and when Titus at first refuses to let Mutius, whom he has killed, be buried in the family tomb. This intrafamilial moment is worth pausing on. It offers insight into the relationship between power and whiteness and between white power and the exclusionary practices that can create intraracial tension. Right before stabbing Mutius within the play's first three hundred lines, Titus refers to him as *"villain* boy" (1.1.291).[33] This phrasing signals the father's clear disapproval and the son's now dark enemy status, a status that is applied to Black Aaron throughout the play by the white characters. When confronted by his son Lucius and brother Marcus for being "unjust," Titus doubles down on his quick extermination of Mutius (1.1.293). Largely due to his tragic flaw, his unwavering loyalty to the state, he then tries to distance himself from the family members whom he now considers to be "traitors" (1.1.297, 350) and "foes" (1.1.367) who "dishonor[ed]" him (1.1.296). In this troubled white moment, the intraracial color-line emerges and so, too, does Titus' *potential* to become the white other. When Marcus chastises Titus and exclaims, "Thou art a Roman, be not barbarous," he attempts to reign in the Andronici's incensed patriarch. Marcus asserts a core difference between what it means to be a good white Roman and a barbarous white other. In fact, it is a difference he establishes in his opening speech, when he informs the audience of "the weary wars against the barbarous Goths" who were ruled by Tamora, the ethnically different white woman who quickly becomes Saturninus' new wife and Rome's new empress (1.1.28).[34]

By becoming "incorporate in Rome," Tamora and her living Goth sons cross the intraracial color-line (1.1.463). Tamora's ascension, to which Aaron calls attention in his opening speech (2.1.1), enables her swift transition in status, a transition that Rome's most powerful male political figure sanctions. Tamora's gender and whiteness afford her the privilege of influencing how things shift with respect to intraracial tension. Bassianus, her now brother-in-law, and Titus' family quickly become viewed as a "faction": the "father and his traitorous sons," as Tamora calls them (1.1.452–453). And Saturninus sees himself as "dishonored openly" by them all (1.1.432). What he perceives as public humiliation and disrespect interestingly amplifies Titus' earlier rhetoric, articulated after the Mutius conflict. In the eyes of Saturninus and Tamora, the two white political figures with the most power, Titus loses respect as well as his previously revered status. At a dizzyingly rapid rate, the opening scene reflects just how confusing intraracial tension is in *Titus*. The opening scene also illustrates how racialized designations, and diminished statuses along the color-lines, are violent power moves the dominant culture uses to sustain its authority.

Upon close reading, then, Act 1, Scene 1 leaves us with very little to say that is good about white people's behavior, that of the dominant culture and the barbarous Goths, whose otherness is initially signaled by their being cultural outsiders and Rome's enemies.[35] While physical and moral whiteness are pedestalized, in relation to Lavinia, for example (1.1.52), those attributes are simultaneously torn down and presented at the onset as chaotic, violent, untrustworthy, "dishonor[able]," (1.1.13) "traitorous," "lawless," (1.1.313) and "quarrel[some]" (1.1.466). Without Aaron to serve as an embankment upon which whiteness can fashion itself and center its victimization in the beginning, it becomes easier to see that white hegemony is hardly as good and pious as it presents itself. It requires Black Aaron, and blackening, as a distracting scapegoat.

The messiness of intraracial relations, and how we are to read the Goths in the opening scene, is further complicated by Tamora's assumption of shared whiteness – what might be understood as the macro-level intraracial conflict that persists throughout the play. The Goth Queen does not immediately recognize that her Goth whiteness is not at first perceived as the same as Roman whiteness, because she invests too much in what Margo Hendricks has referred to as the "idea of commonality."[36] Tamora does not accept that the dominant culture, despite her easy assimilation,[37] could view her as uncivilized and see her for what she is not, as Virginia Mason Vaughan suggests.[38] This failure on her part to understand how "this Rome is also a colonial power,"[39] as Vaughan notes, further denotes the existence of a boundary between the dominant culture and white others, a boundary that becomes evident at this point in the play when the Goth Queen begs the "Roman brethren" to spare her eldest son Alarbus' life from sacrifice (1.1.104).

The usage of "brethren" by Tamora toward the Romans reveals her emphasis on the similarity of racial whiteness, yet it also underscores the significant cultural difference between the two groups that the opening scene reinforces ad nauseam. When Titus, Lucius, and Lavinia use the term "brethren" just a few lines later in reference to the Andronici (1.1.122, 1.1.146, 1.1.160), they clarify that for them the term represents family and that, in the Foucauldian sense, it is exclusionary in its sole consideration of the blood that binds their living and dead kin.[40] Moreover, their usage of brethren establishes a boundary between colonizer and colonized that mirrors "1590s anxieties about the confrontation between a European power and the 'barbarian' peoples it seeks to conquer."[41] The Andronici's rebuttal of Tamora's attempt at unconditional solidarity among white people is clear in its non-reciprocation: from the Andronici's perspective, the Goths are not brethren, regardless of their shared whiteness. There is something about Goth whiteness that automatically distinguishes them from the Romans.

Despite the difference, Tamora's being of the right "hue" (1.1.262) – a recognizably "fair" hue (1.1.264)[42] – enables her advantageous marriage to Saturninus and her and her sons' "advance[ment]" in Rome (1.1.331). Her socio-political ascension suggests she occupied a lower status as an outsider even in her position as freed prisoner of war. Surely her ascension relates to social class, but I would also argue that it is something more than class since, before coming to Rome, Tamora was a queen, as her son Demetrius reminds us in his lamentation about when "Goths were Goths," when they were the dominant culture and had access to ruling-class power and privilege in a non-Roman domestic landscape (1.1.140). The Goth entrance into Rome denotes a potential shift in their racial perception. This shift is affirmed by the sacrifice of Tamora's eldest son. Moreover, the Goth entrance into Rome marks an undoing of their racialized self-perception, which Tamora thinks she reclaims when Saturninus, opposed to the Andronici "faction" in this moment (1.1.405), as he proclaims, sanctions her becoming "incorporate in Rome" – albeit in a way that does not fully erase her othered status (1.1.463).[43]

What results in Act 1 through the two Roman brothers' marriages is a familial mixture of white people and white others. This mixture keeps intact the early modern prioritization of endogamous racial relations and it makes room for the utilization of emblematically blackened white figures to help define comparatively white Roman goodness.[44] Saturninus claims that "lovely Tamora, Queen of Goths, / That like the stately Phoebe 'mongst her nymphs / Dost overshine the gallant'st dames of Rome" (1.1.316–318). His link between the Goth Queen and Phoebe further speaks to endogamy and Tamora's socio-political elevation.[45] What Saturninus implies is that Tamora, while in Rome, is not of Rome. Nevertheless, the distinction does not preclude the acceptability of her attractiveness because she is of the right hue, an exalted hue. As such, the intraracial beauty contest Tamora wins here adds another layer to the various ways whiteness is in conflict with itself in violent and non-violent ways. Much is at stake for whiteness in *Titus*.

Thus, to return to my earlier engagement with Toni Morrison: *Titus* without Aaron, what *is* it? What does Shakespeare create for us to see and hear when he does not center the Black voice and body in Act 1, and other moments where Aaron does not appear, such as Act 2, Scenes 2 and 4 and Act 4, Scene 3? What is left for analysis if one takes seriously the notion that Aaron, a fictional Black sixteenth-century figure who would have been performed by a white actor in blackface, exists primarily as a distraction? What is left if one sees Aaron primarily as a literary device that draws our attention to this play's engagement with the color-lines – Du Boisian and intraracial – in ways that complicate notions of how manmade racial hierarchies and racial whiteness are constructed? *Titus* without Aaron is Romans fighting Romans, Goths fighting Romans, and Goths fighting Goths. *Titus* without Aaron is white people abusing, deceiving, raping, mutilating, cannibalizing, lying to, and fighting with white people, which "Tamora's unbounded [white] power in Rome" frees her to do.[46] *Titus* without Aaron exemplifies how, according to Jack D'Amico:

> The Moor as villain becomes a convenient locus for those darkly subversive forces that threaten European society from within but that can be projected onto the outsider. The destructive forces of lust and violence are thus distanced by being identified with a cultural, religious, or racial source of evil perceived as the inversion of European norms. And yet to the extent that the alien is imaginatively understood, the audience recognizes that the most stereotypical image mirrors those desires and energies that work from within.[47]

Aaron's Black presence conveniently amplifies what we see in the lusty, violent Goths who serve as an intraracial source of evil that is supposed to contrast with normative Roman, or English, behavior. By having the Goths in the play, *Titus* projects racial stereotypes onto the white other and the somatically different Other.[48] Yet, with the Black man isolated in Act 1, away from the action and discourse, we see that whiteness reflects back to itself what it seems to hate most.

In mirroring itself, whiteness illuminates how projection operates. D. Marvin Jones argues in *Race, Sex, and Suspicion: The Myth of the Black Male* that "Black identity through the lens of the dominant perspective is by definition alien and savage. [The black male] is received not as subject, but as an object onto which whites may project their fears."[49] Without Aaron, blame in *Titus* rests squarely on white people's shoulders, even though the play – with Aaron – does its best to put the onus on Aaron for Rome's collapse, as Matthieu Chapman argues.[50] Scrutinizing

Titus without Aaron makes it inconceivable to suggest that he "justly" deserves his torturous death-by-starvation sentence.[51] *Titus* without Aaron renders it impossible to criminalize him and his Blackness, and label him a skilled criminal."[52] And *Titus* without Aaron, especially in Act 1, allows one to call into question the "invisible badge of inherited superiority"[53] white people wear, inside and outside of the play. It is the badge that grants them permission to participate in the white patriarchal and supremacist stereotyping of Black men, Black people, as racially inferior and threatening.[54] Promoting Aaron's "menacing presence in Rome may expose the darker side of Rome, and by extension, England." It is a personal-critical choice with a risky payoff.[55] To be clear: The darker side of Rome exists well before Aaron has a chance to say or do anything other than be a prisoner of war;[56] this makes what seems like a critical hyperfocus on Aaron's Blackness and villainy troubling, especially because it oversimplifies white people's victim status in the play. Aaron has no part in the micro- and macro-level intraracial issues that initiate the play's conflicts. In Act 1, where whiteness is central and centered, Aaron is as innocent as his Black son.[57]

Convertibility: Goth "Friends," Goth "Foes"

In the field-shifting article "White-limed Walls: Whiteness and Gothic Extremism in Shakespeare's *Titus Andronicus*," Francesca T. Royster critiques racial whiteness by suggesting that "Tamora is represented as hyperwhite" because of a distinction in her "hue," a term that appears in the play several times.[58] My own thinking on whiteness in *Titus* is indebted to Royster's pioneering central argument that "Tamora's whiteness is racially marked, is made visible," as her reading of *Titus*, in line with earlier calls by Hall and MacDonald for whiteness to be on the critical table,[59] helped lay the groundwork for a more persistent interrogation of whiteness by premodern critical race studies scholars.[60] Royster directly highlights Tamora's otherness and "alien whiteness," reading the Goth body as marked by "hyperwhite[ness]."[61] Yet, to me, the play suggests the Goths, and even some of the Romans at times, exude a whiteness that is less-than (ideal). That is to say, they embody substandard whiteness, particularly as the cultural outsiders. I agree with Royster that there are levels of racial whiteness, and that the play complicates how we can read whiteness. However, I ultimately offer a different view on *Titus*' engagement with whiteness: In the context of the intraracial color-line, I depart from Royster's reading to recognize that the Goths' racialized difference is

an internal matter enabled by what Leonardo refers to as "flexible whiteness."[62] This racialized difference, which is what makes the Goths foes one
minute and friends the next, has everything to do with how the Romans
interpret the moral character of these cultural outsiders and how they
manipulate their position in relationship to the Goths, based on what is on
the inside. For example, one can consider how the Goths think and
subsequently present themselves as participants, wittingly or unwittingly,
in supporting white hegemony.

In being introduced as white others, Tamora's Goth faction is distinguished from the Romans from the play's beginning, and they are presented as a danger to dominant ideals and idealized whiteness.[63] Tamora is
not a chaste Lavinia; and the former's sexually voracious sons are not
suitable white men for Lavinia. If Tamora and her sons are pale, somatically speaking, as Royster notes, then internally they are as dark as
Shakespeare makes Aaron out to be. Mapped onto and into these Goths'
bodies, and sometimes Roman bodies, is the intraracial tension the play
grapples with throughout. They are white on the outside, but considered
dark on the inside from the racist perspective. As such, it is fitting to read
the Goths as less-than-ideal white people, or hypo-white people, with
respect to their interiority, as defined in Marcus' preliminary description
of the "weary wars" the Romans have fought against these inferior white
others (1.1.28). Presented as barbarous, lascivious, and marginalized, they
are not depicted as better than the Romans in any positive way despite
managing to take over the play's center for a bit. And the fact that another
set of Goths becomes Lucius' "friends" in Act 5, Scene 1 does not change
their barbaric nature, per se. If anything, it is their alleged barbarism, or
maybe his own barbarousness, that Lucius taps into when he seeks help
from them to reclaim Rome for the Andronici. Like the racist or xeno-
phobe who tolerates the existence of Black people when it is convenient,
Lucius accepts the Goths on an as needed basis. His acceptance does
not require him to erase the Romans' overall or initial negative perception
of the Goths, nor does it require him to relinquish his relative
white superiority.

Ideal whiteness depends on how one adheres to the tenets of whiteness
as prescribed by the dominant culture. The consequence of not adhering is
exclusion. Amplifying Thandeka's assertion about white community,[64]
Royster asserts that "white group identity is enforced by the threat of exile
and fundamental shame."[65] I would add that acceptance into whiteness
may also require some form of initiation, as the Goths are only released to
Saturninus and freed after one of them, Alarbus, pays with his life the

group's entry fee into the cult of Roman whiteness. To gain admission, Tamora must lose her eldest son; in effect, he must be excluded from the play. After this occurs, Tamora ascends, and she can masquerade as an imperial Roman white woman who is afforded the protection of white men. Scholar Morwenna Carr posits that this is the case in the forest scene (Act 2, Scene 3), when Tamora's sons defend her motherly honor against the Romans, Bassianus and Lavinia, who "see [Tamora's] proximity to Aaron's Black body as discolouring her [external] hyperwhiteness,"[66] a discoloring that cannot be undone once the baby appears. That Tamora gives birth to a physically Black baby also suggests the notion of hypo-whiteness is at play, in that her diminished whiteness makes way for Blackness.[67] Carr's assertion about discoloring underscores my sense that the Goths' whiteness is diminished, for the Goth brothers also maintain proximity to Aaron, their self-proclaimed "tutor" or surrogate parental figure (5.1.98).[68]

Bassianus' and Lavinia's attacks on Tamora's moral character and "honor" are reminders of her difference (2.3.73). "Dismounted from [her] snow-white goodly steed," Tamora finds herself physically and rhetorically in a liminal space in the forest scene: between her white Roman husband, represented in the steed image, and Black Aaron. This love triangle perfectly elucidates how the racial hierarchy works; Tamora and her Goth sons, the white others, occupy a space between hegemonic whiteness and Blackness – the space dedicated to uncouth whiteness. The white woman's sexual, reproductive body is an integral component of this system, which relies on her to generate white offspring. However, once there is incontrovertible evidence she has failed in that role, proof provided in Act 4, Scene 2 when the Black baby emerges from the "surer side" (line 127), it is undeniably evident she betrays whiteness, or maybe whiteness betrays her. For the offense, she finds herself literally "throw[n] forth" and cast out (5.3.198). All who jeopardize the safeguarding of white supremacy – not just the "colored alien,"[69] as Habib labels such figures, but even white people, too – must be written out.[70]

White Powder, White Power: The White Other Devoured

Goth convertibility is not limited to their being both friends and foes, for it turns out the Goths have a variety of exploitative functions, including culinary uses. In one of *Titus'* most central domestic scenes,[71] the Andronici's revenge takes a gruesome, cannibalistic turn. Having been left in Titus' white hands by their neglectful mother Tamora, Chiron and

Demetrius – disguised as "Rape" and "Murder" (5.2.62) – meet a most horrific fate for their rape and mutilation of Lavinia and for being "a pair of cursèd hellhounds" (5.2.144). The explicit association of the Goth brothers with the demonic, in addition to their dehumanization, is enough to remind us that this play's outsider discourse is nuanced in that it employs a white cultural outsider binary: the good and the bad Goths. And we know these brothers belong to the latter group because of their treacherous deeds, and because Titus labels them "foes" after having them bound like animals (5.2.166). Interestingly, as I noted earlier in this chapter, Titus refers to his own family members as foes in Act 1, Scene 1. These Goths, unlike the ones to whom Lucius appeals for support in Act 5, Scene 1 (lines 1–8), exemplify the type of white others the play seeks to control explicitly, the white other the play must purge due to moral blackness.[72] These Goths, perhaps more so than Aaron, underscore why white hegemony must restore order in Rome if it wants to ensure its survival. A Goth that is a foe is the most dangerous kind of Goth there is. And the Goths' ability to pass as royal white friends is also what makes their presence troubling since they can hide in plain sight. Titus' actions in this scene reveal his awareness of the intraracial threat, but also irreversibly compromise his own whiteness. The Andronici patriarch's deliberate incorporation of the Goth's whiteness into the play's famous pasties make his culinary concoction a noteworthy part of the play's (intra)racial narrative, a point to which I will return shortly.

Before analyzing the white powder Titus produces, I will examine the language and logic that gets him to that point. His discourse is racialized and supports the intraracial color-line's function. With Lavinia by his side, Titus contrasts Roman whiteness with Goth whiteness, or white hegemony and the white other. With palpable anger, he notes:

> Here stands the spring whom you have stained with mud,
> This goodly summer with your winter mixed.
> You killed her husband, and for that vile fault
> Two of her brothers were condemned to death,
> My hand cut off and made merry jest;
> Both her sweet hands, her tongue, and that more dear
> Than hands or tongue, her spotless chastity,
> Inhuman traitors, you constrained and forced.
>
> (5.2.170–177)

Lavinia's predicament echoes *Much Ado*'s fallen woman narrative, although Titus makes it clear Lavinia had no agency. She, like Hero, who is imagined to be stained and blackened because of a lie, is seen as impure; she is, like *Hamlet*'s Ophelia, muddied,[73] albeit figuratively, and essentially socially dead. Yet, the fault for her uncleanliness lies solely with the Goth brothers. Still, Lavinia represents the play's sullied white hegemonic female figure, one whose father still sees her as "goodly" because of her white skin and Roman blood, the latter reflecting her internal whiteness. The mixing of Goth and Roman blood through the illicit sex – the mixing of white female and white *other* male bodies and body parts – reinforces the play's insistence on making and marking the cultural distinction between Goths and Romans at times, and between ideal and less-than-ideal whiteness.[74] Positioning that point in the context of the intra-racial color-line and white other constructions, I would add that the difference between the play's white people is indeed intraracial, not just cultural, given that Shakespeare portrays the Goths and Romans at times as representing diminished whiteness, thus supporting much of the previously mentioned criteria that define the white other.

Centered in Titus' speech are the wrongs done directly to white Roman men – Bassianus, Martius, Quintus, and Titus – with Lavinia, of course, being an extension of those abhorrent wrongs, an image of violated hegemonic whiteness. I will revisit white male protection of the white(ned) woman in Chapter 3. With three Roman white men killed, three white hands cut off and one white woman's tongue cut out, the Romans have been dis-membered in what Scott Lindsey calls the play's "spectacles of violence."[75] However, nothing strikes Titus as being more of a precious loss in this moment than Lavinia's chastity, which was first her father's white property and then her betrothed Bassianus' property that was stolen by Tamora's sons, and nearly stolen by his brother Saturninus. Lavinia becomes less-than-ideal due to her rape and mutilation. These Roman bodies, limbs, and wounds depict the many ways a select group of white others took power – vocal, sexual, physical, psychological – away from white hegemony. In a different Scene in this same Act, when Lucius refers to a set of Goths as "friends," Titus refers to them as "traitors," thus exposing the Goths' unstable position in this play. As a reminder, Titus also treats his son Mutius like a traitor and kills him as a result. The dominant culture uses the white other to perpetuate whatever narrative needs advancing in a given moment; the Goth status as other helps justify the Romans' contradictory rhetorical categorization of them. And since these particular Goths, Chiron and Demetrius, are "inhuman," they will be treated as such, and inhumanely, too.

To right the wrongs committed against his family members, Titus must war with whiteness and try to overpower this set of Goth foes. He must destroy the white other whose adopted Roman royalty significantly jeopardizes domestic stability. As this play suggests, a most delectable kind of revenge is found on Titus' dinner table and lies in one of his key cooking ingredients:[76] a powder-like substance made of Chiron's and Demetrius' bones. The bone-white powder Titus creates by "grind[ing Goth] bones to dust" might be read as a racialized substance that represents the literal physical breakdown of the white others. This breakdown ends when Tamora unsuspectingly cannibalizes her sons and is then herself killed. Mixed with Goth blood, a substance also treated as a racial marker in the early modern period,[77] the bone powder signifies grotesque intraracial violence. It also signifies the reclaiming of white hegemonic power in a moment that echoes the "sacrifice" of Tamora's son Alarbus at the play's start (1.1.124).

Chiron's and Demetrius' murders are the continuation of the white others' extermination that was religiously justified earlier in the play. Brought in as prisoners of the state, these othered figures follow a trajectory that demands their annihilation. There is even more urgency directed at their demise than at Aaron's. He receives a slower, more torturous death. Consequently, he gets to have a disruptive voice that forms nearly half of *Titus'* final seventeen lines.[78] The concluding graphic, bloody violence spares Aaron and his son in favor of a sensational display of white-on-white violence. The "pasties" comprised of Chiron's and Demetrius' blood and bones, and eventually served to their mother, indicate a necessary returning of the white other in*to* the white other (5.2.189). There is no space for this kind of uncontrollable Goth in Rome. Lucius suggests as much with his final order that Tamora's body be discarded like a piece of meat for birds and beasts to devour – no proper burial rights for her (5.3.195–200). Yet, like the lingering presence of the Black baby, who remains somewhere in the Roman landscape, as far as we know, there are also Goths still in Rome, the Goths with whom Lucius formed an army. As such, the threat of future interracial overthrow exists, as critics have pointed out, and so, too, does the threat of intraracial overthrow.[79]

Hyping Whiteness

This chapter concludes by driving home what is the most troubling thing about Goth convertibility as it pertains to their conscious and unconscious role in sustaining white supremacy. Moreover, this chapter speaks indirectly to how white people find it easier to identify with other white people and even with non-Black people.[80] The closer to whiteness, the easier it seems; that is why the intraracial color-line is a useful theoretical concept for reflecting on race, anti-Blackness, white solidarity, colorism, and so on.[81] In *Titus*, no one identifies with Aaron or his son; sympathy and sensitivity are not ever sincerely afforded to the latter. In a way, then, this chapter shows how Goth convertibility speaks to the power of assimilation and internalized racism, the latter of which operates in the service of white supremacy. Among non-white people, internalized racism is one of many methods used for hyping whiteness and sustaining anti-Blackness. Sustaining racial asymmetry is the main function of the white other, too.

As I think about hyping whiteness, hip-hop and rap culture come to mind, because in that culture, a "hype woman" or "hype man" is a figure who enhances a rapper's performance by offering vocal support, helping to invigorate the crowd and reinforce the artist's lyrics through calculated emphasis.[82] The hype man or woman is not the star of the show; they are a foil, much like the Goths ultimately are for the Romans. However, they play a crucial role in facilitating the transmission of the dominant artist's message, sometimes even exerting more energy than the main act. This figure in hip-hop provides a useful counterpoint for considering when someone or something, like the white other, is being used in the service of something else, like white supremacy. Thinking of the "good" Romans, and even Shakespeare, too, as the main artists, I contend that the best hype man or woman for whiteness is the white other who, as a tool to bolster the superiority of whiteness, amplifies harmful messages about the inferiority of those who do not adhere to the dominant culture's standards and those whom the dominant culture vilifies.

This dynamic plays out in Act 4, Scene 2, when the Black baby appears, and also in Act 5, Scene 1, when a "worthy Goth," as Lucius favorably calls him, brings the captive Aaron and his son before the Goth troops and their newfound Roman ally and leader. Once deemed Rome's enemies, a certain sect of Goths becomes Lucius' "faithful friends" (5.1.1), instead of his and Rome's "foes" (1.1.29), as the now much more complicated intraracial conflict rages on between one presumably good Roman-Goth faction (Lucius and his allies) and a presumably bad Roman-Goth white other faction (Saturninus, Tamora, and her sons). We can also read the conflict as white/white other versus white/white other. By displacing blame onto Saturninus and Tamora, Lucius and the good Goths identify a common enemy and band together as a result.[83] This is how racial, white solidarity works, even outside of the play and in the real world. I think about how anti-Black racism can align poor and rich white people's white supremacist interests, for instance.

There is a mutual reversal of frustration in that the Romans are discontent with Rome/Saturninus, as evidenced by letters Lucius receives (5.1.2–3), and the Goths are discontent with their former ruler, whom they now call "cursèd Tamora" (5.1.16). Even outside of Rome proper, Lucius maintains his intraracial, colonial dominance by likening the Goths to "bees" being "led by their master" (5.1.15). Such figurative language highlights the intraracial power relations that persist throughout *Titus* between Romans and Goths, no matter whether they are deemed good or bad people. As hype figures, the less-than-ideal white people represent, for better or worse, whatever is necessary in a given moment to maintain white hegemonic values and justify certain actions. "Friends" in Act 5, Scene 1, the Goths are literal "foes" (specifically, Chiron and Demetrius) in the next scene (5.2.166). The rhetorical variability is a stark reminder that the dominant culture holds the power to describe whoever it wants however it wants, an idea I revisit in the Conclusion through a brief reading of *The Comedy of Errors* in relationship to racial profiling. Retaining and exerting the power to define and redefine others' identities at will is unquestionably the prerogative of whiteness. This is evident, too, in the next chapter on *Hamlet*.

Notes

1 *On Whiteness*, The Racial Imaginary Institute (SPBH Essays, No. 4, 2022), 13.
2 From Claudia Rankine, Beth Loffreda and Max King Cap, *The Racial Imaginary: Writers on Race in the Life of the Mind* (Albany, NY: Fence Books, 2016), 17. By kind permission of Claudia Rankine and Beth Loffreda.
3 Hendricks and Parker argue, "'Race' as that term developed across several European languages was a highly unstable term in the early modern period, a period that saw the proliferation of rival European voyages of 'discovery' as contacts with what from a Eurocentric perspective were 'new' and different worlds, the drive toward imperial conquest and the subjugation of indigenous peoples, and the development (and increasingly 'racial' defense) of slavery." Margo Hendricks and Patricia Parker, *Women, 'Race,' and Writing in the Early Modern Period* (New York: Routledge, 1994), 1–2. Also see Hall, *Things of Darkness*.
4 The critical reception of *Titus Andronicus* has changed over the years, and for good reason. I recommend readers engage with the essays in *Titus Andronicus: The State of Play*, ed. Farah Karim-Cooper (London: The Arden Shakespeare, 2019).
5 Amy Scott-Douglass, "Shades of Shakespeare: Colorblind Casting and Interracial Couples in *Macbeth in Manhattan*, *Grey's Anatomy*, and Prison *Macbeth*," in *Weyward Macbeth: Intersections of Race and Performance*, eds.

Scott Newstok and Ayanna Thompson (New York: Palgrave Macmillan, 2010), 193–202.

6 This is also true in *Much Ado About Nothing*, which I address briefly in the following chapter.

7 All references to Shakespeare's plays come from *The Complete Works of William Shakespeare*, 7th edition, ed. David Bevington (New York: Pearson Education, Inc., 2014).

8 There is a history of Black actors in the role of Macbeth and Richard III, and sometimes in ways that play on stereotypes about Black men and violence. See Lisa M. Anderson, "When Race Matters: Reading Race in *Richard III* and *Macbeth*," in *Colorblind Shakespeare: New Perspectives on Race and Performance*, ed. Ayanna Thompson (New York: Routledge, 2006), 98–101.

9 For an extensive analysis of *Macbeth*, sound, whiteness, and race, see Brown and Stoever, "'Blanched with fear.'" Also see essays in *Weyward Macbeth: Intersections of Race and Performance*, eds. Scott Newstok and Ayanna Thompson (New York: Palgrave Macmillan, 2010).

10 Morrison, *Playing in the Dark*, xii.

11 Hall, *Things of Darkness*, 12.

12 Dyson, *Tears We Cannot Stop*, 82.

13 Ibid., 73–93.

14 Cardon, The *"White Other,"* 2.

15 Despite the flipping of the minority/majority narrative, Disney products such as *Pocahontas* still manage to "reinforce the prevailing status quo." See Patricia A. Turner, *Ceramic Uncles & Celluloid Mammies: Black Images and Their Influence on Culture* (New York: Anchor Books, 2000), 107.

16 Cardon, The *"White Other,"* 147–148.

17 According to Nathan Ron, Erasmus considered "all who are not Christian-European (aside from schismatics, heretics, and Jews) [as] rank barbarians." *Erasmus and the "Other,"* 17.

18 Cardon, The *"White Other,"* 3. If you look at an image of the theatrical release poster for this film, everyone is optically white-skinned. See https://en .wikipedia.org/wiki/My_Big_Fat_Greek_Wedding.

19 The white other occupies a liminal space; what I present as the racial space in between white hegemony and Black in the ternary racial hierarchy that expands the Black/white binary. This liminality helps mark the white other's powerful invisibility as an other. While breaking down the ternary hierarchy with respect to gender is outside this project's scope, I will note that the lens of Black feminism is useful for expanding the ternary system with attention to differences among men and women: (1) white men; (2) white women; (3) white other male; (4) white other female; (5) Black men; and (6) Black women. The white other expands categories of difference and the paradigm that shows how power is unequally distributed and exercised. In the liminal space between Black and white, the white other loses human value and gets pulled toward metaphorical and even literal death. Also outside of this project's scope is full consideration of the position of other racial others, or

non-Black people of color, in the racial hierarchy (and how Black people might other each other intraracially).

20 Engaging ideas posed by feminist Chela Sandoval at a 1982 conference, Kim F. Hall observes how white women can be othered, for example, and thus occupy a precious place in the racial hierarchy that puts them next to white men in terms of color and beneath them in terms of gender. See *Things of Darkness*, 178–179.

21 Francesca T. Royster, "White-Limed Walls: Whiteness and Gothic Extremism in Shakespeare's *Titus Andronicus*," *Shakespeare Quarterly*, 51.4 (Winter 2000), 432–455; 436.

22 Imtiaz Habib, *Shakespeare and Race: Postcolonial Praxis in the Early Modern Period* (New York: University Press of America, Inc., 2000), 2.

23 Margaux Deroux, "The Blackness Within: Early Modern Color-Concept, Physiology and Aaron the Moor in Shakespeare's 'Titus Andronicus,'" *Mediterranean Studies*, 19 (2010), 88, 86–101.

24 Lara Bovilsky, *Barbarous Play: Race on the Renaissance Stage* (Minneapolis: University of Minnesota Press, 2008), 33.

25 Chapman, *Anti-Black Racism*, 158.

26 David Sterling Brown, "Remixing the Family: Blackness and Domesticity in Shakespeare's Titus Andronicus," in *Titus Andronicus: The State of Play*, ed. Farah Karim-Cooper (London: Arden Shakespeare, 2019), 114.

27 Stoever, *The Sonic Color Line*, 7.

28 Brian Boyd posits that the baby, and by extension Aaron, "so patently enriches the play's characters, conflicts, and concerns." "The Blackamoor Babe: Titus Andronicus, Play, Ballad and History," *Notes and Queries*, 44.4 (December 1997), 492–494.

29 See Charlie Rose's interview with Toni Morrison: www.youtube.com/watch?v=5EQcy361vB8.

30 Ibid.; emphasis added.

31 See Anthony Gerard Barthelemy, *Black Face, Maligned Race: The Representation of Blacks in English Drama from Shakespeare to Southerne* (Baton Rouge: Louisiana State University Press, 1987), 91. The metaphorical possibilities for blackness are infinite. Beyond sin and melancholy, blackness in the early modern period could be "deeply synonymous with mental instability, and anger manifesting as violence. Consequently, black becomes a signifier of the potential for destruction, chaos and evil doings, echoing early mythology and manifesting in early modern racial interactions." Deroux, "The Blackness Within," 92.

32 Saturninus calls for his faction to draw their swords again at line 205.

33 Emphasis added. "Villain" appears about twenty times in the play.

34 After the sacrifice of Tamora's eldest child Alarbus, her son Chiron comments, "Was never Scythia half so barbarous" (1.1.131). This commentary on Roman behavior, coming from a marginalized white outsider, also highlights the Romans' potential for savagery, which is connected to the play's racist discourse on Blackness.

35 Smith, *Race and Rhetoric*, 2.
36 Hendricks explains, "Race ensures the idea of commonality by negating or effacing the different interests of a group of individuals. However, there is an inherent paradox in this push for commonality. In order to invest race with meaning, modern societies must frame visible (and, quite frankly, minor) differences among people in terms of antithesis. Consequently, race becomes at once transcendentally immutable and historically mutable." "Surveying 'race' in Shakespeare," in *Shakespeare and Race*, eds. Catherine M. S. Alexander and Stanley Wells (Cambridge: Cambridge University Press, 2000), 1–22; 19.
37 Smith, *Race and Rhetoric*, 130.
38 Virginia Mason Vaughan, "The Construction of Barbarism in *Titus Andronicus*," in *Race, Ethnicity and Power in the Renaissance*, ed. Joyce Green MacDonald (London: Associated University Presses, 1997), 165–180; 165.
39 Ibid., 172.
40 Chapman, *Anti-Black Racism*, 2.
41 Vaughan, "The Construction of Barbarism," 167.
42 See Royster, "White-Limed Walls," 433.
43 Speaking of slaves, which Tamora is not, Orlando Patterson explains "liminal incorporation" and how someone who is socially dead is still considered part of society (*Slavery and Social Death*, 45). Although Patterson's focus is on enslaved people, his discourse maintains applicability to *Titus* with respect to insider/outsider dynamics.
44 Various kinds of endogamy – "social," racial, and "economic," for instance – were important to early modern people, especially with respect to marriage. See Lawrence Stone, *The Family, Sex and Marriage in England 1500–1800, Abridged Edition* (New York: Harper and Row, 1979), 50.
45 Royster, "White-Limed Walls," 433.
46 Christopher Crosbie, "Fixing Moderation: *Titus Andronicus* and the Aristotelian Determination of Value," *Shakespeare Quarterly*, 58.2 (2007), 147–173, 162.
47 Jack D'Amico, *The Moor in English Renaissance Drama* (Tampa: University of South Florida Press, 1991), 2.
48 Virginia Mason Vaughan posits, "When all is said and done, the black characters that populated early modern theatres tell us little about actual black Africans; they are the projections of imaginations that capitalize on the assumptions, fantasies, fears, and anxieties of England's pale-complexioned audiences." *Performing Blackness on English Stages, 1500–1800* (Cambridge: Cambridge University Press, 2005), 5–6.
49 D. Marvin Jones, *Race, Sex, and Suspicion: The Myth of the Black Male* (Westport, CT: Greenwood Press, 2005), 59.
50 Chapman argues, "The final thought of the play, then, is not to offer a plan for rebuilding society, but to place the blame for the collapse of civil structures onto the shoulders of Aaron's incorporation" (*Anti-Black Racism*, 173). The

play does this, indeed, but not successfully so when we consider what *Titus* is without Aaron.

51 Part of Thomas Herron's reading of Aaron hinges on error. For example, he claims, "Aaron's final punishment fits his crime and his 'base' nature: at the end of the play, Lucius will stick Aaron where he justly belongs, that is, in his native element, 'fastened' in the 'earth' where he will be half-buried and starved to death as apt punishment for his excessive appetites (5.3.178–82)." "*Titus Andronicus*, Hell and the Elements," *Shakespeare* 13.3 (September 2017), 239–257, 247. Reading this, I wonder at judgments implied in terms like "justly." Why and how is torturing Aaron, torturing the Black man, just, and according to whom?

52 Meg Pearson notes that "the play presents [Aaron] not only as a villain, but as a criminal so skilled that he teaches others his craft." "'That bloody mind I think they learned of me': Aaron as Tutor in "Titus Andronicus," *Shakespeare* 6.1 (2010), 34–51. Such a reading gives Aaron too much credit, for he only "thinks" Chiron and Demetrius learned from him – he does not know. And such a reading undoes that novelty of Aaron that Shakespeare himself instills in his first Black character by having him contradict certain racist assumptions.

53 Mary Floyd-Wilson asserts: "The erasure of Africa from the civilized world, and the reinterpretation of 'blackness' as monstrous and unnatural, allowed for the construction of a European race that united a wide range of colors and complexions under and invisible badge of inherited superiority." *English Ethnicity and Race*, 19. As I have argued elsewhere, white critics are often thought of as thinking and writing from a non-raced perspective. The blending here of Bartels' and Floyd-Wilson's scholarship in particular shows why it is important to reflect on the implications of white racial identity and perspectives.

54 Gustav Ungerer, "The Presence of Africans in Elizabethan England and the Performance of *Titus Andronicus* at Burley-on-the-Hill, 1595/96," *Medieval and Renaissance Drama in England*, 21 (2008), 19–55; 39–40. Bartels has suggested that the play "does not challenge the racial stereotype," which suggests a limited understanding of how Aaron's challenges are possible. See Emily C. Bartels, "Making More of the Moor: Aaron, Othello, and Renaissance Refashionings of Race," *Shakespeare Quarterly*, 41.4 (Winter, 1990), 433–454; 442.

55 Emily C. Bartels, *Speaking of the Moor: From Alcazar to Othello* (Philadelphia: University of Pennsylvania Press, 2008), 68.

56 Pearson herself acknowledges that "for nearly four acts, Aaron holds sway over the play's action." His absence in Act 1 is not accounted for in this critical interpretation of his influence. "'That bloody mind,'" 39.

57 Imtiaz Habib comments on the somatic and ethnic similarity between Aaron and his child (*Shakespeare and Race*, 107). I would add that Aaron's claiming the child is a "reification" of his own racial innocence in Act 1. Lori Schroeder notes, "As Aaron clutches the baby and vows to defend him against all harm,

he also invites Chiron and Demetrius to read and interpret the baby boy before them, whose innocence Aaron himself carefully inscribes." "The Only Witness a Tongueless Child: Hearing and Reading the Silent Babes of *Titus Andronicus* and *The Winter's Tale*," *Medieval and Renaissance Drama in England: An Annual Gathering of Research, Criticism and Reviews*, 27 (2014), 221–247; 234.

58 Royster, "White-Limed Walls," 432. See Little, Jr., "Is It Possible to Read Shakespeare through Critical White Studies?," 276–277.

59 For example, Hall touches on the "fetishization of white skin" and other matters related to whiteness in *Things of Darkness*, 211. Joyce Green MacDonald, "Introduction" in *Race, Ethnicity, and Power in the Renaissance*, ed. Joyce Green MacDonald (Teaneck, NJ: Fairleigh Dickinson University Press, 1997), 9. Little, following Hall and MacDonald, also puts whiteness on the critical table in *Shakespeare Jungle Fever*, especially in Chapters 1 and 2.

60 Royster, "White-Limed Walls," 433.

61 Ibid., 432–433.

62 Zeus Leonard argues that "*flexible whiteness* has always relied on the creation of levels and shades of whiteness." "Tropics of Whiteness," 6.

63 Royster, "White-Limed Walls," 432–433.

64 Thandeka, *Learning to Be White: Money, Race, and God in America* (New York: Continuum, 1999), 8.

65 Royster, "White-Limed Walls," 436.

66 Morwenna Carr, "Material/Blackness: Race and Its Material Reconstructions on the Seventeenth-Century English Stage," *Early Theatre* 20.1 (2017), 77–85, 85.

67 Barthelemy, *Black Face, Maligned Race*, 95.

68 See Brown, "Remixing the Family," as the essay leans in part on the notion that Shakespeare positions Aaron as a surrogate parent for the white Goth brothers Chiron and Demetrius.

69 Noémie Ndiaye gestures in the direction of threat with respect to the Black baby and white anxiety: "What Lucius sees in the mixed race baby is a menace to the established order of the Roman society, threatening, most exemplarily, to interrupt the rightful royal lineage. Indeed, Aaron's baby is a double threat to the Roman political system, first because he is the fruit of adultery on the part of the empress, second, because Aaron's plan to save his son's life consists in putting a Moorish impostor on the Throne." "Aaron's Roots: Spaniards, Englishmen, and Blackamoors in *Titus Andronicus*," *Early Theatre: A Journal Associated with the Records of Early English Drama*, 19.2 (2016), 59–80; 70.

70 Habib, *Shakespeare and Race*, 94.

71 Other key scenes are 3.2, the fly scene, and 5.3.

72 Vaughan, "The Construction of Barbarism," 174–175.

73 In *Hamlet*, Ophelia famously dies a "muddy death," as Gertrude laments (4.7.184).

74 Brown, "Remixing the Family," 115–116.

75 Scott Lindsey, "'Groaning Shadows That Are Gone': The Ghosts of *Titus Andronicus*," *English Studies: A Journal of English Language and Literature*, 96.3–4 (May 2015), 403–423, 403.

76 Herron asserts, "The just desserts of revenge are served and devoured, as one would expect from the genre: justice demands a hellish end for the protagonists. In *Titus*, the stage enacts these processes on a symbolic (hence loosely allegorical) level: viewers are left at the end of the play agog at the 'hell on stage' the characters have just lived through." "*Titus Andronicus*, Hell and the Elements," 240.

77 There was a range of "meaning and markers" of race in the period. See Akhimie, *Shakespeare and the Cultivation of Difference*, 20.

78 Lindsey explains: "Aaron's talking head disrupts the closing harmony of *Titus* in a way that is even more potent than the 'usurper's cursèd head' (5.7.99) in the final scene of *Macbeth*. Recalling the events of the play's opening, Rome's new leader is haunted not by the 'past honours' of a previous emperor but the 'heinous deeds' of a villainous Moor whose talking head will 'torment Lucius and the Roman public' by "reminding them of his past victories over the Andronici'. If the ghosts of Lavinia and Titus will be laid to rest, then the 'undead' Aaron and Tamora will continue to haunt the play's audiences." "Groaning Shadows," 419.

79 As Royster notes, "other offspring survive" in *Titus,* and so, too, do other adults. "White-Limed Walls," 455. Vaughan also attends to the play's unresolved problems: "*Titus Andronicus* begins with the Roman army's success over the barbaric Goths, but it ends with a new emperor whose power depends upon the loyalty of these same Gothic soldiers. It concludes, in other words, with the triumph of the colonized people and the establishment of a new Rome, an amalgamation of urban and agrarian cultures. In Shakespeare's play, the relation between colonizer and colonized is problematic; the act of gain (conquest) entails a loss of racial and cultural purity." "The Construction of Barbarism," 172.

80 It is no secret that "minorities can without a doubt also identify with and strive to perform whiteness." See Tobias Hübinette and Catrin Lundström, "The Phases of Hegemonic Whiteness: Understanding Racial Temporalities in Sweden," *Social Identities*, 20.6 (2014), 423–437; 426.

81 Sort of like the Irish, who were once considered Black-ish by the English, the Goths are able to capitalize on their whiteness despite being culturally different than the dominant culture. See "An Interview with Noel Ignatiev of *Race Traitor* Magazine, 'Treason to Whiteness Is Loyalty to Humanity,'" in *Critical White Studies: Looking behind the Mirror*, eds. Richard Delgado and Jean Stefancic (Philadelphia, PA: Temple University Press, 1997), 607–612; 608. Barthelemy writes about the linguistic gymnastics the English performed to distinguish themselves from different groups: "Readers of seventeenth-century literature know that while blacks were called 'Moors', all Moors were not black. In fact, almost anyone who was not Christian, European, or Jewish

could have been called a Moor; this includes Asians, Native Americans, Africans, Arabs, and all Muslims regardless of ethnicity." See *Black Face, Maligned Race*, x.

82 For a definition of hype man, see https://en.wikipedia.org/wiki/Hype_man.

83 Vaughan, "The Construction of Barbarism," 176.

CHAPTER 2

Engendering the Fall of White Masculinity *in* Hamlet

> The stupidity that undergirds white supremacy is now perpetuated from one generation to the next through "socialization."
> – *How to Be Less Stupid about Race*, Crystal M. Fleming[1]

In relationship to the intraracial color-line, *Hamlet*'s (circa 1601) negotiations of whiteness make it a problem(atic) play.[2] Shakespeare structures his famous tragedy around white people watching other white people: surveilling, judging, spying, and critiquing. Recall that the play begins with several men on Elsinore's guard platform. From the beginning, the characters, especially the men, are set up in different ways to be on guard. That is what Hamlet is doing when he works to catch Claudius' "conscience" (2.2.606); that is what Rosencrantz and Guildenstern are doing on Claudius' behalf as they observe Hamlet; that is what the Ghost is doing when he reenters the play in the closet scene to chide Hamlet for losing sight of his purpose; and that is also what Polonius, to his detriment, is doing behind the arras in Act 3, Scene 4. All this surveillance allows us to see that *Hamlet* presents the white other's regulation as part of a complicated socialization process linked, among other things, to expectations around whiteness and masculinity. Such expectations are informed by anti-black and anti-Black discourses that "constrain and enable the construction of white masculinities" within Shakespeare's play.[3]

Exploring the association between violence and masculinity, Jennifer Forsyth outlines some early modern period-specific expectations:

> To be masculine implied the ability to become violent since manhood was so strongly correlated with physical defense, whether contributing to a military defense or defending one's name and honor with one's sword [. . .] The ideal man – the honorable nobleman – thus was both continually at risk of violence and prepared to respond appropriately [. . .] Physical force must be employed in a good cause, and other masculine virtues of self-restraint, moderation, stoicism, and honor insist that control is essential.[4]

In *Hamlet*, ideal white masculinity dies with Old Hamlet. The play makes it challenging for any living Dane not to appear weak. This reality has devastating implications for the Danes, and the Danish men who fail to exhibit and therefore achieve ideal masculinity.[5] This reality adds to the play's generically tragic qualities, since Hamlet's unmanliness, signifying his otherness, contributes to his character flaws.[6] Beginning in medias res, with the memory of Old Hamlet recalled through reference to his death, the play reminds us that somewhere in Denmark the dead King's body is going through the decomposition process. The "spirit of decline" and the theme of decay haunt *Hamlet*.[7] All that the King *was* is no more, as Hamlet's lamentation to Horatio proves: "'A was a man, take him for all in all, / I shall not look upon his like again" (1.2.187–188). Indeed, there are no "heroic" men like Old Hamlet in Denmark.[8]

In having been "all," including the Danish exemplar of courtliness, patriarchy, and "manhood embodied,"[9] the dead King leaves a void in his kingdom and household. There is no immediate successor to maintain the martial, masculine, patriarchal qualities of Old Hamlet,[10] deemed "majestical" by Marcellus (1.1.149) and twice referred to as "valiant" for his defeat of Old Fortinbras and for his military prowess (1.1.88, 1.2.25).[11] Old Hamlet is the deceased war hero and patriarch who represents particular racialized power and authority. As a ghost, Old Hamlet's "armed" appearance – with his military apparel evoking "a medieval ethos of violence,"[12] through which "wrath, anger and revenge functioned as expected and lauded royal traits"[13] – offers a comparatively hypermasculine image that appears again in the drama only through the non-Danish figure Young Fortinbras. As critics like Jennifer A. Low acknowledge, "*Hamlet* is framed by the deeds of Fortinbras."[14] And this framing extends, and brings closure to, the celebration of white masculine militaristic strength first presented at the play's onset in the reflection of the deceased Danish father figure. The contrast between the types of masculinity depicted provides balance for our understanding of how gender ideals are constructed:

> Thus [masculine] anxiety is both a negative effect that leads us to patriarchy's own internal discord, but it is also an instrument (once properly contained, appropriated or returned) of its perpetuation. If anxiety were *only* a critical lens showing us the contradictions of the system that produced it, we would not see the function, the cultural work, that this physiological and psychological condition accomplishes – it would merely be an effect.[15]

In *Hamlet*, then, masculine representation has two primary purposes: First, it is meant to ensure patriarchy's survival, which is a reality represented by Young Fortinbras emerging in the end to be Denmark's savior. Second, masculine representation also generates discourse about what needs correcting, how the play must restore an idealized white masculinity that offers stability and order. In this respect, *Hamlet* dramatizes along the intraracial color-line how "explicit and implicit cultural messages about *who* authentic white men are, and expectations for *how* they should behave, together structure identity formation."[16] To be an inauthentic white man is to be the inside outsider, to be he who belongs and does not belong.[17]

White Men, Black(ened) Masculinity

The negotiation of whiteness – notably illustrated through weak, unstable masculinity, and metaphorical and literal blackness – has a developmental trajectory in Shakespeare's tragic oeuvre that begins with *Titus*. Moreover, the interpretation of gender being read differently, and deficiently, for Black men in comparison to white men has historical roots we can locate as early as the slave trade, if not before, a matter I will address in Chapter 4.[18] Portrayed as barbarous, bloodthirsty, adulterous, devilish, and uncivilized, Aaron provides the canonical introduction to the idea of black(ened) masculinity. This introduction initially leads one to believe Shakespeare's first Black Moor is a stock villain figure,[19] until we see him express his melancholic emotions in Act 2, Scene 3 and then become a parent in Act 4, Scene 2. The latter is a pivotal, troubling moment that exposes how parenthood complicates easy assumptions about the Black man, whose "cloudy melancholy," hypersexuality, and uncontrolled emotions mark his effeminacy (2.3.33). Yet, it is Aaron's melancholy that also humanizes him.

Beyond defining himself as the sole protector of and provider for his "firstborn son and heir" (4.2.93), Aaron instinctually envisions himself as a nurturer[20] in an imagined androcentric domestic scenario where he raises his and Tamora's dark-skinned lovechild alone. He envisions nourishing the newborn in ways reflecting sensibilities that would have been more traditionally maternal than paternal in sixteenth-century England.[21] Aaron's maternal nature is perhaps linked to the socio-political and literary history of infantilizing and effeminizing Black men, who are subjected to violent forms of social control in the plays. Othello and the Prince of Morocco are also subjected to this kind of control, for instance.[22] Shakespeare imbues his character with negative attributes that diminish his masculinity, though one can also read his maternal nature positively, since he represents the ultimate parent. However, the paradox is that in being the ultimate parent, in erasing Tamora and constructing a Black household without a mother, Aaron seemingly becomes mother, too. In being father-mother he must, at least, embody some of the woman's qualities to ensure his son's survival and, more generally, the survival of Blackness.

In the early modern period, the continuation of familial bloodlines through legitimate progeny, a biological process linked to sex, served as a marker of one's masculinity. Children – physical evidence of a man's reproductive power, literal proof of his functioning sexuality – could make a man more of a man, so to speak, by affirming his patriarchal prowess through the production of heirs.[23] In *The Merchant of Venice*, the Prince of Morocco loses access to the social-sexual system that would have otherwise granted him lawful heirs because he fails the casket test designed by Portia's late father. Choosing the golden casket, choosing incorrectly, he resigns himself to "never speak to lady afterward / In way of marriage" (*Merchant*, 2.1.41–42). Assuming that marriage would legitimate Moroccan offspring, the Prince's voyage to Belmont denotes the end of this Black man's line. The regulation of his body emasculates him. His unmanliness is also evidenced by his verbosity, as women, who spent much time in the sole company of other women, were stereotypically thought to have the gift of the gab in the period.[24] Moreover, his impotence is yet another sign of his unmanliness since he cannot meaningfully contribute to the patriarchal system in the long term. The Black man is, in effect, sterilized.[25]

Morocco's failure is, in part, due to what Shakespeare presents as his inadequate masculinity. Beyond his dark complexion, the Prince is not a representation of the ideal man, nor is he the ideal suitor for Portia. He is not a white man, a very specific racial and social status he could never hold.[26] The play juxtaposes him with Italian Bassanio, to whom Morocco does not compare, not even with all his Black royal majesty (*Merchant*, 2.1.1). One need only consider the Prince's logic for choosing the golden casket to see that his attraction to the gold is superficial, based largely on a misguided judgment about the exterior fashion of the object. The interior/ exterior and male/female dichotomies "support[ed] the intellectual and legal foundations of patriarchy":[27] It was a way early modern people divvied up masculine and feminine concerns, with the interior (intellect, rationality, education) being aligned with men and the exterior (fashion, cosmetics, domestic work, and even displays of extreme emotion) being more aligned with women. In the end, Morocco self-identifies as a "loser," which is apt given his failed attempt to win Portia and his failed display of masculinity (*Merchant*, 2.7.77).

Undeniably, Othello at times also models unmanliness, which was fashioned through the depictions of his dramatic predecessors Aaron, the Prince of Morocco, and even racially white Hamlet, as I will show in this chapter. Othello's canonical placement, appearing after Hamlet, is a return to the somatically Black man; one might view his character as a consolidation of the mounting signifiers of blackened/Black unmanliness that function as a common denominator between him, Aaron, Morocco, and Hamlet. Identifying Othello's masculine shortcomings is not hard. Shakespeare ensures he is replete with them, as some critics have noted, even if in ways that seem unfair to the General.[28] While the following is not an exhaustive list, some of the textual moments that emphasize the Black Venetian General's unmanliness include his uncontrolled emotions and hysteria; his being ruled by Iago; the illusion of his being a cuckold; the forced reality of his failed patriarchal power and related domestic disorder; his suicide; his instinctual thought to poison his wife; his losing himself in his marriage ("Othello's occupation's gone," he says [*Othello*, 3.3.373]); his authority being usurped by Desdemona, for example, the "general's wife is now the general," according to Iago (2.3.308–309); and his perceived hypersexuality and association with witchcraft.[29] This last point is a salient connection between Blackness and unmanliness, one that draws *Hamlet* into the racialized gender discourse that gets coded as black or, more specifically, the "Violent Black Man type."[30]

The allusion to the Africanist presence in gendered language gives credence to my analysis of unmanliness as a racialized category that denotes difference related to Black/white and inferior/superior dichotomies, with whiteness positioned as supreme. Thus, unmanliness, displayed by the Black or white man, significantly diminishes and perhaps voids the patriarchal, masculine power one might wield. If the exoticism of Blackness is part of what makes Othello attractive, his unmanliness, presented as stemming from his Blackness, has the opposite effect, as do his other attributes that reduce him to one who is Black and bad by the play's final scene. In a fit of rage, the Black man generates domestic destruction by killing his white wife and leaving the remaining characters with "heavy heart[s]" (*Othello*, 5.2.382).[31]

Canonical figures associated with unmanliness – Aaron, Macbeth, Richard III, Hamlet, and Othello – enable the following syllogistic reasoning, reasoning that allows the recognition of discourses about "the failures of masculine performance"[32] to relate to discourses about racial construction in Shakespeare's plays:[33] If questioned masculinity is a marker of metaphorical blackness, then there is also potential for critiqued masculinity, understood as behavior that "does not conform to traditional codes of masculinity," to be socially unacceptable, a symbol of blackness that transmits a stigma about black(ened) manhood.[34] By cloaking rotting, and rotten, white Danish masculinity in literal and figurative blackness, Hamlet's and Claudius' in particular, Shakespeare establishes the white masculine crisis that is the crux of what "is rotten in the state of Denmark" (1.4.90). This crisis unfolds along the intraracial color-line. Shakespeare puts pressure on different kinds of expressions of masculine anxiety embodied by the white others in this play. Furthermore, as Coppélia Kahn would stress, the masculine crisis is indicative of how men in *Hamlet* struggle to stabilize and enact their manliness that always seems vulnerable to the perceived intrusion of womanliness.[35]

Specifically, *Hamlet* demonstrates how the white men's blackening conflicts with the goals of patriarchy. The play enables blackness to be about, yet move beyond, skin color by depicting unmanliness as a kind of dangerous, monstrous blackness one can embody, leading a character like Hamlet to "act black"[36] or be black in a visual or performative sense.[37] As the move toward performative blackness is a contemporary privilege for the white person who gets to seem Black precisely because of their whiteness, so too is Hamlet's move toward blackness, which I interpret as a privilege of his highborn status: In early modern England "only the wealthy could afford the acres of black cloth that went into mourning cloaks and gowns, hangings, draperies, and covers."[38] When attached to the white body (for example, Hamlet's), that blackness, presented as a peculiarity, contradicts the tenets of whiteness that are required for its socio-political superiority. Thus, Hamlet's blackened mood, appearance, and conduct jeopardize whiteness, masculinity, and patriarchy.

In her insightful study, Akhimie links conduct and race to the inferiority/superiority dichotomy by recognizing that "ultimately, conduct is a way of sustaining an underlying belief that some people are more valuable than others, that some are 'of quality', while others are not."[39] Much like literal evil-doing, villainous conduct by white characters is metaphorically black, therefore rendering it, as I argue, an underexamined subcategory of difference within Shakespeare's work. It is a subcategory that necessitates racialization, especially given how race and racism, in the past and now, depend on hierarchically imbalanced power dynamics. Jennifer Feather and Catherine E. Thomas' volume of essays, *Violent Masculinities:*

Male Aggression in Early Modern Texts and Culture, assesses how "masculine ideals are significantly influenced by other categories of difference including not only social status but also age, sexuality, and social context."[40] To that list I would add another category of difference – race – that is important to consider with respect to the construction of "normative masculinity."[41] The racialization of masculinity has not been interrogated comprehensively in key criticism that privileges white masculinity and positions it as universal. Hall's *Things of Darkness*, a seminal text on premodern race and gender that is not cited in Feather and Thomas' volume, could have informed the astute but racially homogenous readings of masculinity.[42] While critics have questioned Hamlet's masculinity before, because of his bond with Horatio and because of his madness and murderous indecision, I contend that the understanding of his unmanliness deepens when we consider how blackness, symbolized by the night and the "inky cloak," among other dramatic elements, enshrouds this tragic hero, transforming Hamlet into the devalued white other whose masculinity necessarily comes into question (1.2.77).[43]

Talking about Race in Hamlet

In 2002, Peter Erickson titled an essay with what undoubtedly was a provocative, productive question: "Can we talk about race in *Hamlet*?" There, he asserted that "the scope of inquiry [in the study of race in Shakespeare] should be expanded to include the broader sphere of rhetoric and imagery" that make it possible to discuss race in plays such as *Hamlet*.[44] Because of Erickson's essay, and other works like it that examine race beyond the five "so-called 'race' plays," it is clear we can talk about race in *Hamlet*.[45] And as I will suggest, *Hamlet*'s engagement with race matters is quite strong, particularly with respect to gender.[46] Therefore, in this chapter I build on Erickson's claims, especially those articulated about "whiteness and weakness."[47] I consider how Shakespeare's tragedy constructs the white other in relationship to gender. I also examine how black imagery is mapped onto white bodies in ways that add to Hall's arguments regarding the early modern usage of "tropes of blackness" as they pertain to "gender differentiation" and to Patricia Parker's ideas about *Hamlet*'s "preoccupation with blackness, soiling, sullying, and dulling" – for example, through unmanliness and the subsequent othering of Danish white men that makes the intraracial color-line visible.[48]

The work of the aforementioned critics, and others like Akhimie, and Lisa M. Anderson with Ayanna Thompson and Scott Newstok, to name a few, reveals how important strides have been made to scrutinize what Shakespeare's works have brought to early modern critical race studies scholars.[49] In other words, my *Hamlet* analysis rejects the field's "pathological averseness to thinking about race," as Erickson and Hall describe it, by showcasing why it is imperative to close-read racialized whiteness and make it visible.[50] The exclusive focus on white figures in a work such as *Hamlet* is especially generative for (premodern) critical race studies scholarship, as *Hamlet* is a dramatic work whose dominant white male characters remind us to, as Urvashi Chakravarty urges, "reassess the presumption that race is, fundamentally, about the faraway rather than about the familiar."[51] A specific focus on the proximate, on somatic similarity,[52] reveals how Shakespeare engages race in *Hamlet*, a text that does not contain somatically Black characters. Rather, to borrow rhetoric from Ian Smith, Shakespeare uses "language as a racial marker" to generate important socio-cultural distinctions between ideal manliness – represented in the play in its desired form by Old Hamlet's and Young Fortinbras' whiteness – and less-than-ideal manliness – represented by the characters who embody feminine traits and/or blackness, a stigmatized color linked to African identity in the period.[53] Shakespeare employs racially charged descriptors to negotiate the varying degrees of whiteness. One example that reveals the racialization of words relative to whiteness is the "equivalence of honor and manhood," as the latter term implies white male representation in the early modern context.[54] According to Low, "Up to a certain time in the English Renaissance, [there was] an almost universal understanding of honor as the spiritual quality that enables a man to gain glory in feats of war."[55] In considering Old Hamlet and Young Fortinbras, one must be mindful of how their militaristic and patriarchal conduct shapes the interpretation of their manliness as well as the unmanliness of their dramatic counterparts.

Hamlet is replete with racialized discourse that revolves around "unmanl [iness]" and that fashions the ideal white masculine self-image in connection to the white other who is blackened throughout Shakespeare's play (1.2.94).[56] This discourse in *Hamlet* is worth attending to since, as Smith asserts: "In addition to proverbs and conduct books, a man trying to shape himself to the expectations of his peers might turn also to the theatre."[57] He adds, "Shakespeare's plays represent masculine identity in ways that must have been recognizable from everyday life even as they set up models of action and eloquence that a man might want to imitate."[58] Popular stage representations, designed to imitate public and private life, had the potential to influence how early modern English people defined and interpreted masculinity. Given the importance of theater as a cultural transmitter and shaper, examining how *Hamlet* manages gender construction and race exposes the intraracial color-line's operation and opens possibilities for understanding the strained relationship between whiteness and unmanliness beyond the confines of this popular white-centric Shakespearean drama.

To this end, I want to address *how* this play does that work, focusing on at least one way of what I believe are many, and outline what unmanliness is and does in this tragedy.[59] So, how can we talk about race in *Hamlet* and how can we use its characters to talk about race? Hall's contention that "the polarity of dark and light is most often worked out in representations of black men and white women" indicates how important opposition is in the definitional relationship between Black and white.[60] As I suggest, white masculinity is imbued with specific meaning that black(ened) masculinity lacks in the period. Through *Hamlet*'s references to unmanliness that function as a rhetorical device, through the way unmanliness serves "as a perversion of a code of manly virtue," *Hamlet* dramatizes Denmark's deterioration through the breakdown, or decomposition, of white masculinity. In so doing, the play codes unmanliness as black, thereby offering insight into the formation of the (un)manly white subject.[61] Aligned with Sky Gilbert, Bernhard Frank, and others, I posit that Hamlet exhibits qualities that call into question how manly he is, especially in comparison to his deceased father and Young Fortinbras.[62] Hall reminds us that black, a negative signifier opposed to white, connotes many things within and outside of Shakespeare's canon (sin, evil, death, melancholy, etc.), and in early modern England.[63] To this list I would add unmanliness, a quality embodied by other white male Shakespeare characters such as Macbeth[64] and Richard III. Their masculinity and conduct are presented as unstable in their respective plays.[65]

Although *Hamlet* does not include Black characters, a fact that makes sighting and citing the white other more challenging, it is precisely this lack of Black that allows the play to enrich the Shakespearean canonical discourse regarding the relationship between whiteness and unmanliness – and how it may even impact contemporary perceptions of Black men, who are often dehumanized, infantilized, emasculated, and effeminized in social discourse.[66] As Rebecca Ann Bach notes, "In texts of the English Renaissance many people whom we would see as men – including boys, men who violate their duty, cowards, Catholics (and atheists and Puritans), Frenchmen (and Italians, black men, Jews, and other non-English people), and men of low status – are depicted as more like women than they are like men."[67] Bach adds that "they are effeminate because they act like women – that is, they are frail, unable or unwilling to fight, or subordinate – and also because they desire women."[68] Through *Hamlet*, I reconceptualize the understanding of Shakespeare's original positioning of blackness as base – and instead think about "base" as meaning foundational and strong – given that negotiations of whiteness depend heavily on blackness, which gets used as a support beam to stabilize notions of the ideal white masculine self.[69]

Dyeing Masculinity

For the Danes, the valorized Old Hamlet is the unattainable height of masculinity and majesty. As Parker observes, Hamlet insinuates this when he berates his mother in the closet scene for leaving the "fair mountain" to "feed and batten on [the] moor" (3.4.67–68).[70] As critics have yet to investigate thoroughly, this is a moment where Hamlet's language overtly signals that Gertrude crossed the intraracial color-line with her new choice of lover and the resulting perverse domestic configuration. Claudius – as inferior "moor" – does not compare to Old Hamlet – the superior "fair mountain," who represents the ideal masculine white patriarch in this juxtaposition. When white characters show disdain for other white figures, it is often because they reject the uncouth whiteness that contradicts white cultural norms and expectations. The rejection is a form of intraracial regulation that happens to the internal audience (the characters within the play) and for the external audience (those reading or watching the play). Such policing of white others exposes the irrationality embedded in the logic that entitles whites to deem people "Other," for the inferior other is still white in this case. And so, the regulation functions as a policing of the self along the intraracial color-line. Exploring whiteness in this way suggests that while Hamlet cannot literally strip Claudius of his somatic whiteness by applying the dual-meaning "moor," the Prince does achieve this effect figuratively, which implies there are levels to white personhood that one can slip in and out of. The same is not true for Black people. The popular premodern "washing the Ethiop white" adage implies at its core the difficulty, if not impossibility, of Black becoming white.[71] As a murderer, sinner, liar, and incestuous proxy for his deceased valiant brother, then, Claudius proves himself to have slipped into a position of social, political, and racial unacceptability. This makes him an early modern representation of the "lowest white man," an identity signified as other if one takes seriously the homonym "Moor."[72]

As such, the loss of "Hamlet, / King, father, royal Dane" is a loss from which Denmark cannot easily recover; hence the state's, and royal household's, rapid deterioration under the rule of the white other, Claudius (1.4.44–45). Through the minor characters Rosencrantz and Guildenstern, we learn that kingly death has corrosive potential. Rosencrantz astutely explains: "The cess of majesty / Dies not alone, but like a gulf doth draw / What's near it with it" (3.3.15–17). This simile indicates why unmanliness swells as the play progresses, for if white kingly greatness can die, then it can subsequently decompose, metaphorically speaking, like the physical royal body, and negatively impact everything that "live[s] and feed[s] upon" it, as Guildenstern warns (3.3.10).

The King's dead body, and the temporary death of ideal white masculinity, represents a fundamental crisis that darkens the play. The invisible background image of the rotting human corpse, with its foul odor emissions and visual evidence of decay,[73] denotes a physical blackening of the white body that enhances *Hamlet*'s anxieties about death.[74] Images of the human decomposition process, for instance, show how the body changes after death, becoming discolored, darkly spotted, and blackened[75] over time during a decay stage called "black putrefaction."[76] Even the Ghost's words imply this when he conveys to Hamlet how the poison affected his body: "A most instant tetter barked about, / Most lazar-like with vile and loathsome crust / All my smooth body" (1.5.72–74). Developing sores, Old Hamlet's white body transforms into something that resembles tree bark, which is usually a shade of brown. The reference to leprosy scabs and the "crust" that overtake the body creates a contrast between the newfound roughness of Old Hamlet's skin and deteriorating stature and the natural smoothness of his once healthy white body.[77] Claudius' evil deed, his choice to poison his brother with "juice of cursèd hebona," introduces blackness, or blackening, to Denmark through sin and immorality; through Old Hamlet's body's physical response to the poison; and through the King's death and the initiation of his decomposition process (1.5.63).

Claudius literally taints Denmark's masculinity both through the murder itself and *how* he murders, since poison was thought to be a feminine, passive way to kill, as *Othello* reminds us when the General suggests he will poison Desdemona.[78] The Ghost's repeated description of the murder as "foul" (1.5.13, 26, 28, 29) and "unnatural" (1.5.26, 29) prescribes Claudius' unmanliness and emblematic blackness, which one cannot help but notice in the remainder of the play. The murder is unnatural and foul, as in corrupt, because the murder*er* is unnatural and foul, as in spiritually soiled with sin. When the Ghost describes Claudius, he others his brother by referring to him as "serpent," (1.5.37) "incestuous," (1.5.43) and "adulterate beast" (1.5.43). Distancing Claudius from a civilized identity, the snake image links the new King to the devil and blackens him morally, as does his monstrous sexuality, the characterization of which aligns him with stereotyped, somatically different characters such as Aaron and Othello. Moreover, the characterization distances him from his deceased brother, who represents white male propriety. The Ghost allies Claudius with "witchcraft" and consequently a stereotype linked to criminality and Black sexuality attributed to characters such as Othello and Cleopatra (1.5.44).[79] Furthermore, he accuses Claudius of having "shameful lust" (1.5.46) and "wicked wits and gifts, that have the power / So to seduce!" (1.5.45–46). As seducer, Claudius plays the woman's role, standing in for the play's absent Black hypersexual seductress. He is a Cleopatra, so to speak.

The Ghost colors Claudius as his dark foil whose personhood pales in comparison to the Ghost's now dead white masculinity and patriarchal magnificence. The brotherly dynamic is represented by familiar binaries such as good and evil, white and black, masculine and feminine, and even the language of high and low. These binaries affirm the stigma about unmanliness, which registers in *Hamlet* as a character flaw. According to the Ghost, Gertrude, like morally weak Eve,[80] began existing in a fallen state once she chose to "decline / Upon a wretch whose natural gifts were poor" in comparison to Old Hamlet's (1.5.51–52).[81] The decline represents a lowering of standards, given that Gertrude chooses to replace the ideal masculine white patriarch with a lesser version of him, the white other. The former presumably possesses the richer natural qualities that represent what is socially desirable. Gertrude's marital move is reductive for the reasons the Ghost explicitly states and for reasons implied in the subtext that presents the new King as having more in common with his spouse than his late brother. The decline from a presumably healthy marriage to one that is incestuous and spiritually unhealthy parallels the state's deteriorating health, deterioration linked to Claudius' rotting masculinity and white otherness.

The play's characters recognize Hamlet's changed state, but most of them do not recognize Claudius' transformation – perhaps with the exception of perceptive Hamlet, who aims to "catch the conscience of the King" (2.2.606). When the Prince insults the King's manliness before he departs for England, he reinforces what the play already articulates as a possibility: that the new monarch is a dysfunctional amalgamation of social roles and a cancerous, inept ruler and patriarch who severely weakens the body politic. Hamlet's intensified disrespect toward Claudius, observed in his resistance to legitimating a father-son relationship, is a result of the tension that exists between these unmanly figures. In catty ways, they call out each other's less-than-ideal masculinity and emphasize the intrafamilial tension that influences the play's intraracial tension. By refusing to refer to Claudius as "father" when leaving for England, Hamlet rhetorically attributes feminine characteristics to his "uncle-father" and denies Claudius the patriarchal power he tries to assert (2.2.376). Their farewell exchange in this pivotal scene reasserts the new King's failure to solidify himself as a surrogate father and patriarch.[82] The "lowest white man", the white other, is rejected as the Prince defines Claudius' position with an ambiguous goodbye that displays "gender confusion":[83]

> HAMLET: Farewell, dear mother.
> KING: Thy loving father, Hamlet.
> HAMLET: My mother. Father and mother is man and
> wife, man and wife is one flesh, and so, my mother.
> Come, for England!
>
> (4.3.53–57)

The one flesh that is Gertrude and Claudius is notably feminine; this is unsurprising given the decomposition of white masculinity and patriarchy, which makes it impossible for Claudius to be seen, like Old Hamlet, as "King, father, royal Dane" by Hamlet (1.4.44–45). "Father," a fundamental social role, would legitimize Claudius, the white other, and affirm his patriarchal position. Hamlet's refusal is a subtle reminder of the difference between the idealized white man, his biologically related deceased father, and the new King. In her comments on the above dialogue, Janet Adelman argues that "in this fantasy, it does not matter whether Hamlet is thinking of his father or his incestuous stand-in."[84] However, I propose it matters greatly, for the erasure of masculinity heightens Claudius' feminization and reduces his patriarchal power; as Adelman rightly claims in another moment: "In this rank mixture [of masculine and feminine], the female will always succeed in transforming the male, remaking him in her image."[85] Hamlet's clever, dismissive farewell address others Claudius by its identification of the King with the incestuous mother figure who, prior to this scene, looks "into [her] very soul / And there see[s] such black and grained spots / As will not leave their tinct" (3.4.91–93). Moreover, the gender confusion Hamlet creates here reflects a disruption of socio-political order, with the living King erased and his absent wife, the Queen, on top.[86]

By the time we truly discover what is rotten in the state of Denmark, ideal Danish masculinity has been compromised by white unmanliness, which is displayed by the play's two most central male figures. Hamlet's own masculine defects are reflected in his misogynistic language toward Ophelia that personifies "frailty" and creates an inextricable link between it and "woman" (1.2.146). According to Hamlet, weakness is a womanly trait, yet the male characters' conduct contradicts this logic by underscoring the possibilities for male feminization at various points in the drama. Displaying signs of weakness, the males exude what was understood in the period as feminine behavior: Upon learning about Ophelia's death, for instance, Laertes becomes emotionally expressive and sheds tears, acknowledging that "when these [tears] are gone, / The woman will be out" (4.7.189–190). That is to say, when presumed frailty is in men then so, too, is the woman, for the metaphorical *she* engages men in an internal power struggle that is understood, according to Andrew D. McCarthy, "as a physical assault on their bodies (that is, 'women's weapons')."[87] Especially since gender is a social construct, McCarthy's claim suggests there is a tenuous boundary between masculinity and femininity that is illuminated through the white other's presence.[88]

Code Black: "Unmanly Grief"

Gendered expectations around grief were commonplace in early modern England. However, a person could be culturally transgressive in their mourning process.[89] As Hamlet experiences the emotional effects of his father's death, Claudius condemns the Prince's "unmanly grief" with a critique containing racial undertones and challenging Hamlet's masculinity (1.2.94). Claudius' criticism produces gendered anxiety[90] and exploits the aural power of masculinity to code Hamlet's black mood as wrong. The critique also denotes Claudius' own weakness by representing what modern readers consider "toxic masculinity." In shaming the Prince, Claudius aims to regulate Hamlet's metaphorical blackness, as expressed or made visible in his emotions, perhaps so they become manly, representative of ideal aristocratic[91] white masculinity and devoid of prolonged grief.[92] In fact, Claudius imbues his criticism with meaning that connects Hamlet's tarnished whiteness to his unacceptably prolonged grief, grief that emasculates him.[93] Those rhetorical moments are worth highlighting because they document the play's evolving discourse surrounding Hamlet's compromised state. Even the Queen notices Hamlet's blackness when she orders him to "cast [his] nightly colour off / And let [his] eye look like a friend on Denmark" (1.2.68–69); in not looking like a friend, Hamlet appears as a threatening black(ened) enemy. His demeanor has negative implications for his relationship with

Denmark, as his nightly color embodies the blackness, also represented by black bile, that consumes him.[94]

Following Gertrude, Claudius specifies how Hamlet's attitude is an affront to Denmark: "It shows a will most incorrect to heaven," he explains, and he reiterates and expands on that assertion by saying that Hamlet's unyielding unmanly grief is "a fault to heaven, / A fault against the dead, a fault to nature, / To reason most absurd" (1.2.101–103). Invoking religion, Claudius reinforces through the "fault" repetition that Hamlet's behavior violates God's will[95] and, in so doing, comes close to being sinful, because it is a neglection of his duty to God.[96] Additionally, the King emphasizes that one also has a moral obligation to honor and not offend the dead and nature by mourning too long. Such logic aligns with Elizabethan and Stuart sentiments "about the propriety and protocols of mourning, in particular who should mourn, how to mourn, and for how long mourning should be observed."[97] Ironically, in honoring his (deceased) father's will, as the Bible instructs children to do,[98] and by having his father's "nature in [him]," the Prince's eventual murderous intentions act as a corrective to the behavior for which Claudius chastises him (1.5.82).[99] Being unmanly due to his incessant grief, Hamlet rejects the rigid boundaries of toxic white masculinity. All of this, as Claudius concludes, is evidence of Hamlet's irrationality and unsound judgment. This would have been understood by early modern people as an inability to reason,[100] which contributes to the Prince's wrongly colored mood and otherness.

But it is not just Hamlet's temperament that is colored black and therefore wrong, it is also Hamlet himself that is the wrong color. As white other, he is a character who defines himself as "too much i'th' sun" (1.2.67);[101] wears an "inky cloak" (1.2.77) and "customary suits of solemn black" (1.2.78); and opts to be the "darkest night" that lets Laertes' star "stick fiery off" as they prepare for the duel, a pastime that cultivated aristocratic manhood (5.2.254–255).[102] Such descriptions point to an undeniable physical, or external, blackness that complements the internal blackness signaled by Hamlet's melancholy and anger; it is as though the black ink from his cloak bleeds, seeping into the play's tragic fabric. *Hamlet* contains a few moments that indicate it is possible for white to be black(ened) internally or externally: Hamlet's allusion to the Greek Pyrrhus' "sable arms" (2.2.452), black "purpose" (2.2.453) and "black complexion" (2.2.455) echoes the Prince of Denmark's own disposition and provides an example of blackness consuming a somatically white being.[103] When Hamlet notes that Pyrrhus "did the night resemble," he reminds the audience, as seen in Figure 2.1, of his own dark appearance at

Figure 2.1   Illustrations to Shakespeare, group scenes (unfinished) by John Massey Wright (late eighteenth or early nineteenth century). Image 35434, used by permission of the Folger Shakespeare Library.

the play's onset and of the fact that even a white man can be a black-like figure (2.2.453).[104]

Beyond the Pyrrhus scene, white otherness defines Hamlet's identity in Polonius' assertion that "the apparel oft proclaims the man," that one's fashion choices are central to how one is perceived, to the judgments others might make and also to one's perception of self (1.3.72).[105] Sartorial choices can convey status, broadly speaking (class, ethnicity, race, gender, etc.), and clothes can outwardly mark one's internal state.[106] Clothing, as Polonius theorizes, speaks for the wearer; thus, Hamlet's clothing distinguishes his otherness.[107] His sartorial choices foreshadow his volatile black emotional state, which oscillates between melancholy, instigated by his sorrow,[108] and revenge/anger, what Claudius labels Hamlet's "dangerous lunacy": a feminizing phrase, given that early modern women were stereotyped as being highly susceptible to hysteria and madness (3.1.4).[109] Hamlet's gender non-conformity – his inability to be the ideal masculine white man, or maintain a distinct masculine identity due to his being consumed by emotions associated with the feminine[110] – links him to blackness and makes him a foil to Old Hamlet.

In this dramatic work sustained by white people watching other white people, one should expect that Claudius is not alone in recognizing "Hamlet's transformation" (2.2.5) as partly a consequence of his compromised manliness. Gertrude laments her "too much changèd son" (2.2.36),

Polonius wants to find "the cause of this defect" in Hamlet (2.2.101), and Claudius claims, regarding Hamlet, "th'exterior nor the inward man / Resembles that it was" (2.2.6–7). Gertrude is concerned with how much the Prince has changed: In her eyes, he is on the verge of possibly losing himself. Hamlet's black makeover alarms the play's other main characters. His "defect" is his deficient, allegedly flawed masculinity that Shakespeare associates with blackness, which, when imposed on the white body, becomes viewed as abnormally white.[111] Interestingly, the defect revelation is made by Claudius, a flawed white man who is himself a defective, failed patriarch.

When these characters evaluate Hamlet, they highlight aspects of his rotting masculinity, which the play underscores just one scene earlier when Hamlet enters Ophelia's closet in Act 2, Scene 1 and displays physical aggression toward her. Hamlet's behavior parallels Othello's hostility toward Desdemona in the moment when the Black man "strikes" her, as the stage direction indicates (*Othello*, 4.1.246). Paradoxically, Hamlet's aggression is a symptom of his masculine fragility, which makes him have more in common with a woman such as Ophelia and less in common with his valiant deceased father, a fact that further distances him from ideal white masculinity. This dynamic is similar to how Claudius' hypersexuality links him to Gertrude, the play's other woman. Figuratively speaking, the rot on Hamlet's masculinity tarnishes it in ways that underscore his unmanliness. As the play progresses, not even Hamlet can deny the irreversible deteriorating condition of his masculinity, for which death is the only remedy: Death is the only way the woman will be out. The play's catastrophic conclusion purges the most prominent representations of white unmanliness and blackened femininity.

As previously argued, Hamlet's defectiveness links him to blackness and femininity, sometimes independently of one another but often in conjunction. When Polonius comments, "How pregnant sometimes [Hamlet's] replies are," he feminizes the fruitful complexity of the Prince's intellect and wit in a metaphor that amplifies Hamlet's dramatic emasculation (2.2.208–209). This might explain why Hamlet says, "My wit's dis- / eased," for he is so troubled with unmanliness (3.2.320–321). For Hamlet's replies to be pregnant, in theory, they must be impregnated somehow: allowing for a literal interpretation of "pregnant," given that this meaning was understood in Shakespeare's time, as Tonya Pollard explains, one can observe the homo-hypersexual undertone here through Hamlet's "potential maternity," which places him in a curious position.[112] Since biologically speaking only women can become pregnant among humans,[113] the implication is that Hamlet's replies have occasionally copulated – with a man – to be as generative as they are. This occasional copulation conveys a sense of casual and otherworldly[114] fornication, linking the Prince to the concept of whoredom, a type of conduct stemming from monstrous female sexuality, which he directly associates with his "adulterous" mother[115] and himself later in this scene.[116] Similar to Claudius, Hamlet acts as a Cleopatra-like figure. And if Hamlet's replies are pregnant, then so, too, is Hamlet, since he births those ideas.

Conversely, when Hamlet's replies are not pregnant, indicated by Polonius' use of "sometimes," one might say they are unfruitful but still fertile. Nevertheless, such replies showcase the multiplicity of meanings found in the term "pregnant"; and such replies are reminders of how sexual and masculine anxiety drive the play's dramatic tension and the gendered tension within Hamlet.[117] Whenever Hamlet makes loaded statements that make his audience think, he taps into his unmanly self or a maternal self, which solidifies him as a character who is "unpregnant of [his] cause" since he is quick to talk and slow to act (2.2.562). Laertes' previously cited line, "the woman will be out," is even more fascinating when considering it an extension of how men in this play can be pregnant. To expel the woman from the body is, in a way, to give birth to her so she exists as a feminine self that is distinct from one's masculine self. When the woman is out, in terms of what *Hamlet* proposes, with her go tears, inconstancy, frailty, fear, monstrous sexuality, hysteria, madness, and so many other qualities that the valiant Norwegian Young Fortinbras does not seem to possess because, as a cultural outsider, he has not been steeped in the corrosive power of white Danish masculinity. From beginning to end, it is the Danish men who are pregnant with the woman. They represent feminine excess through their symbolically grotesque male bodies.[118] Such bodies are products of an authority that was understood as toxic: maternal power, as Adelman theorizes in her analysis of masculinity and the maternal body.[119]

Citing Defective Whiteness

Hamlet best articulates his own embodiment of unmanliness through self-deprecating behavior that immediately follows Polonius' metaphorical critique of the Prince's masculinity. After the Pyrrhus episode, one in which Hamlet's reaction parallels his later response to Young Fortinbras in Act 4, Scene 4, Hamlet berates himself for being "a dull and muddy-mettled rascal," phrasing that acknowledges his weakness (2.2.567).

Although it is part of a hyphenated term, the racial implications of "muddy" cannot go unnoticed, for "muddy" connects Hamlet to Ophelia, who dies a "muddy death" (a darkening of the white body); her reputation is stained by the speculation surrounding whether or not her death was a suicide and therefore a sin (4.7.184).[120] Hamlet's doubts about his masculinity, apparent when he asks himself, "Am I a coward?" remind us that up to this point he has remained a man of no action (2.2.571). His masculine insecurity overwhelms him: In a span of nearly thirty lines in Act 2, Hamlet declares he is "pigeon-livered," as in meek, and "lack[s] gall to make oppression bitter" (2.2.577–578). He chastises himself for being an "ass" (2.2.583). And he self-identifies his "weakness and melancholy," qualities that signify his unmanliness and internal blackness, respectively (2.2.602).

Most strikingly, Hamlet criticizes his delayed action with figurative language and repeats the now familiar idea that there is some resonance between the Danish Prince and morally corrupt, hypersexual women, the kind of women thought to defy early modern social decorum. Accordingly, he expresses his frustration with the fact that he "must, like a whore, unpack [his] heart with words / And fall a-cursing like a very drab, / A scullion!" (2.2.586–587).[121] Claudius also uses similar language when he compares his evil deed to the "harlot's [ugly] cheek beautied with plastering art" (3.1.52). "Whore," "drab," and "harlot," terms describing women with monstrous sexuality – women like Gertrude, who has been "whored" by Claudius, according to her son (5.2.64) – reveal how "Hamlet pinpoints his own effeminacy, characterizing himself as more like a boy or woman than a man [...] Shakespeare could not be clearer that Hamlet is emasculated by his own lack of action," as Gilbert surmises.[122] Furthermore, Hamlet's verbal assault on himself indicates how he projects onto women his self-dissatisfaction. The Prince uses feminized discourse to criticize women and berate himself, as if to insinuate that masculine discourse is inaccessible to him in this moment where he reminds us of his gendered, racialized faults.

The types of women to whom Hamlet compares himself expose his masculine insecurities stemming from his misogyny and sexism, and perhaps his disdain for the blackness he embodies.[123] Hamlet's alignment with women, or even their abstract image, reiterates how he is not a reflection of his father's heroic image, despite bearing the same name, which creates the ultimate contrast: Old Hamlet versus Young Hamlet, the latter being a white other. The Prince is, indeed, his own person, but this does not bode well for Denmark, since he is a weak white man. When

Claudius pronounces that Hamlet is "from fashion of himself," indicating that the Prince's melancholy has drastically altered his personality, the King builds on his previous remark that Hamlet is not what he once was (3.1.178). The Prince is still not in what one might recognize as his usual form, much like Ophelia is not herself after Polonius' death, because something steps in between Hamlet and himself. Identified as the causes of his much-altered state, his "grief" (3.1.180, 186) and "melancholy" (3.1.168), feelings spawned by his father's murder, allow another nuanced parallel between the Prince and Ophelia to surface, since we see her in "deep grief" over her father's murder in Act 4, Scene 5 (line 76). Just as Hamlet is from fashion of himself, "poor Ophelia [is] / Divided from herself and her fair judgment, / Without the which we are pictures or mere beasts" (4.5.8–87). She, too, is out of fashion, yet in ways that contrast with Hamlet, "in part, probably to emphasize the difference between feigned and actual madness, melancholy and distraction."[124]

Nevertheless, it is through this connection that the unmanly construction develops further, since grief and melancholy blacken Ophelia's aura in the play, literally separating her from the *"fair* judgment,"[125] and leading her, like Hamlet, to death.[126] The possibility of Ophelia being beast-like is an allusion to Hamlet's own bestial state, which I will soon explore. Also, Ophelia's psychic division intimates that she may also exist on the "other" or wrong side of the intraracial color-line, as her separation from "herself and her fair judgment" mark a distinction between the image of an idealized virtuous white woman and a lesser, dehumanized white woman – a representation of the white other – who is bestial, uncivilized, and, quite possibly, unhuman. Paradoxically, Ophelia is already socially dead before she dies physically; without a father and without a husband, she ceases to exist, in the early modern sense (as daughter or wife). In other words, she does not have a social role that validates her womanly existence. There are no masculine pillars to uphold her, since emasculated Hamlet proves himself an unsuitable love interest.[127]

Hamlet's myriad instances of masculine fragility repeatedly remind us that ideal Danish masculinity no longer has a pulse, as signaled by Old Hamlet's dead, cold, decomposing body.[128] When the human body shuts down, and the cells die and release their energy, the body's temperature drops rapidly. As one considers what physically remains of Old Hamlet in the grave, one should envision his body as blackened by the decomposition process. The coldness is reflected in the atmosphere of the body politic and Denmark; and the coldness reinforces how much the old King's suspicious death influences the play's tone and setting, which both support my reading of Denmark's masculine crisis: In the opening scene, Francisco, a member of the watch, remarks that it is "bitter cold" (1.1.8); Hamlet begins Act 1, Scene 4 by observing, "The air bites shrewdly; it is very cold" (line 1); when Ophelia grieves her father's death, she says, "I cannot choose but weep to think they would lay / him i'th' cold ground" (4.5.70–71); and during Hamlet's comical exchange with Orsic the former reiterates, "'Tis very cold. The wind is northerly," and the latter concurs, even after he initially claimed it was hot (5.2.96). I am not suggesting Old Hamlet's death caused things to be chilly in Denmark, though one could potentially make that argument regarding Hamlet and Claudius' icy relationship. What I am proposing, however, is that there exists a correlation between the King's dead body and the drama's cold atmosphere, which taken together indicate how white masculinity lacks dynamism and life, an argument that *Hamlet*'s sustained frosty climate sustains.[129]

It is, after all, in this cold landscape where one finds the Danish men who need to let some form of the woman out. Indeed, unmanliness is presented as the condition of white Danish men after heroic Old Hamlet's death. Early on, Claudius mentions that Young Fortinbras, who represents ideal masculine whiteness, "hold[s] a weak supposal of our worth"; the possessive form of the royal *we* renders this moment about Claudius and the general Danish population (1.2.18). Ironically, the Player Queen argues in the climactic act that women express weakness and "fear," but apparently so, too, do men in *Hamlet* (3.2.165, 168). Marcellus and Bernardo watched the Ghost of Hamlet with "fear-surprisèd eyes" (1.2.204) as they "distilled / Almost to jelly with the act of fear" (1.2.205–206). Talking with Polonius, Hamlet asserts that old men have "most weak hams," insulting the alleged physical deficiency of older men (2.2.201). In a metadramatic fashion, Rosencrantz claims, "Many wearing rapiers are afraid / of goose quills and dare scarce come thither" (2.2.343–344). Guildenstern and Rosencrantz display moral frailty as they "soak up the King's countenance" and betray their friend Hamlet in the process (4.2.16). Laertes "weeps" out the woman in him when learning of Ophelia's death; and when Horatio considers drinking what is left of the poisoned drink, he rebuffs his Danish identity, declaring he is "more an antique Roman then a Dane" (5.2.343).

In the context of suicide, though, Horatio further distances himself from ideal masculine whiteness, for to die by drinking poison is not "manly."[130] For the ancient Romans, as Myles McDonnell asserts in *Roman Manliness*, "*Virtus* holds a high place as a traditional quality that played a central part in war, politics, and religion."[131] Hamlet, Claudius, and their Danish dramatic counterparts create distance between themselves and *virtus* by not actively or consistently demonstrating aggressive manly behavior.[132] They break with Old Hamlet's established, more traditional militaristic masculinity. In the Danish white men, then, unmanliness lives; and it arguably lives on through Horatio and through the tragic story he must recount. Even without containing men in women's clothing, *Hamlet* contributes to the anxious notion – expressed in early modern tracts and pamphlets by anti-theatricalists such as Stephen Gosson,[133] Phillip Stubbes, and Willian Prynne – that theater and performance could effeminize men and destabilize the sense of self.[134] It was not just costumes, but also dramatic discourse and character behavior that influenced how anti-theatricalists condemned the theater, for action could lead men, performers and spectators, to question the stability of their own gender identity, so it was thought.[135] And seeming "to lack an inherent gender" identity could theoretically make a man seem like less than a man and more like a woman – and therefore monstrous.[136]

Restoring Ideal White Masculinity

Norwegian Young Fortinbras' masculine aura redirects the play's focus through his leadership and seemingly uncompromised normative masculinity as he commands the play's concluding action and restores a sense of *virtus* (5.2.388–392, 397–405). Even though Fortinbras speaks very little in this scene, his valiant presence, which counters Hamlet's weakness (literalized by his dying and death), is apparent, so much so that it generates reminders of Hamlet's own inaction and masculine deficiency. Rather than avenge the Ghost's murder, which is his primary charge in Act 1, Hamlet thinks and talks, and even puts on an "antic disposition" (1.5.181). Indeed, he acts but he does not act like Young Fortinbras. The play's opening foreshadows Hamlet's contrasting passivity, as Horatio describes Young Fortinbras as "hot and full" of intense manly aggression and strength, characteristics more in line with social expectations. Young Fortinbras' hotness is a necessary counter to the coldness I discussed previously (1.1.100). Distracted by his unmanliness, Hamlet's questionable revenge is slow.[137] It takes witnessing Fortinbras' steadfastness to compel Hamlet to get back on course, albeit passively, for he notes his "thoughts [will] be bloody," but conveys nothing about what his actions will be (4.4.67).[138] With his father murdered and his mother whored, the Danish Prince has more than enough reason to enact his revenge. Yet instead, he illustrates what inaction means, how it makes a human being indistinguishable from a beast, a previously cited term he uses in reference to Claudius in Act 1, Scene 5, when he labels him "adulterate beast" (line 42). Hamlet's passivity and his inability to be manly show us how he and his uncle, as representations of the white other, have more in common with the play's women and each other than they may recognize.[139] In Act 5 especially, we discover that Shakespeare may have been most interested in constructing a play designed to accept and challenge the ideal of violent masculinity, for "Shakespeare's show-stopping climax in *Hamlet* is oddly inconclusive" as it pertains to displaying combat in a way that fully celebrates the art of the duel.[140]

In the denouement, Young Fortinbras returns to avenge his father's murder and, more importantly, to portray what an ideal masculine white man is and to reestablish order, through violent means if necessary.[141] I posit that Young Fortinbras is one answer to Hamlet's question, "What is a man?," an answer that reminds us that the Prince of Denmark has yet to prove his manhood or patriarchal power, something he never gets to do, especially in light of reading him as a failed avenger. Quite possibly, Hamlet fails because he was "rotten before 'a die[d]," as the Gravedigger comically suggests a man can be – rotten because, like Macbeth, he has "diseased manliness" (5.1.162).[142] If ideal Danish white masculinity died with Old Hamlet, who "*was* a man" (1.2.187),[143] then I propose that the lifeblood of unmanliness dies in Denmark through the purging of Hamlet (and Claudius and the women). Fortinbras' assuming the Danish throne revives the image of ideal patriarchy and masculinity that symbolizes strength, valor, rationality, and the potential for aggressiveness.[144] Young Fortinbras *is* a man; and he is *the* most important man in this moment.

The focus on Hamlet's dead body in the end, and therefore the beginning of his corporeal decomposition process, recalls his father's dead body; and Young Fortinbras creates a contrast between the two dead Danes with his treatment of Hamlet's corpse. Norway's Prince orders his captains to: "Bear Hamlet, like a soldier, to the stage / For he was likely, had he been put on, / To have proved most royal" (5.2.398–400). "Like" means Hamlet is, in fact, not a soldier, a social role that might have instilled him with a sense of masculine strength. Moreover, the speculation about what Hamlet could have been further solidifies what he never proved himself as – most royal, most manly, most valiant, most white, like his father.[145] Hamlet proves himself to be something else, something other, that has more in common with his mother than his late father. As white other, Hamlet exemplifies how it is possible to sight the intraracial color-line in a play that exclusively centers white figures. The fifth Act's restoration of normative masculinity rests in Hamlet's silence and in Young Fortinbras' authoritative final words.

When Horatio commits to telling the story of *Hamlet* – all of the "unnatural acts" – he resigns himself to recounting the story of tainted whiteness, Denmark's deterioration, and the decomposition of white masculinity, since, in recounting the play's events, he will have to focus on the two main male characters Shakespeare imbued with unmanliness (5.2.383). Given that a man can be rotten before he dies, as the Gravedigger explains, it makes sense that we can witness the decomposition of Hamlet and Claudius before they physically die. Until the end, Hamlet and Claudius are focal points; they are the most socially, politically, and psychologically prominent men. Similar to *Titus Andronicus'* Aaron, whose highly visible Black body emerges as a vehicle for transmitting fundamental messages about fatherhood and domestic ideals, Claudius' and Hamlet's royal white bodies are encoded with messages about whiteness, otherness, blackness, masculinity, femininity, and domestic (dis)order in this tragedy.[146]

The concluding entrance of Young Fortinbras, an ethnically different white man whom some consider the "anti-Hamlet,"[147] and the presence of myriad dead bodies on the stage, is a restorative measure that reaffirms the play's detachment from unmanliness by returning us to the "esteemed ethnic features" of white maleness that are characteristic of Old Hamlet.[148] The text reinforces this point by constantly highlighting how it is not somatic difference, but Hamlet's sullied whiteness (as in his black mood, fashion, conduct, unmanliness, etc.) that makes him fail to meet the expectations one might have of him based on the precedent set by his heroic father. Thus, how this dramatic work codes unmanliness as black, specifically by stigmatizing it as an inferior category of difference in relationship to ideal masculine whiteness – and therefore styling unmanliness as undesirable, even though it may not actually be so, given that Claudius and Hamlet are still desired by Gertrude and Ophelia, respectively – serves to enlighten our conceptions of race, racial/gender construction, racial power dynamics, and subjectivity. Moreover, it serves to open our eyes to the various ways race, because it is everywhere,[149] intersects with, and is relevant to, discourse on everything:[150] not just gender, class, and sexuality, but also science, social conduct, politics, religion, nature, and, of course, Shakespeare's plays that center on white characters. Despite continued overt and covert professional and public resistance to interrogating whiteness in critical literary ways,[151] we must talk about race in *Hamlet*. For the advancement of antiracism and what I will call "critical racial equity," whiteness must be scrutinized more broadly and more regularly in Shakespeare and premodern English studies. Shakespeare's canon wills it so, even as it pertains to the white figures and under-examined whiteness in a more commonly understood race play such as *Antony and Cleopatra*, the next chapter's dramatic subject.

Notes

1 Fleming, *How to Be Less Stupid about Race*, 15.
2 This chapter adds to a currently limited but growing body of work on *Hamlet* and race. Sonia Massai and Lucy Munro argue that we should "continue to think of *Hamlet* as a key platform, or 'cultural field', within which gaps in our own way of thinking not only about this play but also about the diversity of position-takings of those who engage with it, critically or creatively, come to emerge, telling us as much about the play as the assumptions, world view and expectations that we bring to it." "Introduction," in *Hamlet: The State of Play*, eds. Sonia Massai and Lucy Munro (London: The Arden Shakespeare, 2021), 1–26; 20. A version of the present chapter first appeared in Massai and Munro's edited collection (Brown, "Code Black"). Also see Smith, *Black Shakespeare*, 119–121.
3 Hughey, "Black Guys," 96.
4 Jennifer Forsyth, "Cutting Words and Healing Wounds: Friendship and Violence in Early Modern Drama," in *Violent Masculinities: Male Aggression in Early Modern Texts and Culture*, eds. Jennifer Feather and Catherine E. Thomas (New York: Palgrave Macmillan, 2013), 67–81, 68–69.
5 Bruce R. Smith contends, "In every culture men are expected to propagate, provide, and defend, but the ways in which they are expected to do those things vary from one culture to another. What remains constant across these differences, however, is the fact that masculinity must be achieved. It is not a natural given." *Shakespeare and Masculinity* (Oxford: Oxford University Press, 2000), 2. Also see "Introduction: Reclaiming Violent Masculinities," in *Violent Masculinities: Male Aggression in Early Modern Texts and Culture*, eds. Jennifer Feather and Catherine E. Thomas (New York: Palgrave Macmillan, 2013), 1. Feather and Thomas build on Smith's argument to claim that "masculinity is achieved and negotiated through acts of aggression."
6 Martha R. Mahoney explains, "Like culture, race is something whites notice in themselves only in relation to others." "The Social Construction of Whiteness," 331.
7 William E. Engel, *Death and Drama in Renaissance England: Shades of Memory* (Oxford: Oxford University Press, 2002), 1, 14.
8 Guo De-yan, "Hamlet's Femininity," *Canadian Social Science*, 5.5 (2009), 89–95.
9 Jennifer A. Low, "Manhood and the Duel: Enacting Masculinity in 'Hamlet,'" *The Centennial Review*, 43.3 (Fall 1999), 501–512; 502, 503.

10 See Robert I. Lublin, "'Apparel oft proclaims the man': Visualizing Hamlet on the Early Modern Stage" *Shakespeare Bulletin*, 32.4 (Winter 2014), 629–647, 635, 638.

11 "Valiant" is reserved for Old Hamlet; these are the play's only usages of the term.

12 Lublin, "'Apparel oft proclaims the man,'" 632–633. Regarding the play's relationship to the medieval, Reta A. Terry asserts, "Shakespeare creates characters in *Hamlet* that represent various stages in the evolution of a changing system of honor." Terry suggests Hamlet reflects the tension between these evolving codes while a character like Laertes adheres to the old code. "'Vows to the Blackest Devil': Hamlet and the Evolving Code of Honor in Early Modern England," *Renaissance Quarterly*, 52.4 (Winter 1999), 1070–1086; 1084.

13 Richard W. Kauper, *Medieval Chivalry* (Cambridge: Cambridge University Press, 2016), 353.

14 Low, "Manhood and the Duel," 501.

15 Mark Breitenberg, *Anxious Masculinity in Early Modern England* (Cambridge: Cambridge University Press, 1996), 2.

16 Hughey, "Black Guys," 98.

17 Kelly Stage highlights some of the difficulties Hamlet has with finding his place in Elsinore. These struggles are connected to the challenges Hamlet faces because of the intraracial color-line and his less-than-ideal whiteness. See "'Tragedians of the City," in *Hamlet: The State of Play*, eds. Sonia Massai and Lucy Munro (London: The Arden Shakespeare, 2021), 81–100; 81–83, 93–95.

18 Hortense Spillers, "Mama's Baby, Papa's Maybe: An American Grammar Book," *Diacritics*, 17.2, Culture and Countermemory: The "American" Connection (Summer 1987), 64–81; 72, 77, 80.

19 Eldred Jones, "Aaron and Melancholy in *Titus Andronicus*," *Shakespeare Quarterly*, 14.2 (Spring 1963), 178–179.

20 Deroux, "The Blackness Within," 100.

21 In *Basilikon Doron*, James I positions himself as a mother-like father figure: the ultimate parent who will nourish his subjects. Through this example, it is possible to read Aaron's embodiment of the feminine. See Rachel Trubowitz, *Nation and Nurture in Seventeenth-Century English Literature* (Oxford: Oxford University Press, 2012), 107–108.

22 D. Marvin Jones suggests anti-Black racism normalizes violence toward and the social control of Black men. See *Race, Sex, and Suspicion*, 5, 7.

23 According to Helen Berry and Elizabeth Foyster, "Children [in early modern England] were demonstrable proof of a man's sexual success *and* fertility." "Childless Men in Early Modern England," in Berry and Foyster, 158–183; 170, 182.

24 Clapp, *When Gossips Meet*, 9, 267. See Mark Overton, Jane Whittle, Darron Dean, and Andrew Hann, *Production and Consumption in English Households, 1600–1750* (London: Routledge, 2014), 5. Also see David Cressy on

"gossipings" in *Birth, Marriage & Death: Ritual, Religion, and the Life-Cycle in Tudor and Stuart England* (Oxford: Oxford University Press, 1997), 201–203.

25 I write about Morocco's sterilization in "'The Sonic Color Line': Shakespeare and the Canonization of Sexual Violence Against Black Men," *The Sundial* (August 2019), https://medium.com/the-sundial-acmrs/the-sonic-color-line-shakespeare-and-the-canonization-of-sexual-violence-against-black-men-cb166dca9af8.

26 Manhood, in addition to the assertion of masculinity, "in the early modern period was a status to be acquired." Elizabeth Foyster, *Manhood in Early Modern England: Honour, Sex and Marriage* (New York: Longman, 1999), 28–31.

27 Clapp, *When Gossips Meet*, 6.

28 For example, Karen Newman writes on the feminization of Othello and his alignment with Desdemona. Newman emphasizes Othello's embodiment of Renaissance monstrosity and argues that *Othello* "ultimately fulfills the cultural prejudices it represents." *Fashioning Femininity and English Renaissance Drama* (Chicago: The University of Chicago Press, 1991), 87–88. Ultimately, how can a Black man achieve manhood in the early modern sense if he is, at best, considered a "curiosit[y] or oddit[y]"? Hall, *Things of Darkness*, 11.

29 Newman, *Fashioning Femininity*, 85.

30 Smith, *Black Shakespeare*, 141, 144.

31 Ibid., 163.

32 Jennifer Feather, "Shakespeare and Masculinity," *Literature Compass* 12.4 (2015), 134–145, 136.

33 While *Richard III* and *Macbeth* are not plays I analyze thoroughly in this book, I recognize their potential to do the kind of work regarding whiteness and unmanliness that *Hamlet* does, given the negotiations of whiteness in those plays. For a "black Macbeth" analysis, see Brown, "(Early) Modern Literature: Crossing the Color-Line," 74. Also see Brown and Stoever, "'Blanched with fear.'"

34 Feather, "Shakespeare and Masculinity," 136. Phillip Brian Harper discusses intraracial differences, but within the African-American community, in ways that relate to my *Hamlet* analysis of identity, blackness, and masculinity. On the whole, Harper's book is a generative resource because of the author's concern with the oppressive anxieties that surround masculinity and Blackness. See *Are We Not Men?: Masculine Anxiety and the Problem of African-American Identity* (Oxford: Oxford University Press, 1996), esp. x.

35 Coppélia Kahn, *Man's Estate: Masculine Identity in Shakespeare* (Berkeley: University of California Press, 1981), 1, 12.

36 See "Black Hamlet" in Smith, *Black Shakespeare*, 138–141. Also see Noémie Ndiaye, *Scripts of Blackness: Early Modern Performance Culture and the Making of Race* (Philadelphia: University of Pennsylvania Press, 2022), 2–3, 18.

37 The metadramatic nature of *Hamlet* makes Hamlet no stranger to "role-playing." See Jay Farness, "Character Fictions in *Hamlet*," in Massai and Munro, *Hamlet: The State of Play*, 129–150, 134. Vaughan argues, "On

London's stages, blackness was 'acted out' in ways that profoundly affected images of blacks in English culture." *Performing Blackness*, xii. Feather also observes that "work on racial difference has emphasized the performed and constructed nature of both race and gender in the period." "Shakespeare and Masculinity," 137. See Urvashi Chakravarty, "More Than Kin, Less Than Kind: Similitude, Strangeness, and Early Modern English Homonationalisms," *Shakespeare Quarterly*, 67.1 (Spring 2016), 14–29, 21; and Brown, "'Is Black So Base a Hue?': Black Life Matters in Shakespeare's *Titus Andronicus*," in *Early Modern Black Diaspora Studies, A Critical Anthology*, eds. Cassander Smith, Nicholas Jones, and Miles P. Grier (New York: Palgrave Macmillan, 2018), 137–155; 140–142. For a take on Simon Godwin's *Hamlet*, Blackness and performance, see Sujata Iyengar and Lesley Feracho, "*Hamlet* (RSC, 2016) and Representations of Diasporic Blackness," *Cahiers Élisabéthains*, 99.1 (July 2019), 147–160.

38 Cressy, *Birth, Marriage and Death*, 438.
39 Akhimie, *Shakespeare and the Cultivation of Difference*, 191.
40 Feather and Thomas, *Violent Masculinities*, 6.
41 Ibid., 4.
42 For instance: Hall studies violence, race and gender in her reading of *The Tempest*. See *Things of Darkness*, 142–153.
43 De-yan claims, "30-year-old Hamlet sometimes acts as if he were a child. In words, he is a man of intellect, is a philosopher and a thinker. In deeds, however, he is dominated by feminine emotions." "Hamlet's Femininity," 92. Also see Sky Gilbert, "A Sparrow Falls: Olivier's Feminine Hamlet," *Brief Chronicles* 1 (2009), 193–204; 196.
44 Peter Erickson, "Can We Talk about Race in *Hamlet*?," in *Hamlet: Critical Essays*, ed. Arthur Kinney (New York: Routledge, 2002), 207–213; 212.
45 Ayanna Thompson, "What Is a 'Weyward' *Macbeth*?," in *Weyward Macbeth: Intersections of Race and Performance*, eds. Scott Newstok and Ayanna Thompson (New York: Palgrave Macmillan, 2010), 3–10; 3.
46 Erickson explores the play's male dynamics and depiction of women in "Can We Talk," 209.
47 Ibid., 210–211.
48 Hall, *Things of Darkness*, 2, 6–7, 23, 53; Parker, "Black *Hamlet*," 129.
49 See Akhimie, *Shakespeare and the Cultivation of Difference*; and Lisa M. Anderson, "When Race Matters," in *Weyward Macbeth: Intersections of Race and Performance*, eds. Scott Newstok and Ayanna Thompson (New York: Palgrave Macmillan, 2010), 89–102.
50 Peter Erickson and Kim F. Hall, "'A New Scholarly Song': Rereading Early Modern Race," *Shakespeare Quarterly* 67.1 (Spring 2016), 1–13; 2.
51 Chakravarty, "More Than Kin," 15.
52 Ibid.
53 Smith, *Race and Rhetoric*, 4, 9.
54 Jennifer A. Low, *Manhood and the Duel: Masculinity in Early Modern Drama and Culture* (New York: Palgrave Macmillan, 2003), 97.

55 Ibid., 97.
56 On self-fashioning, whiteness and the Other, see Arthur L. Little, Jr., "Re-Historicizing Race," 92.
57 See Smith, *Shakespeare and Masculinity* (Oxford: Oxford University Press, 2000), 40.
58 Ibid., 41.
59 Emily C. Bartels discusses *Hamlet*, ethnicity and gender, as opposed to a detailed discussion of race; as a result, she does not address what is significant about the play's engagement with and critiques of whiteness. See "Identifying 'the Dane': Gender and Race in *Hamlet*," in *Shakespeare and Embodiment: Gender, Sexuality, and Race*, ed. Valeria Traub (Oxford: Oxford University Press, 2016), 197–210.
60 Hall, *Things of Darkness*, 9.
61 Jarold Ramsey, "The Perversion of Manliness in *Macbeth*," *Studies in English Literature*, 13.2 (Spring 1973), 285–300; 285.
62 Gilbert, "A Sparrow Falls," 196. Also see Bernhard Frank, "'The Rest Is Silence': *Hamlet*, A Closet Case," *Hamlet Studies*, 20.1–2 (Summer and Winter 1998), 94–97.
63 On black/white opposition, see Hall, *Things of Darkness*, 9.
64 Bruce R. Smith declares that Macbeth's "masculinity is constantly on the line." *Shakespeare and Masculinity*, 3.
65 Macbeth, whose wife questions his manliness, is referred to as "black Macbeth" by Malcolm (4.3.53) and Richard III, who is depicted as less than a man because of his deformity, and for other reasons, is referred to as "hell's black intelligencer" (4.4.71).
66 In the period, "to become effeminate was an ever-present possibility" for all men, regardless of social status." Smith, *Shakespeare and Masculinity*, 107.
67 Rebecca Ann Bach, "Manliness before Individualism: Masculinity, Effeminacy, and Homoerotics in Shakespeare's History Plays," in *A Companion to Shakespeare's Works, Volume II: The Histories*, eds. Richard Dutton and Jean E. Howard (Malden, MA: Blackwell Publishing, 2003), 220.
68 Ibid., 221.
69 For more on this interpretation of black as "base," see Brown, "'Is Black So Base a Hue?,'" esp. 143–144. Also see Erickson, "Can We Talk," 212.
70 For a detailed analysis of this scene's racialized language, see Parker, "Black Hamlet," esp. 127–129. Also see Smith, *Black Shakespeare*, 121–122.
71 For more on racial lightening and whitening, see Hall, *Things of Darkness*, 113–115.
72 The white other, coupled with the play's unmanly men, reveals the degrees of whiteness, the types of whiteness that are available for white people to slip in and out of or be pigeonholed into. The idea of there being degrees of whiteness is not just apparent in the early modern literature. Commenting on Donald Trump as "the lowest white man" and suggesting that white tiers exist rhetorically if not also literally, Charles M. Blow asserts: "For white supremacy to be made perfect, the lowest white man must be exalted above

those who are Black." "The Lowest White Man Thinks He's Better," *Miami Times* (January 11, 2018). Also a useful resource on the subject of white male mediocrity and supremacy is Ijeoma Oluo's *Mediocre: The Dangerous Legacy of White Male America* (New York: Seal Press, 2020). Shifting the optic on the lowest white person conversation, Greg Bottoms uses a racial/social class combination – specifically that of the white working class – to acknowledge how degrees of whiteness contribute to racial inequality in *Lowest White Boy* (Morgantown: West Virginia University Press, 2019), 4. In a way that pertains to masculinity (and not race directly), Bruce R. Smith also directs our attention to the "distance" between Claudius and his deceased brother in *Shakespeare and Masculinity*, 49. Michael Neill notes that Claudius and old King Hamlet occupy "rival spheres," which speaks to their oppositional difference. *Issues of Death: Mortality and Identity in English Renaissance Tragedy* (Oxford: Oxford University Press, 1997), 221.

73 Later in the play, Hamlet tells Claudius he shall "nose" the dead Polonius and find his body (4.3.37).

74 Such anxieties are especially noticeable in revenge plays that require the living revenger, "the berserk memorialist," to remember the dead. See Neill, *Issues of Death*, 246.

75 Richard Bautista explains this process and underscores how the body and skin become black. See "Survey of Biological Factors Affecting the Determination of the Postmortem Interval," *Scientia et Humanitas*, 2 (October 2012), 13–22; 17.

76 See https://en.wikipedia.org/wiki/Putrefaction. Black putrefaction begins 10–20 days after death. By the time we meet Hamlet – two months after his father's funeral – the blackening of the dead King's white body has been set in motion by nature.

77 Erickson, "Can We Talk," 211.

78 See *Othello*, 4.1.206.

79 Newman, *Fashioning Femininity*, 82, 86. Within Shakespeare's canon, we see a similar association made between blackness and witchcraft in plays such as *The Tempest*, *Othello* and *Antony and Cleopatra* (and in relationship to the following characters: Sycorax, Othello, and Cleopatra).

80 In her discussion of characteristic differences between males ("active and rational") and females ("emotional and passive") as illustrated in Western history, Myriam Miedzian points out: "Eve's moral weakness is such that shortly after her creation she succumbs to the temptation of eating the forbidden fruit. She is responsible for the expulsion of Adam and all human-kind from the Garden of Eden." *Boys Will Be Boys: Breaking the Link between Masculinity and Violence* (New York: Doubleday, 1991), 7.

81 This discourse that links Gertrude to Eve reduces the former's individuality because, according to Shannon Miller, this is the function of "biblical sub-jectivity," to associate women with a group identity that imbues them with "a series of meanings attached to women in general." See *Engendering the Fall: John Milton and Seventeenth-Century Women Writers* (Philadelphia: University of Pennsylvania Press, 2008), 14.

82 Claudius' failure is wrapped up in his inability to bring order and control to his household, two very important qualities that help define the core ideology of the early modern patriarchal household, as Anthony Fletcher notes in *Gender, Sex and Subordination in England, 1500–1800* (New Haven, CT: Yale University Press, 1996), xx, 204.

83 Marshall Grossman, "*Hamlet* and the Genders of Grief," in *Grief and Gender*, ed. Jennifer C. Vaught with Lynne Dickson Bruckner (New York: Palgrave Macmillan, 2003), 177–196; 177.

84 Janet Adelman, *Suffocating Mothers: Fantasies of Maternal Origin in Shakespeare's Plays, from Hamlet to the Tempest* (New York: Routledge, 1992), 28.

85 Ibid.

86 Miller, *Engendering the Fall*, 2.

87 Andrew D. McCarthy, "*King Lear*'s Violent Grief," in Feather and Thomas, *Violent Masculinities*, 151–168; 154. See Gilbert, "A Sparrow Falls," 197.

88 De-yan, "Hamlet's Femininity," 95.

89 Jennifer C. Vaught, "Introduction," in *Grief and Gender: 700–1700*, ed. Jennifer C. Vaught with Lynne Dickson Bruckner (New York: Palgrave Macmillan, 2003), 1–14; 2.

90 Vaught, "Introduction," 6.

91 Jennifer A. Low acknowledges that conceptions of masculinity may have varied along social rank and that dueling is one way to observe such distinctions – not all groups participated in the practice. See *Manhood and the Duel*, 4, 7, 9.

92 McCarthy, "*King Lear*'s Violent Grief," 154.

93 Vaught, "Introduction," 2–3. Also see Laura Levine, *Men in Women's Clothing: Anti-theatricality and Effeminization, 1579–1642* (Cambridge: Cambridge University Press, 1994), 7.

94 Vaught reflects on humoural theory: "According to Galen's theory of the four 'humours', men who possessed an excess of black bile were vulnerable to melancholy, a word derived from Greek roots meaning 'black bile' and epitomized by Hamlet. Throughout Shakespeare's play, Hamlet is afraid that his tears of grief and melancholia in response to his father's death are less manly than bloody deeds motivated by his choleric desire for revenge. Hamlet is sensitive to his culture's expectations about how men and women should mourn. His notion of grief is intimately tied to gender, a term referring to a social category imposed upon a sexed body. Nevertheless, Hamlet resists and transforms the gender identity constructed for him by his historical moment and becomes a forerunner of men of sensibility in the eighteenth century." Claudius, too, is sensitive to the culture's expectations and actively directs our attention to Hamlet's problematic social behavior. Vaught, "Introduction," 6.

95 For more on the relationship between excessive grief and religion, see Lublin, "'Apparel oft proclaims the man,'" 635.

96 See *OED*, "Fault."

97 Cressy, *Birth, Marriage and Death*, 438.

98 See Exodus 20:12.

99 In his first encounter with Hamlet, the Ghost says to his son regarding the need for avenging his death: "If thou hast nature in thee, bear it not. / Let not the royal bed of Denmark be / A couch for lechery and damnèd incest" (1.5.82–84).

100 Erica Fudge observes how reason was important to "discussions of order": "The human possession of reason places humans above animals in the natural hierarchy. Reason reveals humans' immortality, and animals' irrationality reveals their mortality, their materiality. Reasonable humans are the gods on earth." *Brutal Reasoning: Animals, Rationality, and Humanity in Early Modern England* (Ithaca, NY: Cornell University Press, 2006), 3.

101 Parker, "Black Hamlet," 132–133.

102 Ivo Kamps, "Foreword" in Low, *Manhood and the Duel*, viii. Also see Ibid., 3.

103 Other features of a white person can be black according to the play: "thoughts black" (3.2.253), "bosom black" (3.3.67), and black "soul" (3.3.94).

104 Smith, *Black Shakespeare*, 130.

105 Lublin, "'Apparel oft proclaims the man,'" 636.

106 See Ross Knecht, "'Shapes of Grief': Hamlet's Grammar School Passions," *ELH*, 82.1 (Spring 2015), 35–58; 45.

107 Kaara L. Peterson touches on Hamlet's "alarming sartorial appearance" and "melancholy" in "*Hamlet*'s Touch of Picture," in Massai and Munro, *Hamlet: The State of Play*, 27–50; 37.

108 Robert Burton, *The Anatomy of Melancholy: The First Partition* (London: J. M. Dent & Sons Ltd., 1932), 259.

109 Carol Thomas Neely, *Distracted Subjects: Madness and Gender in Shakespeare and Early Modern Culture* (Ithaca, NY: Cornell University Press, 2004), 93–94. Also see Juliana Schiesari, *The Gendering of Melancholia: Feminism, Psychoanalysis, and the Symbolics of Loss in Renaissance Literature* (Ithaca, NY: Cornell University Press, 1992), 62.

110 McCarthy, "*King Lear*'s Violent Grief," 154.

111 Hamlet constantly highlights his "lack." See Margreta de Grazia, "*Hamlet*" *without Hamlet* (Cambridge: Cambridge University Press, 2007), 2.

112 Tanya Pollard, "What's Hecuba to Shakespeare?," *Renaissance Quarterly*, 65.4 (2012), 1060–1093; 1063.

113 Reproduction is one way women's bodies are invested with meaning. See Newman, *Fashioning Femininity*, 6.

114 Pollard suggests "there is more than one ghostly parent haunting this play," which, in my reading, increases the possibilities for Hamlet's casual fornication. "What's Hecuba to Shakespeare?," 1063.

115 Adelman, *Suffocating Mothers*, 30.

116 Valerie Traub, "Jewels, Statues, and Corpses: Containment of Female Erotic Power in Shakespeare's Plays," in *Shakespeare and Gender*, eds. Deborah Barker and Ivo Kamps (New York: Verso, 1995), 120–141; 123.

117 Adelman, *Suffocating Mothers*, 28–30.
118 Pollard, "What's Hecuba to Shakespeare?," 1081.
119 Adelman, *Suffocating Mothers*, 2, 10.
120 Neely offers a historical perspective: "In England during this period, drowning was the most common type of female suicide and, since it was also a common accident, was the cause of death that made distinctions between accident and volition most difficult." *Distracted Subjects*, 55.
121 As Peterson notes, "Hamlet is an uncommonly thoughtful revenger." "*Hamlet*'s Touch of Picture," 41.
122 Gilbert, "A Sparrow Falls," 197.
123 I thank Arthur L. Little, Jr., for pushing my thinking on this matter.
124 Miedzian, *Boys Will Be Boys*, 53–54.
125 Emphasis added.
126 See Grossman, "*Hamlet* and the Genders of Grief," 178.
127 Marriage was how early modern women made social transformations from daughter and maid to wife, mother, and widow. See Cressy, *Birth, Marriage and Death*, 287–289. In this period, the idea was promoted that "women depend[ed] for their class [and social] statuses on their affiliation with men." See Newman, *Fashioning Femininity*, 87.
128 As Mia Korpiola and Anu Lahtinen explain, there was a premodern understanding that the physical body started to decompose "at the moment of death." See "Cultures of Death and Dying in Medieval and Early Modern Europe: An Introduction," *COLLeGIUM*, 18 (2015), 1–31; 13.
129 Robert Burton explains the ancient connection between coldness and blackness as related to humoural theory: "For Galen imputeth all to the cold that is black, and thinks that the spirits being darkened, and the substance of the brain cloudy and dark, all the objects thereof appear terrible, and the mind itself, by those dark, obscure, gross fumes, ascending from black humours, is in continual darkness, fear, and sorrow." *The Anatomy of Melancholy: The First Partition*, 419. While the deceased King's body may be rotting in the ground, it is not lost on me that his spirit is embodied and present in the play's beginning and in the closet scene.
130 In some ancient Roman writing, suicide is celebrated by writers such as Seneca and Pliny. Stoics believed suicide could be a form of patriotism in order to "save one's country." See Miriam Griffin, "Philosophy, Cato and Roman Suicide I," *Greece & Rome*, 33.1 (April 1986), 46–77, 64, 73.
131 Myles McDonnell, *Roman Manliness: Virtus and the Roman Republic* (Cambridge: Cambridge University Press, 2006), 2.
132 Ibid., 10.
133 Gosson articulated reservations about theater's influence on the male psyche. Charting anti-theatricalist concerns about masculinity in particular, Levine observes: "The first tract to demonstrate any real concern over the issue of gender is Gosson's *School of Abuse* (1579), which accuses the theatre of being both 'effeminate' and 'effeminizing' – an association which is itself suggestive, since it implies that things that are like women are likely to turn into

women. Gosson poses a kind of puzzle. In his dedication 'To the Gentlewomen, Citizens of London', he suggests that looking at women in the audience makes men lose their human identity – they become animals, turn into braying 'wild coultes'. But looking at plays makes men lose not their human identity but their male identity: theatre 'effeminates' the mind." *Men in Women's Clothing*, 19.

134 Ibid., 10–11.

135 See Stephen Gosson, *Plays Confuted in Five Actions in Markets of Bawdrie: The Dramatic Criticism of Stephen Gosson* (Salzburg: Institut für Englische Sprache und Literatur, Universität Salzburg, 1974), 193–194. In his tract examining the professional theater, William Prynne expressed fears and argued that action influenced those performing the actions. *Histrio-mastix: The Player's Scourge or Actor's Tragedy* (New York: Johnson Reprint Corp., 1972), 197. See Levine, *Men in Women's Clothing*, 6, 13.

136 Phillip Stubbes, *The Anatomie of Abuses* (London: Printed by Richard Jones, 1583); Levine, *Men in Women's Clothing*, 12.

137 Adelman, *Suffocating Mothers*, 31. Jacqueline Rose, "Wulf Sachs's *Black Hamlet*," in *The Psychoanalysis of Race*, ed. Christopher Lane (New York: Columbia University Press, 1998), 333–352; 337.

138 This speech, which appears in Q2 and not in the Folio, has also been read as Hamlet critiquing Young Fortinbras' willingness to sacrifice the lives of thousands of men for land that is not worth much. Even so, that critique does not negate Fortinbras' being a man of action. If anything, the violence reaffirms his earned masculinity.

139 Gilbert posits that "Shakespeare was a man who, through what is arguably his greatest character, dared to valorize the feminine" ("A Sparrow Falls," 203). I would push this point further by indicating that it is through the racialized association of the feminine with the masculine that Shakespeare valorizes the feminine with a play on contrasts: white with white other and masculine with feminine.

140 Low, *Manhood and the Duel*, 8.

141 McCarthy, "*King Lear's* Violent Grief," 154.

142 Ramsey, "The Perversion of Manliness in *Macbeth*," 295. In an analysis of *The Judde Memorial*, Kathryn M. Moncrief observes, "The painting itself, commemorating its long-dead subjects who are themselves as 'rotten' as the corpse with which they are associated, is an object of memory, asking the reader to gaze on and remember the couple while, at the same time, prompting viewers to remember, ponder and confront their own inescapable mortality." "Remembering Ophelia," in Massai and Munro, *Hamlet: The State of Play*, 51–80; 52–53.

143 Emphasis added.

144 De-yan, "Hamlet's Femininity," 90.

145 Low expounds on Hamlet's goal and failure regarding the performance of masculinity in "Manhood and the Duel," 503–504.

146 Elsewhere, I have argued how Shakespeare employs his characters' racialized bodies to convey important social, cultural and political messages. See Brown, "Remixing the Family," 111–133; and "'Shake Thou to Look on't': Shakespearean White Hands," in *White People in Shakespeare*, ed. Arthur L. Little, Jr. (London: The Arden Shakespeare, 2023), 105–119.

147 Grossman, "*Hamlet* and the Genders of Grief," 193.

148 Smith, *Shakespeare and Masculinity*, 6. The revelry at court in the opening Act also reminds us things are different in Denmark. See 1.4.19–20.

149 One core sentiment expressed and honored by The Racial Imaginary Institute, founded by Claudia Rankine, is that "no sphere of life is untouched by race." See https://theracialimaginary.org/about/.

150 Akhimie, *Shakespeare and the Cultivation of Difference*, 11.

151 I emphasize "critical" here because at the Arizona Center for Medieval and Renaissance Studies Race Before Race 2 conference, held in Washington, DC at the Folger Shakespeare Library in September 2019, Margo Hendricks made an important distinction between "premodern race studies" and "premodern critical race studies." My scholarship champions the mission of the latter. In her talk titled "Coloring the Past, Rewriting our Future: RaceB4Race," Hendricks boldly declared: "There is, however, a problematic rupture that is worth examining. In this talk, I'm going to refer to it as 'white settler colonizing' of 'premodern critical race studies.' I want to briefly offer a distinction between 'premodern race studies' (PRS) and 'premodern critical race studies' (PCRS). PRS is the practice of attempting race studies as if 'you discovered the land.' Practitioners ignore the pre-existing inhabitants of the land, or if these PRS scholars deign to acknowledge the inhabitants it is with a citation. Nowhere do you truly find recognition of the work done to nurture the land [. . .] What truly distinguishes PRS from PCRS, of course, is the bi-directional gaze: the one that looks inward even as it looks outward. As bell hooks observed, 'spaces of agency exist . . . wherein we can both interrogate the gaze of the Other but also look back, and at one another, naming what we see. The gaze has been and is a site of resistance for colonized . . . people globally' (bell hooks, 'The Oppositional Gaze: Black Female Spectators,' in *Black Looks*, 95)."

CHAPTER 3

On the Other Hand
The White(ned) Woman in Antony and Cleopatra

Question, mark, and check whiteness, challenge its dominance as it operates through default positions of cultural behavior.
— The Racial Imaginary Institute Curatorial Team[1]

In *Hamlet*, the intraracial domestic conflicts depend on the exploitation of symbolic blackness to sustain the façade of the presumed superior value of whiteness with respect to the household, gender, politics, culture, and more.[2] The same is true in *Antony and Cleopatra*, where Blackness, especially in relationship to racial whiteness, is an important dramatic feature — but not for the often uncritical, superficial reasons that racism makes it seem. In the play's discourse, for instance, Cleopatra's Black African alterity, as depicted by Shakespeare's imagination and the imaginations of his contemporaries,[3] garners attention and is the subject of much critique and even ridicule, as Francesca T. Royster acknowledges in *Becoming Cleopatra: The Shifting Image of an Icon*.[4] Yet, the inclusion of this Black, hypersexualized woman protagonist who is white(ned), whose dark body Antony refers to as white, supports and puts pressure on my sense that Blackness — designed onstage to "often trump a character's other identity markers"[5] — is wholly a distraction in Shakespearean works where whiteness is central.

The focus on the Black woman Antony describes as white in Act 3, Scene 13 means *Antony and Cleopatra* offers another way for critics to examine whiteness and intraracial conflict in this commonly understood race play. The intersection of sexuality, class, femaleness, and somatic Blackness, and the split domestic settings between Rome and Africa that mirror the play's larger white/Black contrast,[6] presents a different set of critical challenges than *Hamlet* does for the audience to examine and for the characters to manage. Specifically, it is the uniqueness of Cleopatra's race/gender makeup that makes this tragedy an intriguing site for attending to whiteness. Arthur L. Little, Jr. suggests as much in his chapter centered on Antony in *Shakespeare Jungle Fever*.[7] We can attribute the

96

uniqueness, in part, to how Cleopatra – historically and fictionally – "can never satisfyingly be described or explained because she is always shifting," as Royster claims.[8] In Shakespeare's play, the Egyptian Queen moves between Black and white.

Working through how the depiction of white(ned) womanhood is central to *Antony and Cleopatra*'s intraracial dynamics, and its treatment of race and racism, is key since, as Joyce Green MacDonald reminds us, "Race, gender, and sexuality were yoked together to define subject status in the early modern world."[9] MacDonald's premodern reading of those identity markers gestures toward what Black feminist Patricia Hill Collins and sociologist Sirma Bilge identify as "intersectionality's core insight: namely, that major axes of social division in a given society at a given time, for example, race, class, gender, sexuality, dis/ability, and age operate not as discrete and mutually exclusive entities, but build on each other and work together."[10] The interconnectedness of such identity markers is apparent in early modern English literature and contributes to Cleopatra's complex status, as well as the general status of white women, then and now, who benefit from their privileged proximity to white patriarchal power.[11] White women are hardly innocent when it comes to perpetuating racism, particularly against Black women, as Keeanga-Yamahtta Taylor and others make clear.[12] Furthermore, the interconnectedness of such identity markers underscores why intersectionality – and the "six core ideas that appear and reappear when people use [it] as an analytic tool": social inequality, power, relationality, social context, complexity, and social justice[13] – is an incredibly high-impact resource for decoding the workings of whiteness: Antony's, Caesar's, Octavia's, and all Romans'.

Shakespeare positions Antony outside of his natural domestic environment for much of this play. Through his amorous association with Black Cleopatra and his domestic association with Africa, white Antony represents, similarly to the Goths, a different type of whiteness that is degenerate in the Romans' eyes, like that of the white others in *Titus* and *Hamlet*.[14] One can therefore read him as yet another white other figure because his whiteness is substandard.[15] In the falling action of *Antony and Cleopatra*, the Queen's lover ironically becomes, as Caesar declares with bifurcated meaning, "Poor Antony," a devalued white man (4.1.17): one who does not reflect the kind of idealized patriarchal whiteness Caesar embodies, for "in Octavius's eyes, Antony is humbled and effeminized," as Hall claims.[16] Antony is one whose pure, rich royal blood does not preclude his being poor; and one who "fall[s]" (4.12.48) and loses himself to a "grave charm" (4.12.25). This is a pejorative label he eventually deploys in reference to Cleopatra. Hand in hand with the Queen – that is, allied with her and therefore allied with Blackness – Antony forsakes his political duty as triumvir. He forsakes his domestic duties and his claims to the "lawful race" (3.13.108). He neglects his white Roman wives, Fulvia and Octavia, on whom he cheats. And he dares to fight his white Roman "brother," thus instigating a few of the play's key domestic conflicts (5.1.42).

In so doing, he positions himself as opposed to the model white woman and the conventional patriarchal white man; he contradicts domestic norms and therefore rejects white standards. For the most part, Antony abandons his loyalty to the Romans and subsequently becomes alienated from much of what "proper" whiteness is to represent racially, domestically, and culturally.[17] For this, he fails as an ideal white man and becomes the play's somatically similar white other figure as a result.[18] On the one hand, then, what results in Shakespeare's play is a dramatic work embedded with a conflicted yet carefully constructed narrative that aims to bolster the socio-political and cultural power and mystique of whiteness. On the other hand, however, such a result cannot be fully realized due to the play's intraracial tension. This tension is a direct consequence of the interracial tension that makes *Antony and Cleopatra*, as Imtiaz Habib points out, "an emancipatory myth of the black woman in power," the only example in Shakespeare.[19] The named Black woman – Cleopatra – undermines the myth of white superiority with her fierce domestic, political, economic, intellectual, sexual, psychological power. With the white "hand of death" later in the play (4.9.34), Black Cleopatra upsets the Romans' intended "fair victory" and reveals why it behooves the oppressed to mind whiteness, always (4.7.12). Much like the relationship between the Goths and Aaron in *Titus*, the relationship between Antony and Cleopatra, which positions Antony in between Blackness and ideal whiteness, elucidates this play's levels of whiteness and even complicates ideas about early modern domestic expectations.

Gesturing White Hands

In Shakespearean drama, when the phrase "white hand" appears it is attached to an unmistakably white body, a body unlike Cleopatra's. The phrase's relationship to what hooks calls "the dominator imperialist white supremacist capitalist patriarchal culture" is also unmistakable. With the notable exception of *Antony and Cleopatra* (circa 1607), Shakespeare's white hands manufacture unambiguous meaning that allows the dramatist to compose a subversive socially, politically, and culturally significant narrative about whiteness, masculinity, and femininity. The white hand, which belongs to women physically and men rhetorically, is a highly scrutinized object and recurring motif in the canon, which does not highlight the phrase "black hand," perhaps predictably so. Beginning with *Love's Labour's Lost* (circa 1594) and ending with *The Winter's Tale* (circa 1610), the specific phrase "white hand" appears nine times among seven plays and across all genres:[20] comedy, tragedy, history, and romance.[21] In these other plays, this corporeal extremity is always unmistakably attached to a white body – a woman's body. The white hand functions as a fundamental agent of white self-fashioning that is inherently feminized, always through masculine articulation, in discourse centered on commitment, love, beauty, virtue, honor, validation, modesty, sexual purity, and domestic concerns.[22] Yet, as Little, Jr. observes, "However much whiteness seems to communicate an authentic cultural sense of purity, divinity, and power, it remains a theatrical device," and thus inauthentic.[23] I contend that this dramatic device is deployed for maximum racial and rhetorical impact in *Antony and Cleopatra*.

Besides Antony, who at one point in the play defends his white(ned) Cleopatra, several Shakespearean men allude to the "white hand of a lady," which often provides, or provided, some sense of security and comfort for the male figures (3.13.140–142): In *Love's Labour's Lost*, Shakespeare draws out the connection between whiteness and female beauty when Holofernes reads, "'To the / snow-white hand of the most beauteous Lady / Rosaline'" (4.2.130–132). This point regarding beauty, naturalized by the modifier "snow," is bolstered when Berowne says, "And Rosaline they call her. Ask for her, / And to her white hand see thou do commend / This seal'd-up counsel" (3.1.165–167). It is as though the whiteness of the lady's unstained hand is what makes it and her, by extension, worthy of male attention, a point that *Antony and Cleopatra* also illustrates. In *Troilus and Cressida*, Pandarus moves beyond a superficial reference to the white hand: In fact, his speech showcases a keen fixation on the white hand when he references Helen's hand twice, saying, "But to prove to you that Helen loves him: she / came and puts me her white hand to his cloven chin" (1.2.119–120), and a few lines later, "Indeed, she has a marvelous white / hand, I must needs confess" (1.2.137–138). In addition to complimenting the hand, his concentration on the placement of it suggests it mattered greatly when and how a lady's white hand came into contact with something.

Troilus and Cressida is not alone in its usage of the white hand motif as an object of proof and validation, for *Henry V*'s Orleans claims, "By the

white hand of my lady, he's a gallant / prince," regarding the Dauphin
(3.7.93–94). The white woman's hand is a pedestalized patriarchal fixture
that white men possess in the domestic context; the power of ownership
permits men to channel at will the woman's constancy in order to prove
their own. Similarly, in *As You Like It*, Orlando proclaims to the cross-
dressed Rosalind, "I swear to thee, youth, by the white hand of / Rosalind,
I am that he, that unfortunate he" (3.2.384–385). In this instance, the
hand functions as assurance of, as well as a kind of insurance for, Orlando's
self-identification. In pledges that involve distinguishing something about
oneself, the white hand assumes an instrumental role, as also seen in *The
Winter's Tale*. Reflecting on the past, Leontes reminisces about Hermione's
white hand, noting, "Why, that was [. . .] / Ere I could make thee open thy
white hand, / And clap thyself my love; then didst thou utter, / 'I am yours
forever'" (1.2.101–105). Again, white masculine power prevails, as Leontes
reflects on what he could "make" Hermione do with her body. And even
Twelfth Night's Fool asserts, in an otherwise nonsensical reply to Sir
Andrew, "My lady has a white hand" (2.3.27). Despite its randomness,
his statement denotes how the lady's white hand is a recognizable racialized
symbol whose meaning, which is linked to domestic relations and relationships, transcends class boundaries. The white hand is important to him
just as it is important to Antony. In the canon, then, Shakespeare depicts
the white hand as indisputable white prop(erty),[24] and even male property.
It is property that overtly and covertly validates white patriarchal power
and verifies honor associated with the white identity. When transplanted
onto Cleopatra's Black body, the white hand effectively elucidates crucial
messages about whiteness, about its beauty, its domestic importance, its
need for protection and preservation, and more;[25] Blackness, which is a
diversion in Shakespeare's play, as it is in *Titus* without Aaron, can only be
of tangential importance when it is so purposely displaced by whiteness.[26]

Lending Whiteness, Borrowing Cleopatra

Devalued and disrespected by members of the dominant culture,
Cleopatra figuratively and necessarily evolves into a racially hybrid scapegoat that "layer[s] many social and political tensions onto one body.[27] She,
like Antony, contains whiteness and Blackness, as I suggested above and
will presently show. Her being, and becoming, highlights the incredible
instability of white racial superiority and signifiers, as there is an attempt to
erase her Blackness by imposing whiteness on her.[28] The racial mixing and
tension that her character signifies reflects something the play's title itself

anticipates through its clear signaling of racial hybridity: This is the only Shakespeare play about a white man and a Black woman who is whitened. Chapman, Habib, and Royster, to name a few critics, acknowledge the problematic nature of racial categories and racialized terms. Such indiscriminate term application in the early modern period is reinforced by Cleopatra's being "black" (1.5.29) and "tawny,"[29] adding to the confusion about where to locate her racially in Shakespeare's play (1.1.6).[30] And this racial volatility is, perchance, what leads Antony, and scholars, to transform Cleopatra into a figure whose seeming "racial ambiguity" authorizes (mis)readings of her as other than what Shakespeare so deliberately created her to be – a Black African figure[31] – despite the fact that his "treatment of her is not historical," as some critics and historians note.[32] The non-historical treatment of her is prioritized in this chapter to maximize our understanding of how Shakespeare chose to play with whiteness and exploit Blackness as a stabilizer for domestic and white ideology, which becomes evident when studying this play along the intraracial color-line.

In the play text, Cleopatra's borrowed whiteness permits Antony, who is responsible for lending whiteness to the Queen while appropriating and even domesticating her body, conveniently to describe her bodily hue in opposition to Blackness in the climax when he encounters Thidias, a Roman messenger of Caesar's, kissing Cleopatra's hand.[33] In this pivotal domestic moment of racial conversion, which scholars have not thoroughly explored, she ceases to be Black, as her racial identity is aligned with that of Antony's deceased and living fair-skinned wives, Fulvia and Octavia, respectively:[34] Egypt's Queen curiously becomes a "lady" with a "white hand" and seemingly occupies the liminal space between Black and white (3.13.141).[35] A deliberate dramatic choice, as I argue, the metaphorical white hand generates a color conversion that enables Antony to claim Cleopatra as his white(ned) prop/property;[36] for the primary purpose of articulating the centrality of whiteness, Cleopatra becomes a domestic prop, much like *Othello*'s Desdemona, as she endures the Roman's exploitative and manipulative appropriation of her dark body.[37] As such, putting a critical finger on the white hand scene opens up possibilities for grasping the "kinds of power relations [that] are reproduced within our own discipline" and that allow whiteness and its impact to remain invisible.[38]

Antony and Cleopatra's relationship is one that contains an emerging sense of the Black woman/white master dynamic.[39] This dynamic appears historically and is woven into the drama's fabric regarding what Chapman considers to be a need for "mastery over the Other."[40] The Black woman is Black until circumstances necessitate an emphasis on whiteness, an emphasis that *demands* critique in order to, as Hall posits, actively "engage issues of power."[41] Shakespeare builds the Black woman/white master narrative into Cleopatra's association with the two most central and powerful Roman men, Antony and Caesar, who exude paternalistic whiteness.[42] Although their approaches differ, both men cannot resist the desire to master her. In a play whose plot is largely about conquest, the white male quest for supremacy over Cleopatra, a synecdochic representation of Egypt, reflects how even her majestic body – a body that is high-class, so to speak, and not at all due to its being "white" – is subject to both appropriation and color-coded modification designed to reaffirm white superiority.[43] Furthermore, this white male quest imbues the queen's hand with a multiplicity of meanings that suggests it should be feared because of its presumed white power:[44] visual, (meta)physical, sexual, social, and political, to name a few ways the white hand – when placed on the Black woman – exerts symbolic and real domestic authority.[45]

We can view Shakespeare's Cleopatra as an early modern, metaphorical depiction of the skin-bleached or whitewashed Black woman whose altered presence may facilitate white identification with her.[46] This is what curiously makes her slip in and out of the white other category, thus reinforcing how race is a social construct. In her, white people either see themselves or that which is at least more familiar. Therefore, the white hand smacks of what Barbara Trepagnier calls "silent racism," a consequence of a "historical problem" perpetuated by what I refer to as "racist inertia": a global transhistorical phenomenon that has carried racism and its toxic acceptance through time and influenced the production of the characters at the center of this study.[47] Racist inertia, which acknowledges the unchanging direction and adaptability of racism, takes cues from Isaac Newton's laws of motion, one of which notes that an object in motion (or at rest) will remain in that state unless acted on by an external force. Conscious or unconscious racism, whose effects endure, is the abstract object that has moved throughout space and time, leaving in its wake a toxic residue, embodied by the white other, that reveals the past as contaminated by the racial discourse of inferiority and superiority. This phenomenon has significant implications for how Shakespeare's plays handle matters of race; and it also has serious implications for the conjectures we might make about how whiteness worked on and off the Shakespearean stage.

In *Antony and Cleopatra*, the white hand is ironically, and unfortunately, a veiled backward compliment that makes Black Cleopatra worthy of being Shakespeare's only "female protagonist of color."[48] In this light, the white hand simultaneously aligns her with and separates her from a title figure like Juliet, or other white female characters, such as *The Tempest*'s Miranda, *Othello*'s Desdemona, *Love's Labour's Lost*'s Rosaline, *Troilus and Cressida*'s Helen, *As You Like It*'s Rosalind, and *The Winter's Tale*'s Hermione, because, as Little, Jr. asserts, "More than as static synecdoche for the woman's sexual and racial purity, the white hand *works* as the primary penning and pinning agent – authorizing and flaunting, securing and insisting on the white woman's claim to sexual and racial purity."[49] According to legal scholar Cheryl I. Harris, "The concept of whiteness is built on both exclusion and racial subjugation."[50] As such, we see that the white hand is exclusively white property; for Black Cleopatra, there is no true benefit to Antony's whitening of her hand because the reference's implications are both above and beyond her.

Tracing the specific white hand allusions in Shakespeare's canon exposes how Antony's warning to Thidias stands out among all such references, especially because the rhetorical tone is so dark, comparatively speaking. After having the domestic servant Thidias whipped, Antony chides him, "Henceforth / The white hand of a lady fever thee, / Shake thou to look on't" (3.13.140–142).[51] Shifting whiteness onto Cleopatra legitimizes Antony's opposition to Thidias, a lower-class white man, who stands in for Rome, which is a domestic threat to Egypt. Shifting whiteness onto Cleopatra in this domestic moment also makes her a direct foil that enhances Antony's subpar whiteness. That Antony says this to another white Roman man while in Egypt is interesting because the general phrase "white hand of a lady" is not specific to Cleopatra, though it peculiarly includes her.[52] In the play, characters use "lady" in reference to Cleopatra and Octavia, affirming the focus on whiteness here as a deliberate and strange racialized moment that *re*affirms, as Celia Daileader contends, "the central lie of masculinist-racist power, wherein white women become scapegoats for a system of racial oppression that is almost entirely run for the benefit of white men."[53] For many reasons, Cleopatra's whiteness is unbelievable.[54] Antony's assertion of whiteness in relationship to Cleopatra is as much an attempt to fool others as it is an attempt to fool himself.

Given this, the white hand scene is unsurprisingly perverse in its disrespect toward the Queen. Cleopatra's white hand that is attached to her tawny, Black body is an anomaly in Shakespeare's oeuvre. And it is the only such hand that appears in the plays with major Black characters, the traditionally understood race plays,[55] supporting the notion that "the subject of race is peculiarly visual."[56] This fact should give us pause and make us wonder about the work Antony's rhetoric is doing and the work the Queen's hand is doing. It is misplaced in more ways than one. For the hand to be acceptable, and by that I mean beautiful and therefore worthy of being possessed, by early modern standards, it has to be camouflaged as white. For if, as Gretchen Gerzina claims, "the English only began to see themselves as 'white' when they discovered 'black' people," then Cleopatra's whitening acts as a necessary climactic metamorphosis, one that puts understanding the symbolic weight of binary racial opposition on her already taxed Black "female body [that] itself becomes the ground on which race, culture, and cultural affiliation can be promoted."[57] By trying to erase Cleopatra's Blackness, Antony perpetuates a negative attitude toward Blackness. This behavior is an expected part of *his* white other function. He also attempts to domesticate Cleopatra, so to speak, by gifting her with the presumed civilized status of white womanhood.

As Katherine Rowe and Farah Karim-Cooper reveal in their respective studies, hands were an important symbol in the early modern period, particularly white women's hands.[58] In *The Hand on the Shakespearean Stage: Gesture, Touch and the Spectacle of Dismemberment*, Karim-Cooper offers an astute analysis of this bodily extremity. She argues, "Shakespeare's texts demonstrate how the hand was perceived as a powerful instrument of human exchange, emotional expression, self-scrutiny, character, and identity."[59] As an appendage of white self-fashioning, the white hand carves out a lady's social place and directs her way of being in the world. In thinking specifically about *Antony and Cleopatra* and early modern culture, it is crucial to note that "while the code of manners established for the hand in polite society was in continuous flux, there was a distinctive set of rules advising men, women, children, and servants about their hand behaviour, such as when it is appropriate to kiss the hand of a social superior."[60] Additionally, "kissing the monarch's hand was not only a ritualistic gesture, but it was also a sign of the privilege and honour of the kisser."[61] By knowing what certain hand gestures, or even the placement of hands, mean, we can begin to see why Antony gets so incensed by Thidias' behavior. It is not just Antony's language, which I will soon examine, but also the play's action that sanctions the Roman's self-conscious whitening of the Egyptian Queen and causes great friction, racialized anxiety, and domestic discord.[62]

Handling Hairs

Racial tension in the play appears in "entangled" color metaphors that become deeply racialized and are just as complex as the drama's love triangulation that positions at the apex the white other, the less-than-ideal Roman man (1.3.30). Before Antony says the word "white" in relation to Cleopatra, he uses the term – after abandoning his men at sea – in a speech that is indicative of his own wave of internal and external conflicts deriving from his perceived scandalous interracial relationship with the Egyptian Queen. Reproaching himself for failing to be a true military leader, Antony says,

> I follow'd that I blush to look upon.
> My very hairs do mutiny; for the white
> Reprove the brown for rashness, and they them
> For fear and doting.
>
> (3.11.12–15)

Notably, "white" is only said twice in the play, both times by Cleopatra's lover, whose utterances subtly reinforce racial and domestic domination. Antony's blushing denotes a physical response that is exclusive to pale-skinned people, for as Aaron sarcastically asserts in *Titus*, blushing is the beautiful "privilege" of whiteness, not Blackness (4.2.117). Antony's blushing, and following, his association with Blackness, emasculates him in a way that affirms Cleopatra's more dominant status in their relationship, but not in her overall relationship with hegemonic whiteness.[63] Their relationship echoes the dynamic between Black Aaron and Goth Tamora in *Titus*. Turning our attention to a hair rebellion, Antony expresses metaphorical language that presents his Roman scalp, a figurative domestic landscape, as the battleground for a race war between the white and brown hairs.

In following Black Cleopatra, Antony's own behavior and rhetoric here mirror the drama's larger domestic conflict between Rome and Egypt, which is a direct consequence of Antony's rashness, fear, and doting. As they reprove each other, visually depicting Antony's internal struggle, the white and brown hairs exert authority and demonstrate power, but differently. The white hairs, superior symbols of wisdom and experience, chastise the inferior brown hairs for being reckless, for example. The white hairs embody maturity and paternalism, while the brown hairs exemplify youth and inexperience.[64] On Antony's scalp is the hybridity that is later mapped onto Cleopatra's body in Act 3, Scene 13, through the white hand that paints the Queen herself as a racially hybrid image.[65] This colored hair metaphor is nappy, certainly not straightforward, because it also implicitly pictures the Queen through the sassy brown hair that possesses power enough to talk back to the white hair that functions as a surrogate for

Antony.[66] On and in Antony's head, and through the brown-haired resistance, Shakespeare subtly uncovers the fragility and instability of white racial superiority. He exposes it as merely a mythic ideal, one Cleopatra herself challenges, especially at the play's conclusion.[67]

In her critique of whiteness, MacDonald rightly suggests, "The more [whiteness] remains unannounced, unarticulated, the more it may be said to be in operation. Not merely about skin color, early modern whiteness works to naturalize and normalize the operations of existing hierarchies of race, nation, and sexuality. Whiteness articulates cultural authority."[68] In so doing, whiteness exists as a powerfully prescriptive tool. Antony's "mutiny" speech in Act 3, Scene 11 solidifies the hierarchically racialized connection between "brown" and "white" that Cleopatra initiates with her concerns about Roman Octavia's hair color in Act 2, Scene 5 and Act 3, Scene 3. After learning Antony has remarried, Cleopatra wonders if his wife, Octavia, is true competition. This worry supports the notion that there is tension between the white and Black women. As such, it is crucial that when the Messenger leaves Rome he returns to Egypt with a descriptive report on Octavia for the Queen that does "not leave out / The color of [Octavia's] hair," a rather "mundane [material] item" that is nevertheless "deemed worthy of serious attention" in the play and in this chapter, especially because of the racial implications and the reinforcement of both Black and white stereotypes (2.5.115–116).[69]

Cleopatra sizes up Antony's wife. The matter of most significance is Octavia's hair. The Messenger's discourse with the monarch concludes with the following inquiry:

> CLEOPATRA: Her hair, what color?
> MESSENGER: Brown, madam; and her forehead
> As low as she would wish it.
> CLEOPATRA: There's gold for thee.
>
> (3.3.34–37)

The question "what color?" is asked twice in the play, once about something Roman and once about something Egyptian, showcasing how color even matters in the larger domestic contexts. At the pre-battle banquet, as Lepidus inquires about Egypt, he asks Antony about the crocodile, "What color is it of?" (2.7.47) and Antony replies, "Of it own color too" (2.7.48). Its own color is, of course, a color that represents Africa. François Laroque alludes to the color association when he writes, "In Shakespeare's play, Cleopatra is identified with Egypt and, as such, both with the river Nile and its crocodiles and serpents."[70] The return to white Octavia's hair brings comfort to Cleopatra because Antony's wife is dark, as in brunette, but she is not dark enough to keep her husband away from his darker "Egyptian dish," a reality that contributes to the play's domestic conflicts (2.6.128).[71] In this regard, Octavia, too, functions as a hybrid image, though one that lacks Cleopatra's exotic appeal. The Queen rules that Antony "cannot like her long" (3.3.15) because "this creature's no such thing" (3.3.44). She is, as Charmian quickly agrees, "nothing" much (3.3.44). The brown hair on the white body is indicative of the play's color-coded tension amplified by Antony's hair metaphor. As a racial category in the play, white is portrayed as antithetical to the Africanist "shades of difference": brown, tawny, black, swarthy.[72] However, Cleopatra's unwavering confidence in her superiority to Octavia indicates yet again that being Black does not inherently mean one is less than, despite white dominant culture suggesting otherwise. That is one of the many lessons Cleopatra teaches Shakespeare's audience: to measure oneself according to one's own standards rather than those of the dominant culture, which assumes the prerogative to determine, for example, who is important and why; in this case, the virtuous, domestically obedient white wife.[73] Moreover, the nonchalance regarding Octavia is the Queen's assertion of her own racial adequacy. Cleopatra's confidence is her decisive counter to the narrative of absolute white racial superiority that even the Roman's emphasis on Octavia's beauty transmits.[74]

(Ex)changing Hands

When Cleopatra's hand magically morphs into a white one, it, and the body it belongs to, crosses the color-line and becomes symbolically beautiful and worthy of white male protection, thus reiterating how "whiteness is a construct of convenience and improvisation."[75] Whiteness, too, is provisional, a view that is reflected in white iterations of Cleopatra in popular media.[76] The Black, tawny hand signifies inferiority, which Antony's color conversion reinforces since, according to Hall, "the language of dark and light is part of a white supremacist ideology and persists as a common way of making people [of African descent] inferior."[77] Although Antony claims Cleopatra as "[his] love," his whitening of her makes that love questionable (1.1.26).[78] Karim-Cooper acknowledges that "inferior hands include hands that are deformed, unmanicured, old and withered, mis-coloured or rough from manual labor."[79] In light of that reading, the Black hand is deformed visually. If we think of the "white hand" articulation as a rhetorical gesture emphasizing Cleopatra's swarthy hand as "mis-coloured," as in not white and perhaps older because it is "wrinkled deep in time," then the Thidias scene serves to illuminate Antony's underlying prejudice, which forces him to mutilate Cleopatra figuratively and then attach a white hand to her Black body (1.5.30). Moreover, the Thidias episode reveals how Cleopatra's white hand encapsulates Shakespeare's authorial conformity to the dominant culture's social norms regarding English beauty standards and domestic ideology.[80] Once Antony thinks his relationship with Cleopatra is threatened, or that her honor and loyalty have been compromised, he begins to turn on her at the end of the play's climax. This moment marks a shift in their relationship that, in some ways, echoes how the Goths distance themselves from Aaron after the Black baby's birth.[81]

In this "transaction of power that employs distinct, identifiable personal features as the tools of negotiation," to quote Ian Smith, Antony's rather insulting message to the Queen is clear.[82] Unlike Blackness, whiteness is instilled positively with an intangible authority that is somehow universally recognizable; and unlike blackness, whiteness is instilled, paradoxically so, with powerful stereotypes that reify its alleged superiority in contrast to the accumulated perceptions that preserve Black inferiority.[83] Nevertheless, both racial categories are constructs. The white hand should "fever" Thidias and, moving forward, he should tremble at its sight because violating whiteness, especially the white femininity that Antony presents as an extension of his faux hegemonic patriarchal power, means violence for the violator. For an English audience, Antony's reproval of Thidias in that contentious domestic scene would have been apt: "The Romans were *the* model of an imperial and civilizing masculinity, and their empire served as a nostalgic model for an early modern England that strongly desired to perform (and thereby prove) its own imperial and masculine identity."[84] Antony's reaction, which leads to white-on-white violence, is an early modern example of white intimidation, which is itself a byproduct of white privilege, or white dominance. The Roman triumvir indicates that the very appearance of whiteness should make people shudder.[85] That is to say, Thidias has now learned he must automatically fear the presence of a lady's white hand, especially of one who is high-class. It is Antony's hope that Thidias' being whipped will instinctually condition him to avoid looking at or being "so saucy with the hand of" a lady in the future (3.13.99). The aggression is a socio-cultural assertion of Antony's masculine white dominance over both Thidias, who represents Caesar, and Cleopatra. The class difference between Thidias and Antony is notable as well, especially as one considers the different ways identity impacts one's status in the world.

For the Queen, being white(ned), being able momentarily to lack Black, has a crucial psychological effect, one that could manifest as a subconscious fear of what it means not to be white, what it means to exist in what film director Jordan Peele introduces as the "sunken place," which represents a perpetual state of disempowerment.[86] In *Antony and Cleopatra*, the Black body itself appears as a kind of sunken place, and Egypt, too, because both are inferior sites where the white hand reaches out and emerges through Blackness.[87] Another way to envision this: The white hand, extending outward from the Black body, becomes a foregrounded image that contrasts with, and is therefore illuminated and rendered central by, the Black background image that is the Queen's dark body. The Black body becomes reduced to mere highlighter.[88] As I have argued elsewhere, the negative connotation derived from the so-called baseness of Blackness can be inverted when one recognizes "base" as a term that is synonymous with foundational and strong.[89] While the sunken place functions most obviously as a paralyzing, demoralizing space for Black people, it is a foundational space for whites whose sense of entitlement to racial superiority is its own irrational, unnecessary, self-affirming form of racial uplift. In Peele's *Get Out*, Black people's bodies are overtaken and implanted with white agency. The result is white people embodied in Black bodies that are controlled by white hands and minds, and so the Black mind, too, is controlled by whiteness – all a very pertinent illustration of racism's multifaceted impact. The result is Blackness (race) trapped inside of white agency, a dynamic that *Antony and Cleopatra* exemplifies and a visual that, in part, illustrates the white other's essence: Antony's whitening of Cleopatra's hand and Shakespeare's authorial regulation of the Queen's mind and body.

The white hand scene, where there is a switch in Antony's treatment of Egypt, as he calls his lover, is a dramatic attempt to put Cleopatra in her Black place, the sunken place, so Antony retains his fragile connection to hegemonic whiteness through his performance of anti-Blackness. To miss the social, cultural, political, and theatrical power of this particular white hand moment is to render invisible subtly oppressive behavior.[90] Presumably, the reason Antony intrudes on Thidias and Cleopatra's exchange is that Enobarbus exits, as the stage directions note, to report to Antony what he hears the Queen say: that she submits to Caesar and that her "honor was not yielded, / But conquer'd merely" by her lover, whom she portrays as the master-rapist[91] who has exploited the Black woman and rendered her body readily available, as Black women's bodies are often thought to be, unfortunately (3.13.61–62).[92] Antony's jealous rage prompts him to highlight implicitly Cleopatra's Blackness and explicitly their illegitimate progeny (and relationship) when he asks, "Have I [...] / Forborne the getting of a lawful race, [...] to be abus'd / By one that looks on feeders?" (3.13.107–110). Directly calling attention to their interracial sex is yet another way Antony imagines the superiority of a lawful whiteness to which even he cannot fully lay claims.

His declaration that Cleopatra deceives him underscores how he deceives *her* with his complicated love that, at its core, does not look beyond her Black womanhood and the whoredom associated with her race;[93] he reveals a mindset that is in sync with all the other Romans who reduce the Queen to nothing more than a lusty "strumpet" (1.1.13).[94] Antony cannot resist this inevitable response to Cleopatra because "the pressures of imperialism insist on the control and regulation of female sexuality, particularly when concerns over paternity are complicated by problems of racial and cultural purity."[95] When Antony tells Cleopatra, "I found you" (3.13.118), he gives himself credit for discovering and, in a sense, domesticating her, modeling colonialist behavior characteristic of white people who engage in the act of Columbusing. His rhetoric recalls Enobarbus' earlier charge that if Antony had not seen Cleopatra, he would have "left unseen a wonderful / piece of work, which not to have been blest withal / would have discredited [his] travel" (1.2.160–162).[96] In the role of white visual explorer, Antony positions himself in a place of power over his metaphorically appropriated Egyptian domestic landscape.[97]

The Roman triumvir's attempted ownership of Cleopatra is most evident in the connection I draw between Act 3, Scene 13 and Act 4, Scene 8. Antony succinctly affirms for Cleopatra that he is upset because she allowed a lower-class "feeder" to "be familiar with / My playfellow, your hand," which specifically becomes a white hand just a few lines later (3.13.126–127). As Harris argues, "Possession of property includes the rights of use and enjoyment."[98] The possessive "my" makes the hand Antony's white property. At this point, his prior submission to the Queen appears more like a ruse. Even though they are not married, he views her (white hand) as belonging to him, a move that permits his façade of white masculine dominance. This is another reason why Thidias must "shake" with fear to look, because Antony did not authorize his touching the hand that plays with him sexually and romantically. According to Karim-Cooper, "Fears about profane touches and the ugliness of spotted or deformed hands are embedded in the misogynistic writing about witchcraft, diabolism and in the xenophobic anxieties about foreigners in this period."[99] Such domestic fears emerge in this scene and foreshadow how Antony attempts to mold audience perceptions of Cleopatra in the next dramatic act. Associating the Queen with witchcraft criminalizes her in ways that an early modern English audience would have been sensitive to since, as James Sharpe posits, "witchcraft appeared as a crime on the English statute book."[100] He adds, "In secular courts, the crime of witchcraft, as defined by the statutes of 1563 and 1604, could be tried at quarter sessions, courts held four times annually for each of England's counties."[101] Antony is entitled to berate both Thidias and Cleopatra, punishing one physically and the other verbally, in order to reestablish his unstable white male dominance and to correct behavior that Shakespeare's audience would have deemed wrong.

Indeed, Antony's language in Act 3, Scene 13 contains an air of misogyny, and it is infused with racialized anxiety that reminds the audience Cleopatra is not Fulvia or Octavia.[102] She is not a racially white woman, and she does not hold a legitimate domestic status in Rome's eyes, but she is Antony's choice. As I previously claimed, Cleopatra's tawny hand is mis-colored, as in non-white, and therefore somewhat deformed, visually speaking (witches were often portrayed in literature as "foule," wrinkly and old, for example).[103] Given this, I propose that Antony defines Thidias' actions as disrespectful because of his own deeply internalized beliefs about white racial superiority and Black inferiority that sometimes cause him to see Cleopatra as an undomesticated, "cunning" (1.2.152), "enchanting" (1.2.135) Black "witch" (4.12.47)[104] who has him bound in "strong Egyptian fetters" (1.2.122). Those are his words that implicate him in the Roman bigotry shown toward Egypt;[105] he deploys what Hortense Spillers describes as "the powers of [descriptive] distortion that the dominant community seizes as its unlawful prerogative."[106] Doing so allows him to assess what he interprets as the blackness within and outside of Cleopatra, since color "associations intersect with early efforts to understand the physical body and psychology of the mind."[107] In actuality, however, Antony may very well be projecting his own racial frustrations, putting them on Cleopatra while recognizing his own tainted nature.

The major takeaway is that no one can touch Antony's transformed domestic white property, the Queen, unless he says so. He is the master of this feminine possession, so he thinks.[108] And this is how we know that deep down Antony, as white other, views himself as superior to the Queen, certainly in terms of gender and likely in terms of race. When Antony feels

threatened by other white men whose whiteness is not questionable –
namely, Thidias and Caesar – he reacts aggressively toward Cleopatra to
control her with his histrionic emotions;[109] when these other white men
encroach upon his Egyptian territory, he responds defensively and irrationally. Yet, the power he thinks he holds over Egypt accentuates a fundamental double standard that solidifies how he operates with a peculiar
sense of masculine white racial superiority. I say this because in Act 4,
Scene 8 Antony has no problem with another white man touching his
playfellow, the Queen's hand.

   In fact, Antony encourages it. After returning from battle, he issues an
order to Cleopatra and the wounded Scarus, a soldier whom we might also
think of as a domestic servant of the state: "Behold this man, / Commend
unto his lips thy favoring hand. / Kiss it, my warrior" (4.8.22–24).
Antony's possessive use of "warrior" resonates with the phrase "my con-
queror," which he uses to refer to Cleopatra in Act 3, Scene 11 (65). The
hypocrisy is clear, as is the overt homoeroticism that recalls Enobarbus'
earlier lines when he and Menas shook hands.[110] The imperial hand that
was previously whitened, and claimed by Antony, is now authorized to be
kissed by someone who is not the Roman triumvir (or Thidias for that
matter). Certainly, there are several differences between Thidias and
Scarus: the former is an agent of the enemy, Caesar; the former is a
lower-class domestic servant figure; the former presumably has not fought
in battle or earned the right to be honored by the Queen in this way, or to
honor *her* in this way; and the former initiated contact with her hand in
Antony's absence. The Roman lover wants to watch and observe the
physical interaction between Cleopatra and Scarus, between his soldier
and his "playfellow." Antony plays broker in this transaction and, in so
doing, renews a sense of white equilibrium.

   His sanctioning of, and witnessing, this kiss is an exertion of white
patriarchal dominance over Cleopatra. Moreover, this kiss replicates, and
consequently acts as a corrective to, the previous moment that upset
Antony so much. Cleopatra, queen-whore, cannot deny this request –
and she does not – as Antony now pimps out her "favoring" hand in this
troubled white moment.[111] Since Act 4, Scene 8 occurs after the "white
hand" scene, the implication is that the audience is to see from the outset
the Blackness of Cleopatra's hand until Antony whitens it. In this regard,
Thidias literally and figuratively kisses the wrong hand; conversely, Scarus
is entitled to kiss the white hand that is now the right hand simply due to
its converted whiteness. As Antony's "playfellow," Cleopatra's hand, an
extension of her, is and is not subordinate to Antony. The imbalanced

power dynamic between the two lovers becomes most apparent in Act 3, Scene 13, in conjunction with Cleopatra's enforced racial shifting.

Mastering Whiteness

The Queen's white hand, her limited claim to whiteness, which we could also interpret as a kind of white otherness, makes Octavia her direct foil. The existence of and references to Antony's official spouse remind us that Cleopatra is not a wife; she lacks the stereotypical ideal beauty and "patien [ce]" embodied by virtuous white women (4.12.38); she is viewed as a "gipsy" (1.1.10) and "whore" by the dominant culture's primary members (4.12.13);[112] and she is, most obviously, not Roman.[113] In many ways, she does not represent ideal domesticity. Before Antony falls on his sword in Act 4, Scene 14, his last words to Cleopatra are harsh and confirm the play's negative attitudes toward the Black woman, attitudes that are mediated through Antony's white otherness. Infuriated that "this foul Egyptian hath betrayed [him]" once more, Antony verbally assaults his lover, adding to the play's anti-Black violence (4.12.10):

> Vanish, or I shall give thee thy deserving,
> And blemish Caesar's triumph. Let him take thee,
> And hoist thee up to the shouting plebeians:
> Follow his chariot, like the greatest spot
> Of all thy sex; most monster-like, be shown
> For poor'st diminutives, for doits; and let
> Patient Octavia plough thy visage up
> With her prepared nails.
>
> (4.12.32–39)

The trafficking of Cleopatra's body, first handed to Scarus and then envisioned as being turned over to Caesar, adds to the air of Black whoredom perpetuated by the white characters' rhetoric. Moreover, Antony's use of "foul" racializes this moment since, in addition to meaning physically loathsome, wicked, ugly and morally/spiritually polluted, the term means dirty, soiled, and full of dirt.[114] To see the foul Egyptian is to see the Egyptian as dark – physically, spiritually sullied like the main characters in *Hamlet*.

By this point in the drama, Antony's threats against Cleopatra are unsurprising. The same is true for the fantasy he conjures up about racially white Octavia inflicting violence on his illicit Black lover.[115] Here, Cleopatra and Octavia echo the brown and white hairs that battled on Antony's head. The racialized nature of this womanly quarrel, which recalls *Titus'* previously mentioned beauty contest between Lavinia (ideal white woman) and Tamora (white other), becomes more vivid in the messy scenario featuring white Octavia plowing Cleopatra's soil-colored skin with her nails. Antony's usage of "let" and "patient" suggest Octavia is on standby, ready and willing to enact racist intra-gender violence and be an anti-Black accomplice, a role that Mikki Kendall argues some white women willingly play as agents of white supremacy and white patriarchy.[116] White hands would literally become dirty in this interracial image in which Black skin and blood become married to whiteness. Realizing that he is doomed, Antony – who later imagines his and Cleopatra's souls as "hand in hand" in death – wishes ill upon the Queen when he threatens to mutilate her before she becomes Caesar's prized possession of war (4.14.51).[117] This is yet another moment where the lady's white hand acts as an extension of masculine dominance, albeit hypothetically. Moreover, this is a moment where Antony, as white other, hypes whiteness by serving as the racist connector between Blackness and ideal whiteness.

The threat of disfigurement is interesting because, to an extent, Antony already maimed Cleopatra's body when he rhetorically detached her tawny hand and replaced it with a white one. Or maybe he, like "time," just bleached it.[118] While enraged, Antony derives pleasure from the thought of Caesar imprisoning Cleopatra and making money off her Black physique that would be on display among the common people in the Roman streets.[119] The white man sees the Black woman's body as a commodity and available for economic exploitation in his native land;[120] he does not now show the same concern about class boundaries that he showed in the white hand scene. Like her counterparts of color in Shakespearean drama, Cleopatra is a dual spectacle, an early modern minstrel sideshow within the play or perhaps a "ventriloquist dumm[y]."[121] This sideshow feeds the offstage audience's interests just as much as she feeds the curiosities of the characters around her. We could call the latter group an onstage audience since Cleopatra, the character, was performed on the early modern stage by a white male actor and since Cleopatra, as a character, also performed for the dominant culture the perceived monstrousness and impropriety of Black femininity.[122] Caesar's seizure of Cleopatra would be empowering for the white Roman figures because capturing the Queen typifies successful white dominance. Antony desires to hand her over to his Roman brethren to ensure the perpetuation of violent white supremacy and Black inferiority.[123] Cleopatra needs mastering through the physical violence Antony envisions white hands enacting in the quotation above.[124] This is why he determines Cleopatra "shall die" (4.12.47).

Yet, Egypt's queen knows she cannot wholeheartedly trust the white Roman's questionable intentions; and this is what the audience also knows when considering things from her viewpoint.[125] The apprehension about white aims ultimately works in the Queen's favor; it allows her to assume rightfully that Caesar wants to parade her through Rome as a sign of his masculine strength and white dominance. In so doing, he would literally display "mastery over blackness" and bring to fruition Antony's white domination fantasy.[126] Instead, Black Cleopatra will use the power of the white hand, her hand, to master herself and "by some mortal stroke, / [. . .] defeat [Caesar and Rome]" (5.1.64–65). At the play's conclusion, the Queen of Egypt overpowers whatever white masculine holds might exist on her. She calls attention to this when, imagining her future in Rome, she winces at the thought of "some squeaking Cleopatra boy [her] greatness / I'th' posture of a whore" (5.2.220–21). In not wanting to see or experience this, Cleopatra offers another reason why she must commit self-harm and inflict violence with her own hands.

The alteration of "boy" into a verb sheds light on the white boy actor who would have played her part on the early modern stage. Implied in her lines is that she is too much woman for a white boy; she is too magnificent for Caesar, too, and the actor underneath who plays her.[127] By killing herself, Antony's lover asserts through action that the Black Queen will not be played, as in mocked in Rome's streets, ever.[128] She employs her white hand, which adheres to her Black authority, to fight the encroaching white male power that wants to assume control of her body yet again. Until the end, the tension between Black, white and white other (and white and white other), is evident, but paradoxically reconciled through Cleopatra's self-destruction. When Caesar finally encounters the dead Cleopatra, he does not see the white boy actor; rather, he "see[s] performed that dreaded act which [he] / So sought'st to hinder" (5.2.331–332). He did not intend to prevent the Queen's death for her benefit. That was all for his advantage. This fact helps explain why Cleopatra does not "shake" at the sight of the white hand because said hand is hers. Antony gave it to her. In the end, the Egyptian monarch has the royal authority to "ruin" her "mortal house," to cause the ultimate domestic destruction, and consequently undermine white supremacy (5.2.50), so she uses that power to play Roman Caesar and mock his "ass / Unpolicied" in order to, as Marianne Novy sees it, "die with glory in Roman as well as Egyptian terms" (5.2.307–308).[129]

As a more traditional race play, and as a counterexample among the appearances of Shakespeare's canonical white hand motif, *Antony and*

Cleopatra stains the incessantly conquering white hand as a dangerous thing. For all that *Antony and Cleopatra* articulates about whiteness, by the play's conclusion we discover that violence, murder, and suicide may always be attributed to white hands regardless of one's bodily hue, for "if black Cleopatras seduce[, then] white ones kill themselves," according to Little, Jr.[130] Returning to Act 3, Scene 13 and Cleopatra's white hand, it is possible to see this moment as both physical Black-to-white conversion and Antony's recognition of the literal white part of the Queen's hand, the palm side.[131] Through the latter reading, the Black body is always hybrid and "the hand of death" is white (4.9.34). As a symbol, the white hand should instill fear in all because of its inextricable connection to violence and death. In instances of brutality and bloodshed in the play (where characters do not die of a broken heart, illness or natural causes), the white hand is at work, constantly reminding Shakespeare's audience how intra-racial tension and violence are driving forces in this play: Cleopatra beats the Messenger and pulls a knife on him, when she learns Antony remarries; Ventidius kills Pacorus; one of Lepidus' officers kills Pompey; Caesar has Alexas hanged; Eros stabs himself; Antony commits white self-harm and dies, eventually, by that "self hand" after a botched suicide attempt (5.1.21); and Charmian and Cleopatra place asps on their bodies and die by poisonous snakebites. The white hand's work in these examples is aggressive, savage, and (self)destructive. If for no other reasons, this is why one must "shake to look on't."

Moreover, the white hand's penchant for violence foreshadows Cleopatra's own death, a death that is powerfully executed on Cleopatra's terms. The Queen's failed first attempt to slay herself in Act 5, Scene 2 occurs when she learns Caesar's men have stormed her monument; here, the stage directions read, "drawing a dagger," signaling Cleopatra's suicidal agenda as she says, "Quick, good hands" (38). The address to the hands highlights what such hands are capable of. Rather than allow the Romans to take her, Cleopatra prefers to take her own life because, for the overpowered Egyptian, to borrow from Frantz Fanon's discourse on natives, "violence is a cleansing force [that . . .] makes [her] fearless and restores [her] self-respect."[132] Ironically, these "hands [that] lack[ed] nobility" for striking the Messenger (2.5.83), and attempting to kill him earlier in the play, become "good hands" after Antony whitens them; Cleopatra is also referred to as a "good lady" after that scene, too, and "lady" bestows respectability upon her (5.2.193).

As is true in various early modern texts, such as Ben Jonson's *The Masque of Blackness*, whiteness – despite its less than flattering associations with violence here – paradoxically becomes equated with goodness, beauty, and innocence because that is how the racist system works.[133] We are conditioned to see the virtuousness that fosters positive assessments of what undeniably amounts to white brutality because that is how whiteness and anti-Blackness work.[134] That is to say, destructiveness transmutes into constructiveness. The Romans, the white people and therefore their white hands, are depicted negatively as untrustworthy; however, Cleopatra's hands, symbols of the play's racialized anxiety, still encourage a positive critique of whiteness because they are, according to the Queen, the only hands she will "trust" (4.15.51).[135] At best, whiteness maintains unstable, and confusing, meanings in *Antony and Cleopatra* and in contemporary times as well: By killing the Queen, the bad/good white hands do something destructive that is presented and interpreted as constructive. As such, the hands expose the automatic ability for intention to be *always* debatable as one of the quintessential privileges of whiteness.

Playing the Race Cards

In *Antony and Cleopatra*, Antony's behavior, in the white hand scene in particular, validates the perception that white people, with the myriad privileges that automatically accompany whiteness, possess the ultimate race card – the ace of spades in the invisible race card deck. As a reminder: One of the greatest privileges of whiteness is, perhaps, the equation with goodness, the assumption of goodness, the freedom to move without consistent suspicion about, and because of, that presumed goodness. Yet, if ever there were a strong counter to the perception that whiteness equates with goodness – that it is an epitomized reflection of virtuosity – that counter exists unquestionably in white hands, for what have white hands *not* destroyed and pillaged over the centuries?[136]

Manufactured daily, white hands just might be the most prevalent and deadliest biological weapons that exist. Looking at history, even recent history,[137] we can see the colossal damage white hands have caused, for any act of violence one might immediately recall was undeniably committed by white hands. Looking forward, then, we have to wonder: What will those billions of little white hands that come into the world eventually do? In what new, or reinvented, ways will they demonstrate the evolution of global society's most ubiquitous weapon of mass destruction? If history is an indicator of anything as it pertains to the future actions of white hands, then we know: White hands will continue the cycle of destruction. They will destroy whatever they can grasp, and use whatever they can grasp to destroy, confirming again and again that whiteness is not inherently as good, beautiful, innocent, honorable, gentle, and fair as white hegemony would have us believe. When imbued with agency and power, what won't white hands do?

Contradicting the presumption of white goodness: White hands – literal, figurative and synecdochic white hands – will rape children,[138] women[139] and men;[140] white hands will steal;[141] white hands will vote for and elect racists; white hands will ratify and endorse with a signature racist, sexist, Islamophobic, homophobic laws;[142] white hands will craft corruption and write books that perpetuate, even if unwittingly, racism, stereotypes, and bigotry;[143] white hands will kill.[144] Moreover, white hands will mutilate bodies;[145] white hands will shoot up schools,[146] malls,[147] movie theaters,[148] churches,[149] concerts,[150] mosques,[151] and synagogues;[152] white hands will murder minorities;[153] white hands will work relentlessly to stabilize the invisible "color-line";[154] white hands will physically assault and assassinate;[155] white hands will abuse and reject the "Other";[156] white hands will even deliberately spread deadly viruses.[157] And in so doing, white hands will continue to prove Black lives don't matter, not nearly as much as white lives.[158]

White hands will start futile wars;[159] white hands will colonize, segregate, and gentrify;[160] white hands will appropriate;[161] and as Antony and Cleopatra demonstrate in their respective ways, white hands will destroy white hands, exemplifying what makes racism so deadly, since the perpetrators of racism can harm themselves by inadvertently becoming collateral damage for their own offenses. With all the chaos caused by these fair weapons of domestic and mass destruction, it is hard to fathom how white supremacy even exists as a metric with which to assess the alleged inferiority of racially different "Others"; it is hard to fathom why it is only Blackness that is imbued with the most pervasive negative symbolic meaning; and it is hard to fathom how white superiority can be taken so seriously, and so fiercely drive white people's social, political, and personal ideologies, for all have white hands but, alas, all white hands are not created equal – not even Shakespeare's. Wherever somatic whiteness exists and prevails, it inevitably teaches us about the nuances of white ideology and identity formation, matters that pertain directly to the pain, violence, and humiliation white people insist that Black people endure.

Notes

1 MacDonald, *Race, Ethnicity, and Power*, 7.
2 A shorter version of this chapter titled "'Shake Thou to Look on't': Shakespearean White Hands" first appeared in *White People in Shakespeare*, ed. Arthur L. Little, Jr. (London: Arden Shakespeare, 2023), 105–119.
3 Habib, *Shakespeare and Race*, 165. Also see Hall, *Things of Darkness*, 154–155.
4 Francesca T. Royster describes Cleopatra's energy as "formulated by others in the play as anti-Roman, anti-western and uncivilized." *Becoming Cleopatra: The Shifting Image of an Icon* (New York: Palgrave Macmillan, 2003), 13.
5 Jean E. Howard, "Is Black So Base a Hue?" in *Shakespeare in Our Time: A Shakespeare Association of America Collection*, ed. Dympna Callaghan and Suzanne Gossett (New York: Bloomsbury, 2016), 107–114; 110.
6 For Marianne Novy, "The Changing of Places Emphasizes that Antony Is an Outsider in Egypt and Cleopatra in Rome," *Shakespeare and Outsiders*, 15.
7 Little, Jr., *Shakespeare Jungle Fever*, 102–142.
8 Royster, *Becoming Cleopatra*, 2, 17.
9 MacDonald, *Race, Ethnicity, and Power*, 11.
10 Patricia Hill Collins and Sirma Bilge, *Intersectionality* (Cambridge: Polity Press, 2016), 4.
11 Mikki Kendall, *Hood Feminism: Notes from the Women that a Movement Forgot* (New York: Viking, 2020), 2–5.
12 Keeanga-Yamahtta Taylor, ed. *How We Get Free: Black Feminism and the Combahee River Collective* (Chicago: Haymarket Books, 2017), 5–6.
13 Collins and Bilge, *Intersectionality*, 25–30.
14 See John Michael Archer, "Antiquity and Degeneration in *Antony and Cleopatra*," in MacDonald, *Race, Ethnicity, and Power*, 151. Also see Little, Jr. *Shakespeare Jungle Fever*, 102–107.
15 Little, Jr. asserts that Antony experiences a "fall from white grace." He adds, "Rome fears Antony has gone black, gone nonwhite" (123). My reading of Antony differs from Little's in that I see the Roman's whiteness as diminished rather than wholly "lost." See *Shakespeare Jungle Fever*, 124.
16 Hall, *Things of Darkness*, 158.
17 Little, Jr. proposes that "in going primitive Antony goes Egyptian, in effect African." He goes on to say, "But Antony's English and ostensibly white body, a body that is presumably still physically white at the end of the play, betrays him to be a kind of white African," thus adding to the notion that his whiteness has degenerated (given the widespread early modern perception of Africa as an inferior land in comparison to England). *Shakespeare Jungle Fever*, 104. Also see Little, Jr., "Is It Possible to Read Shakespeare through Critical White Studies?" 277; Royster, *Becoming Cleopatra*, 52.
18 Little, *Shakespeare Jungle Fever*, 148–149; Royster, *Becoming Cleopatra*, 34, 53.
19 Habib, *Shakespeare and Race*, 158. Also see Royster, *Becoming Cleopatra*, 35.

20 In a *Shakespeare Studies* Forum (Volume 50, Autumn 2022), which I co-edited with Patricia Akhimie and Arthur L. Little, Jr., more work on Shakespeare's *other* race plays was published. Attention to white women's hands exists in other plays, though the phrase "white hand" might not be the exact language used. For example, Romeo mentions "the white wonder of dear Juliet's hand" (3.3.36). Elsewhere, in *Troilus and Cressida*, we encounter the line: "O, that her hand, / In whose comparison all whites are ink" (1.1.55–56). And in *Titus*, Marcus refers to Lavinia's "lily hands" as he studies her body in the scene where we find her ravished and mutilated (2.4.44).

21 As Matthieu Chapman acknowledges, "Dramatists wrote black characters in no fewer than seventy plays." "The Appearance of Blacks on the Early Modern Stage: *Love's Labour's Lost*'s African Connections to Court," *Early Theatre*, 17.2 (2014), 77–94, 86.

22 See Habib, *Shakespeare and Race*, 4; Little, Jr., "Re-Historicizing Race," 91–92.

23 Little, Jr., *Shakespeare Jungle Fever*, 161.

24 Building on Cheryl I. Harris's work, Little, Jr. discusses "whiteness as a form of property" in "Re-Historicizing Race," 89. These "white hand" passages indicate that for both white and black people, "racial identity remains an important component of social appraisal." Robert M. Entman and Andrew Rojecki, *The Black Image in the White Mind: Media and Race in America* (Chicago: University of Chicago Press, 2001), 1.

25 Considering that "Shakespeare's plays refer back and forth among themselves" (Danson, *Shakespeare's Dramatic Genres*, 7), the placement of the white hand in *Antony and Cleopatra* is even more fascinating and fitting, especially in terms of genre, since the most prominent Black Shakespearean figures – Aaron, Othello, and Cleopatra – are bound to the tragedies.

26 As a very specific kind of distraction for Antony, Cleopatra's blackness, and her affair with the Roman triumvir, calls "attention to the sexual dimension of politics." Melissa E. Sanchez, *Erotic Subjects: The Sexuality of Politics in Early Modern English Literature* (Oxford: Oxford University Press, 2011), 11.

27 In her study on Cleopatra, Royster considers "the tactical borrowing of the Cleopatra image in African American popular culture," in addition to white culture's borrowing of the Egyptian Queen (*Becoming Cleopatra*, 5). Building on this idea, I suggest here that we can implicate Antony in the business of borrowing the Queen to commoditize her, albeit not for financial profit.

28 Little, Jr. asserts, "When Rome does not explicitly reference her racial black-ness, it affects still as part of a more imperious and broader cultural code of alterity as Rome conjures her up as non-Roman, nonwoman, black woman, witch, slut, serpent, bitch, Egyptian, African" (*Shakespeare Jungle Fever*, 145). Rome, as in Antony, also conjures her up as "white" (3.13.137). Additionally, since "the countries bordering the Mediterranean[, including Egypt,] were another frequent source of supply [of black slaves]," I want to propose that this reality may have influenced Shakespeare's choice to blacken the Egyptian Queen; Blackness aligns her with people white hegemony desires to dominate.

See Ungerer, "The Presence of Africans," 31. Virginia Mason Vaughn reminds us that "as early as the 1570s black Africans were in England, working as household servants, prostitutes, and court entertainers." *Performing Blackness on English Stages, 1500–1800* (Cambridge: Cambridge University Press, 2005), 77. Lastly, Anthony Gerard Barthelemy posits, "Attitudes toward black people in the seventeenth century were formulated in an environment that had not distinguished between the traditional Christian view of black people as devils and the then not entirely unfamiliar African." *Black Face, Maligned Race*, ix.

29 Cleopatra may have been played by a boy actor in brownface. See Royster, *Becoming Cleopatra*, 33.

30 Chapman, *Anti-Black Racism*, 8. Also see Habib, *Shakespeare and Race,* 3; Royster, "White-Limed Walls," 448; Royster, *Becoming Cleopatra*, 48; Thompson, "Did the Concept?," 2. Dympna Callaghan reads Cleopatra as a "symbol of woman, of female sovereignty, of racial difference." *Shakespeare without Women: Representing Gender and Race on the Renaissance Stage* (New York: Routledge, 2000), 7.

31 Despite the unambiguous indications in the text, and the Queen's own self-identification, some critics have wanted Shakespeare's Cleopatra to be white and have therefore denied her Blackness. See Royster, *Becoming Cleopatra*, 36.

32 Robert Sandler, ed. *Northrop Frye on Shakespeare* (New Haven, CT: Yale University Press, 1986), 124. See also Celia R. Daileader, "The Cleopatra Complex: White Actresses on the Interracial 'Classical' Stage," in *Colorblind Shakespeare: New Perspectives on Race and Performance*, ed. Ayanna Thompson (New York: Routledge, 2006), 205–220, 205, 209, 213; Royster, *Becoming Cleopatra*, 17–20. Little, Jr. calls attention to the debate about Cleopatra's race when he notes, "Whether white or black Cleopatra finds herself the object of racial passing." *Shakespeare Jungle Fever*, 24. Also see Farah Karim-Cooper, who argues, "While Shakespeare suggests the readability of hands, he simultaneously alludes to the elusiveness of the self upon the surface of the body when people misread hands and their gestures." *The Hand on the Shakespearean Stage: Gesture, Touch and the Spectacle of Dismemberment* (London: The Arden Shakespeare, 2016), 24. Commenting on racial instability, Vanessa Corredera claims that "today's conceptions of race are no more stable or biologically based than those constructed in the early modern period." "Not a Moor Exactly: Shakespeare, *Serial,* and Modern Constructions of Race," *Shakespeare Quarterly*, 67.1 (2016), 30–50, 43.

33 Blackness enables Shakespeare's Cleopatra to fulfill the "common stereotype of black women as particularly promiscuous and sexually immoral." Antony's whitening of her hand is a calculated rhetorical move that, in theory, makes the Queen honorable, if only for a moment. See Melissa V. Harris-Perry, *Sister Citizen: Shame, Stereotypes and Black Women in America* (New Haven, CT: Yale University Press, 2011), 54.

34 Little, Jr. briefly acknowledges this moment but does not offer an extensive critique of it in *Shakespeare Jungle Fever*, 168.

35 Although "female 'blackness' [could be] metaphorical" in the Renaissance, Cleopatra's physical Blackness makes her holistically, and therefore unquestionably, Black. See Bovilsky, *Barbarous Play*, 39.

36 For more on "white property" (my quotation marks added), and white transformation, see Harris, "Whiteness as Property," 1709. Also see Little, Jr., "Re-Historicizing Race," 88; Andrew Bozio, "'Whiteness as Property' in *As You Like It*," *Shakespeare Studies*, 50 (2022), 24–32. For more on Cleopatra's color conversion, see Little, Jr., *Shakespeare Jungle Fever*, 163. As Lara Bovilsky comments, "Shakespeare's lines, we would assume, say only what he wishes." "The Race of Shakespeare's Mind," in *Shakespeare in Our Time: A Shakespeare Association of America Collection*, eds. Dympna Callaghan and Suzanne Gossett (New York: Bloomsbury, 2016), 114–117, 116.

37 Daileader, "The Cleopatra Complex," 207.

38 Thomas K. Nakayama and Robert L. Krizek, "Whiteness: A Strategic Rhetoric," *Quarterly Journal of Speech*, 81.3 (1995), 291–309; 303.

39 Both slavery and colonialism were historical enterprises that reveal the appropriation, commodification and sexualization of Black women's bodies. See Natasha Gordon-Chipembere, *Representation and Black Womanhood: The Legacy of Sarah Baartman* (New York: Palgrave Macmillan, 2011), 7.

40 Chapman, "The Appearance," 89. Also see Boose, "'The Getting of a Lawful Race,'" 41–47.

41 Hall, "Beauty and the Beast," 461.

42 In 5.2, Cleopatra says of and to Caesar, "My Master and my lord I must obey" (115). Although she feigns obedience, the Queen understands, perhaps because of her own "double-consciousness," how the Roman triumvir perceives her; consequently, she plays her part as the submissive captive so as not to reveal her desire to beat Caesar at his own game. For a description of double-consciousness see Du Bois, *Souls*, 3. Also see Kevin K. Gaines, *Uplifting the Race: Black Leadership, Politics, and Culture in the Twentieth Century* (Chapel Hill: University of North Carolina Press, 1996), 9–10.

43 Kim F. Hall expands on the relationship between whiteness and hands: "Whiteness (and white hands) are very often a sign of class, and the language of whiteness and fairness thus simultaneously articulates ideologies of race, class, and gender." In her discussion of portraits, Hall adds, "The emphasis on hands in many of these portraits may foreground class status in that it echoes the emphasis on fair hands in courtly love tradition." *Things of Darkness*, 209, 248.

44 Karim-Cooper, *The Hand on the Shakespearean Stage*, 2.

45 Shakespeare's conscious engagement with black/white language colored and "reflect[ed] popular taste." James Walvin, *Black and White: The Negro and English Society 1555–1945* (London: Allen Lane/The Penguin Press, 1973), 23–27.

46 Even before the early modern period, blackness was imbued with firm negative connotations: "During the medieval period, this belief was made evident in stories, such as the myth of washing the Ethiope white and the

biblical tale of the curse of Ham [...] Another widely held belief among the English was that the darkening of the skin was a sign of sin, and they often depicted devils or demons, both in art and in medieval cycle plays, as having black skin or faces." Chapman, "The Appearance," 78.

47 See Barbara Trepagnier, *Silent Racism: How Well-Meaning White People Perpetuate the Racial Divide* (New York: Routledge, 2010). I first deployed "racist inertia" in my free-standing book chapter, "'Is Black So Base a Hue?': Black Life Matters in Shakespeare's *Titus Andronicus*," in *Early Modern Black Diaspora Studies: A Critical Anthology*, eds. Cassander Smith, Nicholas Jones, and Miles P. Grier (New York, NY: Palgrave Macmillan, 2018), 137–155. Racist inertia connects the modern and early modern periods while acknowledging that we cannot accurately identify when racism began or when it was set in motion. We do know, however, that is has moved throughout time for centuries, and continues to do so.

48 Jennifer Park, "Discandying Cleopatra: Preserving Cleopatra's Infinite Variety in Shakespeare's *Antony and Cleopatra*," *Studies in Philology*, 11:3 (Summer 2016), 595–633; 609.

49 Little, Jr., *Shakespeare Jungle Fever*, 48.

50 See Harris, "Whiteness as Property," 1737.

51 Antony's language shows how "discourses of race and gender are not fully separable in the early modern period and indeed possess numerous identity features" (Bovilsky, *Barbarous Play*, 39). The Queen's hand represents a complicated intersection of blackness, whiteness, masculinity, and femininity.

52 In *Antony and Cleopatra*, the Egyptian Queen makes references to her "bluest veins" and being "pale." These references have served as support for some scholars, such as Royster, seeing Cleopatra as "explicitly emphasiz[ing] her whiteness" (*Becoming Cleopatra*, 18). This is a point of view I struggle with because it is possible for Black people, depending on how dark they are, to become pale and it is also possible for some Black people to see the blue of their veins, myself included. Not only is the blue of my veins visible on the palm side of my hands but it is also visible beneath my darker skin. Cleopatra's blue vein and pale skin references are insufficient evidence of her whiteness, just as references that might mention tanned skin would be unreliable markers of unquestionable whiteness, as it is possible for Black people to become darker when exposed to the sun.

53 Daileader, "The Cleopatra Complex," 211.

54 When Cleopatra says, "I am pale, Charmian" (2.5.60), I read this not as confirmation of her being pale, not as confirmation that her Blackness is only symbolic, but as a sign that her angst makes her weak in that moment. In addition to meaning white, whitish, and ashen in the early modern period, "pale" could mean lacking healthy color, bloodless, feeble, weak, faint, and without spirit.

55 Thompson, "What Is a 'Weyward' *Macbeth*?," 3.

56 See Entman and Rojecki, *The Black Image in the White Mind*, xv.

57 Gerzina, *Black England*, 5. Also see Joyce Green MacDonald, *Women and Race in Early Modern Texts* (Cambridge: Cambridge University Press, 2004), 23.

58 Katherine Rowe, *Dead Hands: Fictions of Agency, Renaissance to Modern* (Stanford: Stanford University Press, 1999).

59 Karim-Cooper, *The Hand on the Shakespearean Stage*, 4.

60 Ibid., 6.

61 Ibid., 45.

62 Erickson, "'God for Harry,'" 331.

63 Little, Jr., *Shakespeare Jungle Fever*, 108.

64 In response to Cleopatra's surprise at his return from battle with Caesar, Antony says, "Mine nightingale, / We have beat them to their beds. What, girl, though grey / Do something mingle without younger brown, yet ha' we / A brain that nourishes our nerves, and can / Get goal for goal of youth" (4.8.18–22). Antony makes it clear the brown hair symbolizes youth; the indication is that Caesar is younger, as Antony also calls him a "Roman boy" (4.12.48). In lieu of white hair, he now refers to grey hair, thus making it retrospectively evident that we can interpret his earlier hair rhetoric as racialized. In both hair metaphors, Antony infantilizes the brown hairs, which reflect a kind of longstanding non-white "struggle for equal adulthood" and respect. See Corinne T. Field, *The Struggle for Equal Adulthood: Gender, Race, Age, and the Fight for Citizenship in Antebellum America* (Chapel Hill: University of North Carolina Press, 2014), 1, 4. For a slightly different reading of the hair metaphor see Jan Blits, *New Heaven, New Earth: Shakespeare's Antony and Cleopatra* (Lanham, MD: Lexington Books, 2009), 132. "Paternalistic assumptions" are also a form of silent racism. See Trepagnier, *Silent Racism*, 6, 36.

65 In "Remixing the Family," I noted how Shakespeare's physically Black characters maintain racial hybridity.

66 "Cleopatra represents," as Hall explains, "the twin fears of foreign difference and female sexuality that resists European patriarchal standards." *Things of Darkness*, 126.

67 In part, this hair reading was inspired by work Eric De Barros has done on *Titus Andronicus*: "'My fleece of woolly hair that now uncurls': Shakespeare's *Titus Andronicus*, 'Black' Hair, and the Revenge of Postcolonial Education," *College Literature*, 49.4 (Fall 2022), 628–651. If, as I argue above, whiteness is instilled with universally recognizable ideal authority, then we might read blackness as maintaining universally recognizable resistance. As Mary Frances Berry asserts, "White oppression and black resistance has been a persistent part of the American scene since the colonial period." *Black Resistance/White Law: A History of Constitutional Racism in America* (New York: Meredith Corporation, 1971), 235. Since Berry acknowledges colonization, to which the English were no strangers (as we see in *The Tempest*), we might apply Berry's claim as we consider Shakespeare's *Antony and Cleopatra* – Berry's American scene an analog for England. Building on this last point, Danson

argues, "*Julius Caesar*, *Antony and Cleopatra*, and *Coriolanus* are so-called 'Roman plays', but they are very English in staging the conflict between the singularly remarkable individual and the demands of the political realm." *Shakespeare's Dramatic Genres*, 36. Bovilsky pushes the English connection further: "The associations of Italy with racial diversity, literary sophistication, alluring sensationalism, and a simultaneous awareness and fluidity of self make Italy an especially fruitful and momentous site where the English can project, claim, and experiment with formations of their own national identity" and, of course, whiteness. *Barbarous Play*, 133. And Little, Jr. observes, "The Romans were also of course England's model for civility, for *civitas*." *Shakespeare Jungle Fever*, 102–103.

68 See MacDonald, *Women and Race*, 36–37.

69 Jonathan Gil Harris, "Shakespeare's Hair: Staging the Object of Material Culture," *Shakespeare Quarterly*, 52.5 (Winter 2001), 479–491, 480, 484.

70 See François Laroque, "Italy vs. Africa: Shakespeare's Topographies of Desire in *Othello*, *Antony and Cleopatra* and *The Tempest*," *Shakespeare Studies*, 47 (2009), 1–16; 9. Little, Jr. also analyzes the crocodile language in *Shakespeare Jungle Fever*, 143.

71 Park, "Discandying Cleopatra," 617–618.

72 Sujata Iyengar, *Shades of Difference: Mythologies of Skin Color in Early Modern England* (Philadelphia: University of Pennsylvania Press, 2004), 1–12. Toni Morrison speaks of the "Africanlike (or Africanist) presence" in *Playing in the Dark*, 6.

73 Kari Boyd McBride, ed. *Domestic Arrangements in Early Modern England* (Pittsburgh, PA: Duquesne University Press, 2002), 6. In early modern England, "obedience to husbands, fathers, and masters was considered the principal duty of women, children, and servants, and rebellion within the family was viewed as synonymous with rebellion against the state." Such behavior was important for the maintenance of order, hence why Cleopatra registers as unruly and Egypt registers as completely out of order. By English audience standards, the Queen does not "abide by ideologies of civility and private life." Viviana Comensoli, *"Household Business": Domestic Plays of Early Modern England* (Toronto: University of Toronto Press, 1996), 17, 21, 66.

74 As Kimberly Poitevin explains, "In the early modern period, skin color had become an increasingly important signifier, not just of beauty, but of class, nation, and race. Though there are some exceptions, women were not, for the most part, trying to darken their complexions or paint their skins green or blue. In domestic manuals and 'how-to' books for manufacturing cosmetics, the artificial red-and-white complexions of English women were often set in contrast with those of darker-skinned peoples." "Inventing Whiteness: Cosmetics, Race, and Women in Early Modern England," *Journal for Early Modern Cultural Studies*, 11.1 (Spring/Summer 2001), 59–89; 70.

75 Susan Briante, "Seeing White: The Painful Ways the World Teaches Race and Color," *Guernica/A Magazine of Global Arts & Politics* (October 9, 2017), www.guernicamag.com/seeing-white/. The ability for the color of Cleopatra's

hand to shift also speaks to the fact that skin "was a contested and unstable boundary" in the early modern period. Poitevin, "Inventing Whiteness," 78.

76 Royster, *Becoming Cleopatra*, 19.

77 Hall, *Things of Darkness*, 266. For more on Cleopatra's "racial and sexual conversion" also see Little, Jr., *Shakespeare Jungle Fever*, 163.

78 Ania Loomba acknowledges how "early modern plays about the East remind us that the discourses of 'modern' racism were shaped by vocabularies of love and war appropriated from worlds that are today regarded as being on the 'other' side of temporal, ideological, and geographic borders." "Periodization, Race and Global Contact," *Journal of Medieval and Early Modern Studies*, 37.3 (Fall 2007), 595–620; 614.

79 Karim-Cooper, *The Hand on the Shakespearean Stage*, 62.

80 Roman Octavia's beauty, alluded to twice in the play, is always couched in positive terms (see 2.2.136 and 2.2.240, for example).

81 Reinforcing my point, I turn to Laroque, who argues, "Like the 'o'erflowing Nilus' (1.2.46), Cleopatra, as Africa, threatens Antony and the whole Roman world with dissolution and with the erasing of identity in its 'colonial economies of desire.'" "Italy vs. Africa," 10. Also see Francesca T. Royster, "Cleopatra as Diva: African-American Woman and Shakespearean Tactics," in *Transforming Shakespeare: Contemporary Women's Re-Visions in Literature and Performance*, ed. Marianne Novy (New York: St. Martin's Press, 1999), 103–126; 106. And for a general take on the idea of the threatening Black woman see Boose, "'The Getting of a Lawful Race,'" 49.

82 Smith, *Race and Rhetoric*, 8.

83 We know that "the English population considered Africans lazy, criminal, and irresponsible with an inherent inclination to drunkenness and sexual promiscuity, all traits that the early modern English associated with 'uncivilized' cultures." Chapman, "The Appearance," 79.

84 Little, Jr., *Shakespeare Jungle Fever*, 103.

85 This white hand scene, particularly the whipping, makes me think of Emmett Till, a young Black boy who was lynched by two white men in Mississippi in 1955 for allegedly whistling at/flirting with a white woman. The horrific consequence for his supposed transgression was meant to instill fear in Black people, especially boys and men, and illustrate the white male exertion of authority over the white female body that is, according to history, always in need of protection.

86 "Sunken place" refers to a low space – metaphorical and real – in which the marginalized find themselves; the sunken place is featured in the Academy Award-winning 2017 racial horror film *Get Out*, directed by Jordan Peele.

87 For more on whiteness appearing out of blackness see Royster, "White-Limed Walls," 452. See also Little, Jr., *Shakespeare Jungle Fever,* 164. Vanessa Corredera explains that *Get Out* "literalizes the horror of Othello's racial experience by stressing white supremacy's physical and psychological appropriation of and violence against black bodies, as well as the strategies that weaken black selfhood in order to make it susceptible to this white bodily and

mental appropriation." "Get Out and the Remediation of Othello's Sunken Place: Beholding White Supremacy's Coagula," *Borrowers and Lenders*, 13.1: 1–19 (April 2020), paragraph 2.

88 hooks, *Black Looks*, 28.

89 See Brown, "'Is Black So Base a Hue?,'" 144.

90 See Trepagnier, *Silent Racism*, 3. Eduardo Bonilla-Silva also addresses how white supremacy is folded into daily actions: "Racial domination necessitates something like a grammar to normalize the standards of white supremacy as the standard for all sorts of everyday transactions rendering domination almost invisible." "The Invisible Weight of Whiteness: The Racial Grammar of Everyday Life in America," *Michigan Sociological Review*, 26 (Fall 2012), 1–15; 1. Also see Nakayama and Krizek, "Whiteness," 291.

91 Little, Jr. argues that "a white man raping a black woman becomes the evidentiary playing out of the dominant society's fantasies of its self-assured and cool stranglehold over these representative foreign bodies [. . .] his raping a black woman becomes one way that *he* may be initiated into whiteness." *Shakespeare Jungle Fever*, 148.

92 Royster, *Becoming Cleopatra*, 9.

93 Habib, *Shakespeare and Race*, 174.

94 "Strumpet" is how the Romans typecast the Queen, as Emily C. Bartels notes in *Spectacles of Strangeness: Imperialism, Alienation, and Marlowe* (Philadelphia: University of Pennsylvania Press, 1993), 7.

95 See Hall, *Things of Darkness*, 148.

96 See Archer, "Antiquity and Degeneration," 157.

97 Harris-Perry argues that "the problem for marginal and stigmatized group members should be obvious. These citizens face fundamental and continuing threats to their opportunity for accurate recognition [. . .] An individual who is seen primarily as a part of a despised group loses the opportunity to experience public recognition for which the human self strives. Further, if the group itself is misunderstood, then to the extent that one is seen as a part of this group, that 'seeing' is inaccurate" (*Sister Citizen*, 38). Harris-Perry's claims also aid our understanding of the white other's social position. D. Marvin Jones offers another way to think about misrecognition: "Like a veil, the dominant perspective hides or obscures the human face of the person who wears it. Unlike a veil, the mechanism of the dominant ideology embedded deeply in culture, which is to say language, within our very understanding of race, remains invisible" (*Race, Sex and Suspicion*, 57). In colonial discourse, the land as "maiden" rhetoric seems somewhat commonplace. See Vaughn, "The Construction of Barbarism," 175. Laroque also writes about "the intriguing links between travel, body and landscape" found in *Antony and Cleopatra*. "Italy vs. Africa," 1.

98 See Harris, "Whiteness as Property," 1734.

99 Karim-Cooper, *The Hand on the Shakespearean Stage*, 63. Chapman points out that "for hundreds of years, at least since the crusades, the English held a widespread belief that fairness or whiteness was equivalent with beauty,

modesty, and good and blackness was equivalent with ugliness, promiscuity, and evil." "The Appearance," 78. For more on African sexuality, and the meaning of whiteness and Blackness, see Winthrop D. Jordan, *White Over Black: American Attitudes toward the Negro 1550–1812* (Chapel Hill: University of North Carolina Press, 1968), 5–8, 33.

100 By the time Shakespeare wrote *Antony and Cleopatra*, England had seen a wave of witchcraft charges, which would have put this subject into the public discourse: "Such charges rose steadily in number from the 1560s, peaked at a total of 180 in the 1580s, stayed high in the 1590s, and then fell away precipitously in the early seventeenth century, with less than twenty indictments in the 1630s. There was a small peak in the 1640s and 1650s, with maybe 130 indictments in the two decades combined [...] After 1660, indictments returned to their 1620s level, the last known trial on this circuit, involving a Hertfordshire woman named Jane Wenham, coming in 1712." James Sharpe, *Witchcraft in Early Modern England* (London: Longman, 2001), 16, 25. Also see Christina Larner, *Witchcraft and Religion: The Politics of Popular Belief* (New York: Basil Blackwell, 1984), 41–43; and Alan Macfarlane, *Witchcraft in Tudor and Stuart England: A Regional and Comparative Study* (London: Routledge & Kegan Paul, 1970), 14–15.

101 Sharpe, *Witchcraft in Early Modern England*, 23–24. Also see Larner, *Witchcraft and Religion*, 71.

102 Antony's anxiety is multifaceted, and it is historically understandable given that "sexual intercourse between members of different groups was the kind of crossover that generated the greatest anxiety." Ania Loomba, "'Delicious Traffick': Racial and Religious Difference on Early Modern Stages," in *Shakespeare and Race*, eds. Catherine M. S. Alexander and Stanley Wells (Cambridge: Cambridge University Press, 2000), 203–224; 213.

103 Macfarlane, *Witchcraft in Tudor and Stuart England*, 158.

104 The racializing of witchcraft is implied in the color symbolism that distinguishes the two kinds of witchcraft: "The crime of witchcraft was defined in various ways. Civil or Roman Law distinguished between black and white witchcraft. Black witchcraft or *maleficium* consisted of causing deliberate harm through the conjuring up of evil powers by a curse of the manipulation of objects (sorcery). White witchcraft consisted of socially useful performances such as healing, fortune-telling, or finding lost property through sorcery or incantation. The first was punishable by death; the second was not." Larner, *Witchcraft and Religion*, 1, 37–38.

105 Archer posits, "Antony himself assumes the Roman discourse that renders Cleopatra whore and trickster, a darkened remnant whose false soul turns antiquity into a conjurer's cheat, like the rigged game of fast and loose." "Antiquity and Degeneration," 151.

106 Spillers, "Mama's Baby, Papa's Maybe," 69.

107 Deroux, "The Blackness Within," 86.

108 His words and actions are a reminder that early modern images of Black women, in art and literature, have "little to do with actual black women." See

Kim F. Hall, "Object into Object: Some Thoughts on the Presence of Black Women in Early Modern Culture," in *Early Modern Visual Culture: Representation, Race, Empire in Renaissance England*, eds. Peter Erickson and Clark Hulse (Philadelphia: University of Pennsylvania Press, 2000), 315–345; 346.

109 Royster, *Becoming Cleopatra*, 14.

110 Enobarbus says to Menas of their hands, "If our eyes had / authority, here they might take two thieves kissing" (2.6.96–98). In 4.8, Antony says to Scarus (line 11) and Cleopatra (line 29), "Give me thy hand." Through the hand and the kiss, these two figures are aligned and the hand, in particular, touches on the "symbolic universe" that contained male-male desire. See Alan Bray, *Homosexuality in Renaissance England* (London: Gay Men's Press, 1982), 21. And see Mario DiGangi, *The Homoerotics of Early Modern Drama* (Cambridge: Cambridge University Press, 1997), 3–4. Also, in *Antony and Cleopatra*, Caesar's giving of his hand to Antony in order "to join [their] kingdoms and [their] hearts; and never / Fly off [their] loves again" adds to the play's homoeroticism (2.2.161).

111 Witches were also thought to be lustful; this personality trait reinforces Cleopatra's association with witchcraft. See Macfarlane, *Witchcraft in Tudor and Stuart England*, 158.

112 Barthelemy recalls that "the popular notion that black women were whorish could be heard on the English stage as early as Shakespeare's *The Merchant of Venice*." *Black Face, Maligned Race*, 124.

113 As Royster articulates, "Moderation and restraint were to Elizabethans the quintessential Roman virtues" ("White-Limed Walls," 448). As such, it would be odd for Shakespeare's Cleopatra to be white from the play's start; in the role of white whore, she would seem a contradiction (too much for a title figure) and alienate the early modern audience.

114 "foul, adj." *OED Online*, Oxford University Press.

115 To be clear, Antony's behavior and discourse toward Cleopatra turn violent. And while this violence appears in the context of an early modern play, it does make me think about the realities of contemporary domestic abuse and how "Black women are 35 percent more likely to be victimized by domestic abuse than white women and 3.5 times more likely to experience intimate partner violence than nonblack women of color" (Fleming, *How to Be Less Stupid about Race*, 58–59). Antony shows no such aggression toward his white wives.

116 Mikki Kendall asserts that twenty-first-century white women, particularly as evidenced by their political support for Donald Trump, have failed to live up to feminist ideals since they consider intersectionality, if at all, only when it is convenient for them. See *Hood Feminism*, 13.

117 After much confusion, "an eternal union with Cleopatra" eventually becomes Antony's goal. See Laura B. Vogel, "Cleopatra: Antony's Transformational Object," *PsyArt*, 19 (2015), 23–20; 29.

118 Daileader highlights the historical whitening/lightening of Cleopatra: "That time bleached her is an ideologically useful accident, but an accident all the same." "The Cleopatra Complex," 209.

119 Antony's behavior demonstrates how "imperialism can[not] be understood without reference to ideologies of race." Ania Loomba, "Early Modern or Early Colonial?" *Journal for Early Modern Cultural Studies* 14.1 (Winter 2014), 143–148; 147.

120 hooks, *Black Looks*, 24.

121 Robin Mitchell, *Vénus Noire* (Athens, Georgia: University of Georgia Press, 2020), 140.

122 For more on the performativity of Blackness and character profiling, see Brown, "'Is Black So Base a Hue?.'"

123 Frantz Fanon, *The Wretched of the Earth*, trans. Constance Farrington (New York: Grove Press, 1963), 43.

124 Saidiya Hartman suggests that "history is an injury that has yet to cease happening." "The Time of Slavery," *The South Atlantic Quarterly*, 101.4 (Fall 2002), 757–777; 772. Given the pervasiveness of global anti-Black violence, I agree with Hartman's assessment of the metaphorical open wound that is the Black existence, which remains subject to violent mastering today.

125 Royster asks: "What could we see if we took the point of view of Cleopatra instead of Antony? In what ways can the tactical appropriation of Cleopatra create insight, freedom and power for real women?" *Becoming Cleopatra*, 15.

126 Deroux, "The Blackness Within," 94.

127 Antony refers to Caesar as a "boy" a few times in the play (see 3.13.17; 4.1.1; and 4.12.48).

128 Joseph Roach claims, "Performance [. . .] stands in for an elusive entity that it is not but that it must vainly aspire both to embody and replace". *Cities of the Dead* (New York: Columbia University Press, 1996), 3. The young actor boy-ing Cleopatra's greatness vainly plays the woman who cannot be played. See also Callaghan, *Shakespeare without Women*, 12. Also see "play me" in *Urban Dictionary*: www.urbandictionary.com/define.php?term=play%20me.

129 Novy, *Shakespeare and Outsiders*, 15.

130 Little, Jr., *Shakespeare Jungle Fever*, 170.

131 The doubly racialized reading of the white hand is possible here because, as Peter Erickson and Kim F. Hall posit, "Early modern race studies places more emphasis on race, not less, and increases the opportunities for discussing race by focusing on new directions for analysis." "'A New Scholarly Song,'" 5. For early modern critical race studies, then, Cleopatra's white hand is a deeply valuable object.

132 Fanon, *The Wretched of the Earth*, 94. With self-respect restored, "there is finally no frivolous or politically irresponsible queen in Shakespeare's play. Throughout, she poses her theatrical body against Rome's inevitable conquest of Egypt." Little, Jr., *Shakespeare Jungle Fever*, 155. Habib describes Cleopatra's suicide as "the subaltern's act of posthumous self agency within

the discourse that is writing it, its ultimate denial of its own scriptability."
Shakespeare and Race, 16.

133 Speaking in relationship to the mid-nineteenth century, Robin Bernstein notes that by that historical point "innocence was raced white." *Racial Innocence: Performing American Childhood from Slavery to Civil Rights* (New York: New York University Press, 2011), 4. I propose that *Antony and Cleopatra* also presents the symbolic equivalent to racial whiteness as innocence and goodness, suggesting, as other critics have, that racial innocence is also a premodern phenomenon. Also see Royster, *Becoming Cleopatra*, 40–41.

134 The view of virtuousness occurs because we have also been conditioned to see that "white violence against blacks is not immoral but natural, normal, and inevitable" (Jones, *Race, Sex and Suspicion*, 88). Patricia J. Williams comments on how Black people are conditioned to see themselves in a white society; and I want to build on her language slightly by arguing that whites in a white society are conditioned from infancy to see in themselves all the positive qualities to which Black people are generally denied automatic access. Goodness and virtue, for instance, are mythically intrinsic aspects of the white identity that allow white people's bad behavior to be always questionable. See *The Alchemy of Race and Rights* (Cambridge: Harvard University Press, 1991), 62.

135 The white hand scene is a literary "exploited distorted representation of [the] black [woman]" that hands her a sliver of acceptability. See Turner, *Ceramic Uncles & Celluloid Mammies*, 11.

136 American slavery and the Holocaust are two distinct examples of significant senseless mass violence perpetrated by white hands.

137 On March 13, 2020, Breonna Taylor, a 26-year-old EMT worker, was killed by police who forcefully entered her Louisville, Kentucky home while she was sleeping: www.cnn.com/2020/05/21/us/breonna-taylor-death-police-changes-trnd/index.html.

138 In 2019, a 53-year-old white man raped a five-year-old girl: www.bbc.com/news/uk-scotland-glasgow-west-50053873. In 2005, Sandra Beth Geisel, a 42-year-old Albany, New York teacher, pled guilty to criminal sexual conduct with minors: www.lawfirms.com/female-teacher-sex-crime-offenders-and-scandals.html. Also see Chapter 3, for a reference to Jerry Sandusky.

139 In 2015, Brock Turner, a former Stanford University swimmer, sexually assaulted an incapacitated woman: https://en.wikipedia.org/wiki/People_v._Turner.

140 See Chapter 4 and the discussion of sexual violence against Black males.

141 In 2008, it was discovered that Bernie Madoff had defrauded thousands of people who chose to invest money with him: https://en.wikipedia.org/wiki/Bernie_Madoff.

142 For example, California Prop 8 created issues surrounding same-sex marriage between 2008–2013; this law was ultimately deemed unconstitutional: https://en.wikipedia.org/wiki/2008_California_Proposition_8.

143 Harriett Beecher Stowe's *Uncle Tom's Cabin* (1852) is an example of a popular text that helped give life to racist stereotypes, despite the novel being written in the interests of anti-slavery.

144 Charles Manson, a white man who allegedly fantasized about starting a race war, was an infamous convicted murderer in the United States: https://en .wikipedia.org/wiki/Charles_Manson.

145 A figurative early modern example of white hands conducting mutilation is, of course, Shakespeare's *Titus Andronicus*, discussed in Chapter 1. An infamous non-fictional example that fittingly follows *Titus* is Jeffrey Dahmer, an American serial killer who murdered and mutilated his victims, killing seventeen men and boys between 1978 and 1991. See https://en .wikipedia.org/wiki/Jeffrey_Dahmer.

146 For example, see "Columbine High School Massacre": https://en.wikipedia .org/wiki/Columbine_High_School_massacre;
"Sandy Hook Elementary School Shooting": https://en.wikipedia.org/wiki/ Sandy_Hook_Elementary_School_shooting; and "Stoneman Douglass High School Shooting": https://en.wikipedia.org/wiki/Stoneman_Douglas_High_ School_shooting.

147 See "Westroads Mall Shooting": https://en.wikipedia.org/wiki/Westroads_ Mall_shooting.

148 See "2012 Aurora, Colorado Shooting": https://en.wikipedia.org/wiki/ 2012_Aurora,_Colorado_shooting.

149 See "Charleston Church Shooting": https://en.wikipedia.org/wiki/Dylann_ Roof#Charleston_church_shooting

150 See "2017 Las Vegas Shooting": https://en.wikipedia.org/wiki/2017_Las_ Vegas_shooting

151 See "Christchurch Mosque Shootings": https://en.wikipedia.org/wiki/ Christchurch_mosque_shootings

152 See "Pittsburgh Synagogue Shooting": https://en.wikipedia.org/wiki/ Pittsburgh_synagogue_shooting

153 See "2019 El Paso Shooting": https://en.wikipedia.org/wiki/2019_El_Paso_ shooting

154 For a critique of the color-line and the "sonic color line" in an early modern context, respectively, see David Sterling Brown, "(Early) Modern Literature: Crossing the Color-Line," *Radical Teacher*, 105 (Summer 2016), 69–77; and "(Early) Modern Literature: Crossing the '*Sonic* Color Line,'" in *Shakespeare and Digital Pedagogy*, eds. Diana Henderson and Kyle Vitale (London: The Arden Shakespeare, 2021).

155 On March 3, 1991, Rodney King was a victim of police brutality when several white police officers beat him: https://en.wikipedia.org/wiki/ Rodney_King.

156 I have written at length about the rejection of the "Other" in *Titus Andronicus* in "Remixing the Family," 118–123.

157 See the following article on Jason Roger Pope, a white man who allegedly has AIDS and deliberately infected Black female victims: https://newsone.com/

3890787/jason-rogers-pope-family-police/. Additionally, in 2020, it was reported (based on FBI intelligence) that white supremacist groups were encouraging their supporters to spread Covid-19 to cops and Jewish people: https://abcnews.go.com/US/white-supremacists-encouraging-members-spread-coronavirus-cops-jews/story?id=69737522.

158 Elsewhere, I examined Black Lives Matter in an early modern context. See Brown, "'Is Black So Base a Hue?,'" 137–155.

159 The American Civil War, sparked by the confederate states' desires to sustain the institution of slavery and retain Black people as human chattel, was, indeed, a futile war.

160 Historic Harlem (New York City), which is home to a lot of Black history, has lost some of its defining cultural and racial character due to gentrification: See "On Every Harlem Corner: Big Money and Bulldozers Threaten Black History": www.theguardian.com/us-news/2019/jun/23/harlem-historic-churches-new-york-city-personal-essay.

161 In 1851, the Indian Appropriations Act permitted the eventual appropriation of Native American Lands and the creation of Indian reservations: See "Indian Appropriations Act": https://en.wikipedia.org/wiki/Indian_Appropriations_Act.

CHAPTER 4

"Hear Me, See Me"
Sex, Violence, Silence, and Othello

I am not wrong. Wrong is not my name.
             – June Jordan, "Poem about My Rights" (1980)[1]

As *Titus Andronicus*, *Hamlet*, and *Antony and Cleopatra* illustrate, exclusion defines the white other's place. The white other is a necessary factor in the negotiation of whiteness and the related perpetuation of anti-Blackness across the intraracial color-line. And this reality leads me to ask a serious question about a significant problem: If white people cannot exist in accord with one another or even with themselves at the individual level, then what hope is there for non-white people – especially Black people who occupy the bottom of the racial hierarchy – to exist in accord with white folks? In society and in Shakespeare's dramatic literature, white matters often get prioritized because of the presumed superiority of whiteness and because of the alleged inferiority of blackness, which is used to define the white other's presence spiritually, sexually, psychologically, emotionally, morally, and even sartorially.

Therefore, as long as white people continue distracting each other in their centuries-old quest to uphold white supremacy, nothing else, no one else can matter as much. Since "learning to listen is a virtue whiteness has often avoided,"[2] as Dyson asserts, I devote space here for the often unheard and I use *Othello* to critique whiteness along the intraracial color-line. I devote space in this chapter to explore further the deep gap between Black and white by seeing and centering Black personhood, all the while considering the interplay among violence, silence, sex, and race instigated by white conduct. Specifically, I want to highlight an underdiscussed issue that reveals how the distance between Black and white, a wedge stabilized by the intraracial color-line and the white other, has major psychological and physical consequences for a minority group often portrayed not as victims but as the perpetrators of sexual violence – that group being men, specifically Black men.

White self-harm, white privilege, white dominance, and "herd invisibility,"[3] key components of white identity formation, have ensured and insured the racial asymmetry that favors white people when it comes to identifying and defining who gets to be victim. By way of *Othello*, then, I want to reflect on what the reality of de-victimization means for Black males by contemplating questions whose answers have tangible psychological and social impact: How do Black males scream for centuries about their psychological, physical, and emotional pain – yet remain unseen and unheard? How do Black boys and men simultaneously hold their collective breath – buried alive for centuries – yet not die?[4] And what is the psychological price Black males pay, and have paid, for being gagged victims of violence (physical, sexual, emotional, domestic, etc.)?

The answers, in part, lie in Jennifer Lynn Stoever's theorization of the "sonic color line": a phenomenon that builds on W. E. B. Du Bois' articulations in *The Souls of Black Folk* and suggests race is a fundamentally important ocular and *aural* signifier that dictates how all racialized bodies are presented, perceived, processed, and even policed.[5] Du Bois specifically homed in on the separation of the lighter and darker races of men as the crux of the racial divide at a time when the influence of American slavery's effects were still sending visibly damaging aftershocks through society, especially in the form of legal segregation (*Plessy v. Ferguson*, 1896) and anti-Black violence (such as lynching) fueled by white supremacy. These aftershocks continue to shake the global landscape today.

I explicitly consider Du Bois and Stoever, here, because their theoretical interventions, which center the divide between Black and white, are implicated in the wider division among white, white other, and Black denoted by the intraracial color-line. Furthermore, the social, psychological, and historical problems that their respective works address are inseparable from the matter I want to cover regarding victimized Black males and their voices, which often remain unheard when it comes to their being victims of violence: murder, police brutality, rape, intimate partner violence (IPV),[6] and even adverse childhood experiences (or ACEs) such as neglect and molestation.[7] *Othello* is a useful entry point into this conversation because, much like *Titus*, this play involves a lone Black male character in a narrative that depends on the presence of a nefarious white other, Iago, who instigates the drama's engagement with white supremacy, sex, violence, and racialized anxiety. *Othello* dramatizes how the intraracial color-line and white other sustain Black subjugation, sometimes with lethal consequences that are no less relevant to real Black men outside of the play.

Othello thrives on its villain's ability to generate racial discord and manipulate and coerce psychologically all those around him, not just Othello. While critics have noted Iago's skill in this regard,[8] they have yet to reflect on it with consideration of the intraracial color-line, specifically in terms of white-on-white violence (or perverse intimacy between white men); Iago's role as the play's primary white other, as a "hype man" for white supremacy like the Goths in *Titus* (as discussed in Chapter 1); and how his role as the white other allows him to use sexualized discourse with or about white men to facilitate his abuse of Othello. As the villain and as a white man, Iago's mediation of emblematic blackness, signified by his morally and ethically corrupt behavior, is quite evident, based on the criteria I outlined in the Introduction. With that discourse in mind, I want to highlight a few key moments from *Othello* before transitioning to a discussion that more broadly centers Blackness in relationship to whiteness. As *Othello* illustrates, and even warns: It is dangerous for Black people not to pay attention to whiteness and it is equally dangerous to center whiteness without critique. That is the lesson Othello fails to learn by trusting the white other too much and by not trusting himself enough.

In being "far more fair than black," as the Duke suggests he is, Othello registers as an assimilated Black man; yet, the racist trauma he experiences in the opening scenes indicates the limits of the whiteness he is perceived to embody (1.3.293). To the detriment of his household and himself, and the state, too, Othello internalizes the anti-Black racism that surrounds him in Venice and Cyprus and, as a result, he lives a life and a lie of self-doubt molded by myriad experiences with racism. As such, I reinforce in this chapter another of this book's central arguments: that examining whiteness, from an antiracist perspective, requires the simultaneous analytical centering and decentering of whiteness. From the critical promised land that Othello does not reach – partly because it would have been impossible for Shakespeare, a white man, to lead him there and more importantly leave him there – I define the play's sex-violence system as a structure that is deeply dependent on blackness and, in this play especially, the Black man and his body. This premodern white dependence on somatic Blackness and figurative blackness in order to establish the parameters of the ideal white self and white other is a troubling precursor for so much violence and trauma that historically followed *Othello* with respect to interracial relations.

In Bed with Iago: Mindfucking White Men

Iago's mindfuck game is good.[9] With skill, he performs like the kind of partner who satisfies himself, as well as those with whom he engages, in what I call his intercourse discourse. The meaning of this section's title is multifaceted: it establishes how a white man, Iago, is a mindfucker;[10] it establishes how white men in this play can be mindfucked; it queers and calls attention to Iago's figurative, and somewhat violent, sexual activity with a few of the play's white men; and it signals how there is a perverse psycho-racial component to the narratives Iago creates around race and sex, narratives that eventually allow him to master Othello and seduce him mentally. In the examples I explore below, the "bed" is a literal and metaphorical intimate material object tied to Iago's intercourse discourse that is designed to perpetuate the play's intraracial tension and anti-Black racism. Iago's intercourse discourse is itself rooted in racism and designed to produce violent outcomes in the public and private spheres.

When we hear of Iago in bed with Cassio in Act 3, Scene 3 (429–442), a moment where we and Othello essentially become aural voyeurs left to imagine an impassioned sleep-talking Cassio sensually touching and kissing Iago as if he were Desdemona, we witness the play's conflation of the erotic, homoerotic, homosexual, intraracial, and interracial.[11] As noted, Iago literally claims to have been in bed with Cassio, but in a sense he also brings Desdemona into that bed. Under the guiding Christian assumption that man and wife are one, by proxy this imagined Iago-as-Desdemona also invokes the presence of a jealously displaced Othello (recalling Hamlet's "mother" language that merged Claudius into Gertrude, see Chapter 2). Iago becomes the embodied intersection of race, gender, and sexuality. In multifaceted ways, the white man displaces the lawful Black husband and marginalizes him, removing his spousal patriarchal power. In bed with Iago, Othello can only be the white woman, Desdemona, if he can be anything at all, as Iago's words imply – the interracial marriage gets whitewashed in this fantasy. Relaying his fabricated tale about occupying the same bed as Cassio, Iago fills Cassio's mouth with words and speaks them to Othello:

> In sleep I heard him say, "Sweet Desdemona
> Let us be wary, let us hide our loves!"
> And then, sir, would he grip and wring my hand,
> Cry, "O sweet creature!", then kiss me hard,
> As if he plucked up kisses by the roots
> That grew upon my lips; then laid his leg

> Over my thigh, and sighed, and kissed, and then
> Cried, "Cursèd fate that gave thee to the Moor!"
>
> (3.3.434–441)

In our minds, we imagine Cassio uttering his sweet words to Iago, a white man. Yet, Iago positions himself as a surrogate for the white woman, Othello's wife.[12]

Iago's erotic whet dream, that is to say, the sexualized dream vision he concocts to whet, or sharpen, Othello's desire to kill Desdemona and "tear her all to pieces," is itself an example of how sex, race, silence, and violence merge in this play (3.3.446). Using the white man Cassio to facilitate his sexual manipulation, Iago coerces Othello into believing his wife Desdemona cuckolds him. By not resisting Cassio's advances in his story, Iago becomes a willing, whorish Desdemona who violates domestic decorum by succumbing to and therefore confirming Cassio's intense desire for her, as evidenced by the aggressiveness, if not outright violence, of his touching and kissing. Manufacturing this story allows Iago to transform Othello into a figurative cuckold while performing emotional and psychological rape on the Black man whose vehement call for "black vengeance" signifies the success of Iago's mindfuck, for he gets Othello to come to the conclusion that he must kill his wife (3.3.462). This dream vision serves other purposes as well: to define Cassio, whom Iago hates, as a betrayer of their General and to elevate Iago's professional and social status as he transitions from being Othello's "ancient" to being his lieutenant and confidant (3.3.494). In pitting Othello against Cassio and Desdemona, Iago successfully fractures the interracial household and orchestrates a complex scenario that involves intraracial violence designed to induce interracial violence, as white male dominance so often does.

Again, I say: Iago's mindfuck game is *so* good. It is, in fact, what helps set the play's intraracial, and interracial, conflict in motion through the villain's relentless insistence on Othello's supposed barbarous difference that marks him as outsider in Venice.[13] Mindfucking is what Iago excels at. He creates and/or capitalizes on white people's psychological malleability and instigates intraracial tension in ways leading to the interracial conflicts that make Othello into a pathetic victim of racism and racial exclusion. As the play's pornographer, so to speak, Iago's sexual imagery gets everyone wet with anxiety. In *Othello*'s first scene, Iago activates the play's racial conflict when he charges that Brabantio's domestic possession, his daughter, has been stolen by a Black Moor. Iago removes Desdemona's agency and stereotypically criminalizes Othello's actions; and he complicates the issue when he calls attention to the interracial aspect of Desdemona's union, which occurred without her father's consent, a move that ignored traditional social expectations related to the courtship and marriage processes. Iago's anti-Black rhetoric fuels Brabantio's racial paranoia by promoting a false narrative about theft. Moreover, he capitalizes on Brabantio's concerns about Blackness through his sensational, sexual imagery when he says,[14]

> Even now, now, very now, an old black ram
> Is tupping your white ewe. Arise, arise;
> Awake the snorting citizens with the bell,
> Or else the devil will make a grandsire of you.
> (1.1.90–93)

Less detailed but no less vivid than his elaborate dream-vision seduction of Othello, Iago's manipulation of Brabantio is alarming nonetheless, because it directly relies on exploiting the racial tension (intraracial and interracial) between white and white (father and daughter) and white, white other, and Black (Brabantio, Iago, and Othello). Forcing Brabantio to visualize the Black man having sex with his white daughter Desdemona, Iago succeeds in generating intraracial domestic conflict that is a byproduct of interracial tension, specifically his "hate" for Othello (1.1.7, 158).[15] There is even an air of homoeroticism in Iago's language given that "ewe" sounds like "you" – in other words, the white self. By extension, Brabantio, the white man, is also being tupped by the Black man, given that Iago's language furthers the uncontrollable Black phallus' reach and given that an early modern audience would have understood Desdemona as her father's property and thus a part of him.

Iago's association of Othello with the devil, and his suggestion that Brabantio's lineage will be blackened in various ways, reveals how much he understands both the familial implications of the interracial marriage and the power of anti-Black racism. According to Ariane M. Balizet, "Because of the understanding that lineage is physically manifest in the blood or 'bloodline', then as now, children were often described as literal extensions of a father's blood."[16] In essence, Brabantio's family line would become stained through Othello and Desdemona's progeny, through the mixed blood, thus reflecting badly on Brabantio's patriarchal power, since the imagined grandchild would serve as incontrovertible proof he could not control his daughter's "wayward passions."[17] His household is out of control. Moreover, Iago's repeated usage of "now" coupled with "awake" creates a sense of urgency because peace has been disrupted by the white, not Black, "devil." The anti-Black animalistic description of interracial sex deepens the anxieties produced by this speech because boundaries of all kinds are crossed, with race being the most central. Iago subtly highlights age as another factor defining the couple's incompatibility beyond race; and Roderigo soon compounds the perceived problems with this union by emphasizing class and cultural differences with attention to sexuality. For instance, he calls Othello a "lascivious Moor" (1.1.129). Furthermore, Iago's physical position in the street symbolizes the integration of the public-private spheres, since he orders not just Brabantio to awake but the common citizens, too. He publicizes this private household conflict, making it relevant to all Venetians, to all white people in the broader landscape. As white other, Iago exists to stoke fears and instigate a divide between the Black man and the white Venetians.

Brabantio echoes Iago's racially divisive sentiment when he reasons that Desdemona has committed "treason of the blood" (1.1.173). By crossing the Du Boisian color-line, Desdemona betrays the white race. Since blood was thought of as a marker of class as well as race in the period,[18] Desdemona betrays the very essence of who she is as a Venetian, as a white woman, and as Brabantio's daughter. The treasonous accusation casts her as opposing her familial, racial duty and presents her as Othello's immoral accomplice. Moreover, the accusation positions Brabantio, head of his household, as a kind of white sovereign figure or master to whom allegiance is owed.[19] Desdemona's attraction to and association with Othello makes her household status contradictory (a fact that helps illuminate the illogical nature of racism); her father simultaneously views her as a dehumanized stolen object and a being capable of betraying any man. Recall that he warns Othello: "Look to her, Moor, if thou hast eyes to see. / She has deceived her father, and may thee" (1.3.295–296). Brabantio's understanding of Desdemona's betrayal anticipates Othello's later concerns about her fidelity, concerns stirred by Iago in several scenes, including the moment where he presents the dream vision analyzed above.

Although the combination of sex and violence I examine here is primarily rhetorical and not physical, that does not mean it is not harmful, for sexual violence is also psychological and emotional, as I will argue in this chapter's remaining sections. Sometimes words, or even just a single word, are all that is needed to inflict severe damage. Iago's deliberate choice to conjure up sexually explicit images through his language puts him – and everyone, including the audience – in bed with Othello and Desdemona while we all envision Brabantio's daughter "covered with a Barbary horse" (1.1.114), as Iago puts it,[20] and "making the beast with two backs"

(1.1.119). Before Act 5, Scene 2, which critics tout as the central domestic scene because the penultimate action occurs in the bed(chamber),[21] and because Othello kills Desdemona in their bed, we have already been in bed with the newlyweds a few times because Iago lures us there. In this respect, Act 1, Scene 1 is all about mindfucking and violating the senses; this opening scene is significant for how it introduces a mode of psychological manipulation that carries on throughout the play.

The force of Iago's non-physical sexual violations makes them akin to rape, which is not about sexual intimacy but about exerting power over one's victim. The opening scene is all about deeply penetrating white patriarchal fears and stabilizing Othello's abject status before we even meet him. Iago plays his role of white other quite well: For example, he shapes negative attitudes about blackness; he perpetuates dangerous stereotypes about Black males; and he participates in the negotiation of whiteness by inspiring Brabantio to defend white ideals and values such as purity, superiority, endogamy, female innocence, and proper domestic conduct. Most of all, Iago reminds us how the ternary racial hierarchy works, for despite Othello's status as a military general and despite his royal lineage, Iago's villainy defeats him. More than the Black/white binary, the ternary racial hierarchy that includes white, white other, and Black shows how distant the Black man is from the top, how the nominally inferior white other, the subordinate soldier, affirms the precariousness of the Black General's authority and status in relationship to white hegemony. Although the Black man may appear on top, he is in actuality far from the valued form of whiteness that doubles as the human standard.

Like *Titus*, *Othello* is a play that uses the Black presence as a means to facilitate white-on-white violence. And similar to Aaron in Act 1 of *Titus*, Othello is silent and silenced, not just in the opening scene but in other moments in the play, too. The silencing of Othello is itself a form of violence because it allows Iago's initial racist construction of the Black man's identity in 1.1 to linger. His demeaning description of Othello cannot be erased from the play. Thus, Iago colors our perception of Othello in a way that functions like a self-fulfilling prophecy, since Othello eventually transforms from the confident, assured General to a violent Black brute who commits mariticide. More subtly than the Du Boisian and Stoeverian color-lines, the intraracial color-line marks the boundary of what it means to be a white figure and a Black figure in a Shakespeare play. And the intraracial color-line even delineates the boundaries of what it means to be a Black person living in today's world, given the pervasiveness of anti-Black racism, which the intraracial color-line is specifically designed to reinforce.

Premodern literature and history have much in common with the present; and unfortunately, Black people have much in common with tragic Othello, still. Living in a predominantly white and racist society, he is a character who does not know the first thing about what it means to be privileged or dominant because he is a dehumanized figure who, like Black people today, is not truly seen or heard because racism and the intraracial color-line limit the possibilities for uncompromised humanization. One might think the senate scene in Act 1 is an exception, but Othello is valued there for what he is, a general, and not who he is, a Black man and newly minted patriarch. There is no antiracist ally or, better, antiracist accomplice to counter the narrative that says he is racially less-than.[22] As such, Othello's racialized erasure by Iago and the play's other white people costs him his sanity. It costs him his dignity. It costs him his marriage. And, ultimately, it costs him his life. When white people deny Black people the right to be respected as human beings, as has been the case for centuries and as continues to be the case, the consequences are dire. The many consequences – emotional, psychology, physical, economic, social, political, professional – help affirm the illusion of white superiority and Black inferiority, allowing white people to mindfuck the masses.

Into the Street: Crossing the Line

Through Iago's meddling and his intercourse discourse, Othello, in an uneasy, uncomfortable way, blurs the boundary between public and private concerns that shape the play's engagement with race and racism. More pointedly, the text suggests there is no real boundary between public and private because, unlike whiteness, racism is not so carefully regulated in white consciousness. Rather, it is more often than not nurtured wherever it can be nourished. We find Iago, a less-than-ideal white person – the white other – calling for support from the "snorting citizens" as he takes his anti-Black racism to the street (1.1.92). A white person, a white man, taking racism to the street, then, is a phenomenon with centuries-old roots, for it is the intraracial regulating of whiteness that can lead to the policing of Black people and Blackness by the law and the common citizens within Shakespeare's tragedy and outside of it. Long before the popular "Karen" meme that represents all that is wrong with racism, there was Iago. What helps Othello's relevance for the present moment is the play's demonstration of how tied racism is to human development. When racist ideologies are fed, they grow, thus allowing racists to successfully nurture their white dominance and oppress others. So, since racism has no off switch, what happens when those who internalize racist and white supremacist ideologies go out into the world? What happens when we step outside of a play like *Othello* and into the real world where it is practically guaranteed that anti-Black racist ranting like Iago's will attract an audience that is willing to listen or, worse, act in order to protect white hegemonic values?

As an unnecessary reminder that builds on this chapter's attention to *Othello*, anti-Black racism has defined what it can mean in today's world to: drive,[23] walk,[24] sleep,[25] party,[26] BBQ,[27] play rap music,[28] sell water,[29] use a coupon,[30] cut grass,[31] canvas (as a state representative),[32] wear a police uniform,[33] eat lunch,[34] attempt to have a business meeting at Starbucks,[35] fly,[36] check out of an Airbnb,[37] vote,[38] wait for a friend,[39] perform routine work inspections,[40] golf,[41] work out,[42] move into an apartment,[43] hire and fire help,[44] worship God,[45] protest, and more – while Black. As these unfortunate examples suggest, the invisible knapsack Black people carry is not replete with the goodies of privilege. It cannot be because, as these various examples reveal, Black people's disenfranchisement, their position below the white other in the racial hierarchy, stabilizes Black inferiority and white dominance; the "bad" cop who murders goes free, the bad "good Samaritan" who calls the cops and makes false accusations is not a criminal, etc. And white supremacy and centrality are what entitle white people to pick up the phone, call the police, and have their concerns be heard and received with the utmost urgency.[46] So what does it mean, what has it meant (if it has meant anything at all), to be heard while Black or, conversely, to listen while white? More pointedly, what does it mean to experience, like Othello, violence as a Black male at the hands of uncouth, morally, ethically corrupt white people whose actions white hegemony sometimes supports and simultaneously distances itself from? In other words, I am suggesting that today's unapologetically racist white people function as Iagos, for in the public realm they so clearly hype whiteness, anti-Blackness, and white supremacy in ways that have lasting socio-political consequences.

Without question, silence renders history unknowable. This is true for personal histories as well as communal social histories that inform us about the past. In my effort to better understand the historical silence surrounding sexual violence against Black men, it is imperative I acknowledge the past and what I see as a kind of macro-level "family-of-origin" issue that, in a way, makes Othello's fictional experience with sexual and racist violence reflective of a particular lived reality.[47] In "The Sexual Abuse of Black Men Under Slavery," Thomas A. Foster informs us that "black men were sexually assaulted by both white men and women," for example, and the "sexual assault of enslaved men took a wide variety of forms, including outright physical penetrative assault, forced reproduction, sexual coercion and manipulation, and psychic abuse."[48] As human chattel in racist environments, Black male minds and bodies were unprotected, and Black women's even more so (though they are outside the scope of the argument I am making here). Similar to Iago, antebellum white folks had a predatory fixation with Blackness; and they responded to this fixation with the kind of violence that reinforced their white dominance. White men and women, plantation masters and mistresses, exploited the Black male body in a variety of ways for their own sexual, emotional, psychological, and financial benefit, not at all hearing the metaphorical, and real, screams of the Black males whose own sexual, emotional, psychological, and financial well-being remained unfulfilled by interactions that rendered them visible only as Black bodies and not autonomous Black human beings with real psyches, emotions, and desires in need of protection. The racialized silence reflects a long history, as seen even in *Othello*, that includes but is not limited to Black powerlessness, hypermasculinity, fetishization, objectification, eroticization, exoticism, heterosexuality, and homosexuality, terms that resonate with some of the earlier descriptors I used to describe Shakespeare's Black male characters in Chapter 2. This is a history we must know and consider in relationship to the silence of Black male victims of sexual violence in order to begin truly hearing those voices – from the past and in the present – and recognizing how physical and mental abuse affects Black boys and men.

The Du Boisian color-line, the separation of Black and white or dark and light, was a problem that defined the transatlantic slave trade and related racial relations and hierarchies.[49] The color-line also represents a division between the powerless and the powerful, a type of imbalanced dynamic reflected in sexual assault cases. As is widely known, rape is about asserting power and dominance over the victim, as Iago successfully does, while demoralizing and even dehumanizing that person; rape is about making one's self feel superior and in control at another's expense.[50] Given this fact, it is unsurprising that, for example, a seventeenth-century Connecticut man named Nicholas Sension "sexually preyed on his male servants. [And it is no surprise that] virtually all of the cases of sodomy that came to the courts in early America involved individuals violating status boundaries – instructors on students, masters on servants. None involved peers."[51] Sension's uncivilized conduct was rooted in racism and the ability to mindfuck his social, racial, economic inferiors. The animalistic act of preying reinforces the predatory nature of sexual violence as it reinforces the vulnerability of the Black male "servant," or enslaved person, who was unable to exert agency in a white supremacist, white patriarchal society governed by perverse white logic and white methods. As part of the household, the servant was property and therefore available for objectification and abuse. Thus, when Iago masters Othello, he takes advantage of the vulnerability that permits him to neutralize the General's authority.

Even abolitionists, often painted historically as nice, innocent, good-intentioned, anti-slavery progressive white people who held positions of socio-political and racial power in relationship to Black people, were also complicit in the sexual violation of Black men: Foster acknowledges that "numerous abolitionist images also fixate on the black male body as perfection, highlighting muscular bodies and, in almost pornographic detail, exposed buttocks, enduring unjust abuse and degradation."[52] From racist and abolitionist angles, Black men were used as props to satisfy the white gaze, to quench the thirst of the white desire for dominance. Both "good" and bad white people crossed the line. These points about the private and public sexual abuse of Black men under American slavery allow us to see a historical trajectory of sexual violence and silence unfold as the racially hierarchized nature of antebellum and postbellum society meant there were no real outlets for Black men to express their physical, psychological, and emotional pain, not even among some of their abolitionist allies, whose own unconscious or repressed racism found a way to surface these white people's true sexual desire for Black men. For white and non-Black people, proximity to Blackness equaled, and equals, power;[53] it did not, and does not, equal being antiracist, not even when interracial bodies retain close contact, as Desdemona herself proves.

As a form of punishment or perverse bonding/bondage, white usage of sexual violence against Black boys and men is intertwined with multiple other issues and legacies stemming from transatlantic slavery.[54] And today, sexual violence against Black males is intertwined with so many issues that plague the Black community at large, matters that also connect to slavery's history and its effects, such as mental illness, poverty, and familial/domestic instability. If we consider the fact that slaves were not thought to be people but property,[55] and that what we understand as, and what they understood as, their familial ties were not treated as legitimate familial ties at all by their white masters and mistresses, then the macro-level family-of-origin problem I am highlighting here becomes easier to identify, since families are thought to influence who people are and who they end up being.[56] I contend that the Black slave family, or family unit, had several influencers. Therefore, the exposure to and transference of different forms of trauma could happen from within and outside of what one might think of as the family unit, broadly speaking, proving the plantation itself to be a dangerous space. The multidirectional nature of different trauma transference likely contributed to the Black male silence around antebellum and subsequently postbellum sexual violence, since no one with power stopped inducing Black male screams. But how can anyone intervene if no one can hear, if no one wants to hear? I wonder who heard Othello, a Black man who himself was "sold to slavery" at some point in his life and then redeemed (1.3.140).

To think about this more explicitly yet hypothetically: If *my* Black great-great-great grandfather's father was enslaved and was repeatedly sodomized by his master and/or forced to procreate with female slaves,[57] vulnerable Black women, how could he understand and articulate his positionality without access to language that legitimized his victim status, since he himself was considered illegitimate? I think of *Othello* here, too, a character treated as illegitimate once he marries a white woman and attempts to solidify his patriarchal power by expanding his household. Postbellum and antebellum American laws were designed to protect white people, whose whiteness was viewed as a kind of property (see Chapter 3), while said laws subjugated Black people and consistently denied their humanity.[58] How did the Black man, how *could* he, communicate his trauma, and to whom? Perhaps more importantly, what happened when the enslaved Black woman he was forced to rape told her Black son she did not know who his father was because her son was the product of an enforced sexual interaction with a man with whom she could not create a legitimate, legally recognized family? How did her own ancestral trauma transfer to her Black son and in what ways did that trauma manifest in him for the world to see generations later? How did her trauma teach him about racialized sexuality, understood in Black male studies as "a category of historical (sexual) vulnerability?"[59] And who managed that Black boy's trauma, the trauma of my great-great-great grandfather? Because he was not real, because he was not legally considered a person, no one with authority truly heard his screams; rather, they watched, unfazed by how he held his breath in silence, passing down his trauma to another Black boy who would turn into a Black man who could not breathe because society would not let him. And one day, that Black boy would become my father Kevin and then become me, a product of the loud silence surrounding historical and institutionalized anti-Black violence and rape.

Unfortunately, the color-line still contributes to the disparities in Black male disclosures of sexual assault and subsequently Black male willingness to seek professional help for victimization today – "the world simply does not believe men and boys are victims of sexual violence."[60] If "it is often difficult to conceptualize male bodies as being victims of sexual violence, and even more so when the perpetrator of that sexual violence is female," it is even more difficult to see male bodies as being victims of sexual violence when those bodies are Black, as even *Othello* criticism has made clear through its lack of attention to Iago's anti-Black intercourse discourse.[61] Race explodes the dimensions of the issue, since Black people and Black pain are often rendered invisible, as bell hooks stresses in *Black Looks: Race and Representation*.[62] For instance, studies have been conducted on the long history of discrimination within the medical profession, showcasing how treatment by medical professionals, and even their responses to overtly articulated pain, can vary across racial lines, with there being less sensitivity to or acceptance of expressions of pain by people of color, especially Black people.[63] Black pain is unbelievable, literally.

Since society largely disallows Black men and boys to be viewed as victims, it consequently disallows them opportunities to experience and process their pain; the language to construct the self as a victim, to construct one's experiences as a result of victimization, is limited if not non-existent. This has been the case for some time. And if it is impossible to see a reflection of oneself in the world, then how can one actually see oneself? How can one see an independent victimized self that society says does not exist? Othello does not have a reflection; his pain does not exist. Historically and stereotypically, Black males have been cast as brutish, as rapists, as sexually aggressive, as insensitive, as un-nurturing, and more, and these stereotypes are reinforced by the intraracial color-line and white other.[64] The general socio-cultural narrative surrounding the Black male existence in America, and globally, is one that amplifies myths designed to rationalize white fears of Black masculinity and sexuality. *Othello* is a play that rationalizes those fears, even today. It is a play that exemplifies how easily racism shapes society's perceptions and treatment of Black men.

Touching on the Pain

The white/white other/Black ternary racial hierarchy reinforces how Black people's concerns can be easily neglected when the negotiation of whiteness takes precedence because of white supremacy. Recall when Brabantio tells Roderigo, "Oh, would you had had her!" (1.1.179) shortly after saying, "In honest plainness thou hast heard me say / My daughter is not for thee" (1.1.100–101). A representation of white hegemony, Brabantio undoes his previous rejection of Roderigo. Desdemona's father quickly converts a less-than-ideal white man into a potentially suitable suitor for Desdemona just because Roderigo is white and not Black like Othello. Brabantio's behavior illustrates how the ternary system reveals racism as a distraction designed to create distance between Black and white.

With a little of slavery's legacy and impact in mind, I will now gesture toward some of the reasons why contemporary Black males are largely silent about sexual assault and why their requests for professional help are lacking and not heard. For many Black boys and men, as Tommy J. Curry and Ebony A. Utley explain, "Concepts of masculinity are built on independence and coping with racism by being cool";[65] such a response to racism means that Black males tend to manage racial injustice improperly. They do not manage it in productive ways that would give them strength to handle the powerlessness they might feel in the face of sexual abuse. This sense of independence is problematic because it often leads to isolation, the development of internalized anti-Black racism, a warped understanding of masculinity, and an inability to cope effectively with negative feelings that are a result of the powerlessness and loss of personal control Black boys and men may feel. Without a proper outlet for their pain, these Black male victims of sexual abuse are left to fend for themselves as they confront the psychological, emotional, and physical consequences of a bifurcated issue that involves the intersection of sexual assault and racism. The screams of these untreated victims are not heard within society – as with sounds of the highest frequency, their pain does not register, much like Othello's.

Because Black males are not truly being heard, there are significant consequences that accompany their suffering. Curry and Utley remind us that "while studies have generally noted the increased psychological stress, anxiety, depression, and self-harm of male victims, Black males who are precariously situated in a white supremacist and white patriarchal society are much more likely to be criminalized and thereby victims of fatal force by law enforcement if they display any of the symptoms common to sexually abused victims."[66] Here, I think of Brabantio's instinctual reaction to label Othello a "thief" for taking possession of Desdemona through marriage. I also think of what appears to be an instinctual white male desire to pursue Othello in lynch mob fashion (1.1.185–186), to "subdue him at his peril" (1.2.82). The criminalization and adultification of Black males does not afford us a fair chance.[67] I cannot help but wonder if anyone had ever sexually assaulted any of the unarmed Black men and boys who have been killed in recent years by police in America.[68] I wonder if those Black males' responses to the aggressive, unwanted touches of authority figures somehow triggered their own post-traumatic stress disorder, and triggered a past they remained silent about until their dying days. Have you ever stopped to think about *that* when people mention Trayvon Martin,[69] Michael Brown,[70] Freddie Grey,[71] Tamir Rice,[72] or Black Lives Matter?

We will likely never know if any of them were victims of sexual assault, but given the statistics and the fact that "in the United States [alone], one eighth of children are sexually, physically, or emotionally abused prior to the age of 18," it is entirely plausible that one or a few of the dozens of murdered unarmed Black men and boys were inappropriately touched or spoken to by someone who held power over them in some way during their youth.[73] On some level, my wondering about these unarmed Black males' potential exposure to sexual violence does not even matter because:

> To many, Black males are solely perpetrators of violence. When Black men or boys are discussed regarding sexual violence, far too often they are cast as the rapist, never the victim of rape or sexual exploitation by the men and women in their communities. Whereas previous research has shown the difficulty of recognizing males as anything more than perpetrators of sexual violence, for Black men their recognition as victims is practically impossible.[74]

Therefore, even if a Black male displays symptoms common to sexual abuse victims, the symptoms will likely be ignored or misdiagnosed because the potentially true cause of the symptoms remains invisible, masked by the response to the Black brute stereotype that screams, "He did it. He is not the victim!" In other words, if society understands males (with the default understanding being white males) as raised and socialized to be "naturally aggressive and violent," adhering to the "boys will be boys" adage, then such a reading of maleness is amplified for Black males, whom society automatically presumes to be dangerous, aggressive, and criminal.[75] I am reminded again of the racist assumptions Iago and Brabantio make so easily about Othello (see 1.1.81–83 and 1.2.63–72).

Although both sexual violence and racism can produce psychological stress, such stress may not be appropriately managed within the Black community due to a variety of factors. For one, the stigma around seeking mental health support still remains, though seeking care does appear to be a bit more acceptable nowadays.[76] However, the notion that one has a mental problem can often evoke fear and shame. That fear and shame can result in resistance to seeking support, especially given that "concepts of Black masculinity are built on independence," as I mentioned previously. To be a strong Black male is to be able to handle "it," whatever *it* is. Society constantly bombards Black men, and everyone, with messages about what it means to be an ideally masculine Black man. Anything that defies that contrived standard renders one socially and/or culturally inferior, in theory, especially in relationship to white logic and white methods. The inability for Black males to cope with the mental strain that accompanies their existence registers as a potential sign of weakness. The alleged defective masculinity might then be associated with femininity, which might *then* lead to stigmatization or ostracization within and outside of one's community. And so, silence ensues.

A dangerous byproduct of, and catalyst for, the silence is ignorance of all kinds. If Black boys and men are not discussing their sexual assault experiences, then a lot remains undiscovered on a personal level for them and on a larger social level for the broader community. If Black males, especially Black youths, do not know the language of sexual assault, do not know how to identify what an inappropriate touch is or do not articulate their experiences with such occurrences, then such violations likely remain undisclosed and/or unacknowledged, and the serious consequences of such experiences do not get dealt with in timely, healthy, or appropriate ways. I cannot help but think about the Black boys who were sexually abused by white Penn State University football coach, Jerry Sandusky, who was convicted of several charges of rape and child sexual abuse. Taking advantage of both his economic dominance and white male privilege, Sandusky used a non-profit he founded for at-risk and underprivileged youth as a way to increase his proximity to his desired victims, some of whom were Black boys (this is a prime example of how proximity to Blackness does not equal antiracism). His proximity equaled power, the power to abuse over forty boys and psychologically harm, or mindfuck, them during a fifteen-year period.[77] "Honest" Iago's proximity also equaled power (1.3.297). Undoubtedly, Sandusky likely took advantage of both his victims' ages and inexperience. Preying on fatherless boys, Sandusky also took advantage of domestic situations and he, as white savior, exploited society's general idealization of the trusted white patriarch. Once a revered "good" white man, Sandusky's sexually predatory behavior, upon exposure and conviction, transformed him into a criminal who subsequently lost his status as an ideal white man.

So, what kinds of matters do silent Black male victims of sexual abuse remain uneducated about? In a study on African American college students' perceptions of sexual coercion, LaTonya D. Mouzon and her coauthors discovered that Black students, both male and female, at a large Midwestern university were unclear on how sexual coercion is a form of psychological and physical violence where "one is exposed to pressure and persuasion to engage in undesired sexual activity."[78] Contrary to what participants in this study thought, engagement in unwanted sexual activity is a form of rape that stems from one being manipulated or even guilted into participating in undesired sexual activity. The guilt tripping is an exertion of psychological power, the kind of power Iago wields over Othello. In this study,

> participants denounced physical coercion as rape and only addressed verbal forms of coercion in their discussions. Participants viewed verbal sexual coercion as a normative behavior and often referred to it as "running the game." They acknowledged the reciprocal nature of coercion as well as the fact that women use it and experience it as much as men. Poor communication skills were identified as a potential cause of sexual coercion.[79]

The ignorance about and denial of what constitutes rape helps explain why many of Sandusky's young Black male victims might not have come forward about their abuse earlier, because they did not necessarily understand it as such. Or perhaps because Sandusky's whiteness and his position as a good, benevolent white man leading a non-profit to help the "needy" made him, in his victims' young minds, into a pedestalized patriarchal figure who was making a difference in their lives: even if they had to pay a price with their innocent Black bodies and endure psychological and emotional damage in the process. This brings me back to my point about how important access to the language of sexual assault is, especially within the Black community.[80] I find it remarkable that Shakespeare's seventeenth-century play, through its treatment of Othello as a kind of rape victim, can facilitate such an important conversation.

Sexual coercion being thought of as a game, and one that Iago plays very well, contributes to the notion that there is a lack of serious attention to and concern about how detrimental the effects of sexual violence are. Moreover, that both men and women engage in coercion suggests that among African Americans, for instance, Black males are especially vulnerable given that less attention is paid to their experiences with victimization – at the hands of either men or women, and regardless of race. There seems to be an almost inherent expectation that "running the game" is a customary part of Black males' sexual and gendered identities, identities that, as Mouzon et al. explain, view "pressure, manipulation, persuasion, and even lying [as] acceptable and part of playing the game."[81] Being socialized to understand sexual violence as a game minimizes the seriousness of the issue and underscores why Black male silence is so personally damaging. Furthermore, if sexual violence is interpreted as a game, then it also makes sense why seeking professional help is not the natural response to this kind of undesired, inappropriate sexual activity. The game is meant to be played, not critiqued. And seeing a psychotherapist would open the game up for analysis, which would both defeat the purpose of the game and expose the aspects of Black youth's sexuality that may need addressing from mental health professionals and other appropriate authority figures.

Another outcome of untreated sexual violence is that one can become predisposed to intimate partner violence or IPV, either as a victim or aggressor. Because of Iago's manipulation, Desdemona becomes a victim of IPV and Othello becomes an imagined victim, made to feel jealous by his wife's alleged infidelity. Information offered by the Center for Disease Control and Prevention indicates IPV, which often transpires behind closed doors in the household, is a serious public health issue, which makes it an urgent matter that needs attention, especially with regard to Black male victims. In a study on IPV victimization in LGBTQ young adults, for example, Tyson R. Reuter and colleagues discovered that significant demographic differences arise. And the impact of IPV is substantial. As Reuter explains,

> IPV typically refers to abusive behavior occurring within the context of romantic relationships. More conservative definitions of IPV are often confined to physical and sexual abuse (e.g., hitting, punching, forced sex), while more liberal definitions typically extend IPV to include non-physical behaviors (e.g., isolating, ridicule, verbal threats, provoking jealousy). Importantly, both forms of abuse (i.e., physical and non-physical) are linked with depression, conflict, aggression, and numerous physical health outcomes, with some studies finding that victims report psychological abuse as equally or more damaging than physical abuse.[82]

IPV's connection with psychological abuse makes it a troubling issue, especially when we consider that Black males' emotional, physical, and psychological pain often does not register. This means that the issues are compounded for Black gay males. The silence amplifies these victims' racially disadvantaged status since, "in addition to stressors associated with a sexual minority status, youth of color and female-identified individuals are perhaps at even greater risk for negative health outcomes due to cumulative stress from a combination of gender, racial, and/or sexual minority identities" (in 4.1 and 4.2, for instance, the stress Othello experiences, as a result of Iago's intercourse discourse, becomes physically evident).[83] If a Black male is taught that IPV, under the "conservative definition" or not, is an acceptable form of love or relationship behavior, and if one is *not* taught to speak about sexual encounters (particularly inappropriate ones), then that raises one's tolerance level for IPV and sexual abuse. For Black boys and men growing up in a white patriarchal, white supremacist society where they are not heard, for myriad reasons, the tolerance level for IPV and sexual abuse is too high. That puts Black males at great risk.[84]

And this leads me to my final point about the factors that can contribute to Black male silence regarding sexual assault and the severely limited disclosure of such encounters. As noted above, the ideals that society has outlined regarding masculinity, white and Black masculinity, have a negative impact on how Black male victims choose to respond to sexual violations. Males, especially Black males, are taught from a young age the "values of the masculine mystique":[85] to be strong, to be hard, to be independent, to cope however they can without compromising the tough masculine exterior, even if it is just a façade. Some of the findings from Charles Amos' collaborative examination of the link between sexual abuse and drug use among African American male college students provide a general explanation for why toxic masculinity is such an influential factor as it relates to Black male silence:

> When male sexual experiences are recognized as abuse, the victims may be viewed as having been "weak" or "not man enough" because they were unable to stop it, defend themselves, or put it behind them. Moreover, many young men who were sexually abused are locked in silence, self-loathing and shame. Young men who dare acknowledge that they were sexually abused are cruelly laughed at and humiliated [...] Most do not dare say a word about it because of the fear of feeling more ashamed than they already feel. Sadly and mistakenly, they believe that there must be something profoundly wrong with them that they were abused in this manner.[86]

Given the potential for ridicule and emasculation, it almost seems as though it is better for Black males to remain silent, independently managing their humiliation, shame, and self-hatred, like Othello. That such victims have potential to be mocked for their exposure to sexual violence introduces another way this matter functions like a game, in that the experience with sexual violation is not treated seriously; rather, it has real potential to become a source of amusement for those who learn about such assaults. This kind of psychological abuse, on top of the experienced physical sexual abuse, magnifies the largely isolated social positions of Black males. Thus, the intraracial color-line manifests, as we see in the case of Sandusky, affirming why Black males may rationalize their silence as an appropriate solution for their victimization. Silence is the price we pay.

White Violence, Black Male Shakespearean Silence

As a BlacKKKShakespearean,[87] I advocate turning to Shakespeare's dramatic oeuvre when contemplating contemporary issues, whether they be personal, political, social, or even psychological. And so, I want to propose that Shakespearean drama, as well as the reception to and criticism of it, reveals what is at stake when the "listening ear," as Stoever terms it, is of the dominant hue.[88] I will touch on this matter mainly by thinking historically about the Black existence and by alluding to Shakespeare's *Titus Andronicus* and *The Merchant of Venice*, considering these plays in the context of the intraracial color-line and the discourse around sexual violence against Black males.[89] I use Shakespeare's fiction to amplify the seriousness of the issue at hand, specifically, how what is transmitted through the literature shapes perceptions that people develop of blackness and, subsequently, Black people. I view Shakespeare's characters, especially the iconic ones, as useful cultural tools constructed by the white imagination, tools that offer a glimpse into early modern English engagement with and ideas about Blackness and its value. The following concrete examples from Shakespeare shed light on how a cultural-psychological[90] approach could be beneficial for putting Shakespeare into the larger world and not just the world of academia, given that sexual violence is an issue that has an impact on people within and outside of formal educational settings.

In Shakespearean drama, and in the real world, as I have suggested, sexual violence occurs in a variety of ways and critical attention to race adds complexity to that issue. Sexual violence can be solely psychological and emotional, for example: In *Titus*, the newly crowned Roman empress Tamora (white other) finds her illicit Black lover, Aaron, in the forest and asks: "Wherefore look'st thou sad, / When everything doth make a gleeful boast?" before suggesting in the same breath that they have sex

(2.3.10–11). Aaron does not share in Tamora's "glee" at this moment, for his self-proclaimed "silence, [and his] cloudy melancholy" "are no venereal signs," as he assures her (2.3.33–36). Moreover, Aaron's sad emotional state – what we might read in modern terms as an indicator of his mental health status – is inconsequential to Tamora.[91]

Rather, she wants to use his Black body, which Shakespeare depicts as stereotypically savage and hypersexual (descriptors that are quite similar to those cited earlier with respect to Othello and the modern Black male), and then immediately enter "a golden slumber" following their orgasmic climax ... or maybe just *her* orgasmic climax (2.3.26). It is hard to tell if Aaron's sexual relief matters here. Regardless, Aaron-as-victim experiences a dual assault coming from within and outside of the play: Tamora does not *hear* this Black man's sadness despite affirming she sees it. Furthermore, scholars have largely ignored Aaron's sadness in terms of reading it as an earlier dramatic moment that reveals his humanization, a moment preceding his often-discussed paternal sensitivity displayed in 4.2, which I have written about at length, as have other critics.[92] Aaron's pain, whatever form it takes, remains silenced.

As *Titus* and contemporary matters show, dehumanization and imbalanced power dynamics are at the heart of sexual and racial violence . In *The Merchant of Venice*, heterosexual interracial desire is, for the Black man, a game to lose because the "casket test" outcome is rigged, if not by Portia then by Shakespeare himself, and because racially white Portia declares, in response to the Black Prince of Morocco's casket selection failure: "Let all of his complexion choose me so" (2.7.79). In other words, let no Black man be successful in this game that involves the white woman's body. Portia wants only Bassanio: a less-than-ideal, fair-skinned man who borrows money from his sugar-daddy-like friend, Antonio, and who, on paper, pales in comparison to the Prince. Yet similar to *Othello*'s Roderigo, Bassanio's racial status situates him above the Black Prince.

Morocco is set up to desire and sexualize unattainable whiteness, given that his pursuit is ridiculed by Portia and mocked by the white external audience. In the end, he is punished for aspiring to be close to whiteness, for desiring to integrate whiteness into his life through marriage. Contrastingly, the racist social system seems to reward Iago with power because of his closeness to Blackness. The consequence for Morocco's failure is a kind of sterilization[93] or symbolic castration: Unable to marry anyone in the future, he cannot produce a legitimate heir. This punishment is problematic because of the physical constraints placed on his procreative Black body. It goes without saying that his departure in the play is, quite frankly, sad; yet his "too griev'd a heart" is the least of Portia's concerns (2.7.76).

Why is it that Tamora's and Portia's respective treatment of Aaron and the Prince of Morocco has not generated much critical conversation about Black male victimization? Why is it that Shakespeare critics have not focused on this matter, and its relationship to psycho-sexual violence, with the same energy and rigor they have used to define Aaron as a villain and Morocco as pompous? Why haven't these two Black male characters been heard or seen in this way? One possible answer: Since neither character benefits from racial privilege nor perceived racial innocence, they are not set up to be seen as suffering since they exist in dramatic contexts that prioritize whiteness – feelings, thoughts, actions, etc. Additionally, the white scholars critiquing these characters as villainous and pompous benefit from their own racial dominance and white innocence that may hinder their ability to see Black victimhood as clearly as they would see white victimhood.[94] In other words, despite general shared humanity, they do not easily identify with Aaron or the Prince of Morocco, whom Shakespeare presents as savage and alien, respectively.[95] The scholarship that demoralizes the Black man and ignores his pain champions white centrality; such scholarship is designed to reinforce the white self-concept whose core values consist of exuding goodness, innocence, and/ or superiority.

The superiority factor is apparent outside of the fiction, too, in field-related responses to the literature. Once, while I was participating in a Shakespeare symposium, someone remarked during the Q&A that Desdemona's tragedy is "worse than Othello's," even though the play's title alone suggests otherwise; in that person's mind, the innocent, good white woman suffers more than the Black man, who directly endures racism and intense psychological mindfucking by Iago for the play's entirety. Even in terms of time spent on stage and engaging with other characters,[96] Othello endures more psychological trauma than his white wife. When people make such defensive comparisons regarding Desdemona, they center whiteness and privilege white femininity without considering the intersectional impact on Othello. The comparative reading championing white privilege completely ignores racism's enduring effects and undermines Shakespeare's complicated, uneasy centering of Othello. Such a reading erases Othello's pain, which readers and audiences should absolutely wrestle with. See him. Hear him.

Actor and playwright Keith Hamilton Cobb, also director of the Untitled Othello Project, brilliantly makes his audience hear and see the

Black man's (early) modern plight in *American Moor*, a play that begins by centering the domestic origins of Othello and Desdemona's love. Cobb's dynamic work gives a powerful voice and a stark visuality to Black male pain induced by racist behavior, which licenses a white man in Cobb's play (the Director character named Michael Aaron Miller) to contend with the utmost conviction that he knows the Black man better than the Black man knows himself.[97] But Cobb's Actor character knows this is not true, as evidenced by the haunting words he utters to the white Director at the play's end: "Hear me. See me," which functions like a prayerful refrain for the Black existence.[98] Hear *me*. See *me*. In so doing, the Actor emphasizes the challenges he has experienced throughout the play, which Black men and boys know all too well – challenges that are a result of the color-line.[99]

The abovementioned Desdemona/Othello juxtaposition, which signifies a cliché white reaction, reflects how Othello's pain – linked to sex, sexuality, and Black hypersexuality – is not heard; or, if it is heard, it only registers as a whisper, whereas Desdemona's suffering is a scream. Yet, Othello's tragedy, and *Othello*'s tragedy, must be considered in its full context rather than with a narrow concentration on, say, the fact that Othello engages in IPV and strikes his white wife and then strangles her in the final domestic scene.[100] I wonder what some people hear and see throughout the play *before* Othello becomes in their minds the stereotyped bad Black male criminal. I wonder what metrics are used to assess Othello's and Desdemona's individual tragedies. I wonder why people insist on separating the marital, familial unit and refuse to see the couple as suffering one shared tragedy at the hands of a racist Venetian society and a manipulative white other, Iago, who himself is implicated in Othello and Desdemona's IPV episodes. And I wonder if at this symposium anyone actually saw me, the only Black male scholar in the room, sitting there and being unexpectedly forced into the role of Othello in an academic Venice. As Stoever reminds us, and as Anchuli Felicia King illustrates in *Keene*,[101] her satirical dramatic riff on *Othello*, white people's listening ears are not trained to hear Blackness (let alone see it), since white listening ears prioritize white sound.[102] This produces a double erasure for the souls of Black folk, an erasure that does not help our mental health or alleviate our psychological pain.

At the symposium, I processed the Black erasure, for and of myself and, more importantly, for and of the Black students in the education system who are likely subjected to and believe this kind of unjust, biased reading of Othello, of criminalized Blackness. As Ayanna Thompson and Laura

Turchi argue, students' bodies – their "race, gender, ability, and sexuality" – are important in both the study and performance of Shakespeare. Yet, scholars, theater practitioners and teachers (who commit pedagogical malpractice by gaslighting their students)[103] often ignore such fundamental individualizing differences in order to push harmful universalist agendas that, among other things, erase Blackness and evade general discussions of race.[104] White people – students, general readers, scholars, practitioners, clinicians – must filter their thoughts before they speak and write them: filter them not through white logic but through antiracist logic, or at the very least through a heightened consciousness of whiteness and white supremacy, which allows them to identify when whiteness is at work on and in the mind. Whiteness never forgets to till and water the soil that nurtures the unseen seeds planted in racism's infinite garden – a vital source of nourishment for delicate white egos.

Across the Color-Line: Psychologizing the Psychology of Racism

According to race and ethnicity research done by the American Psychological Association, between 2005 and 2013 "the active psychology workforce was primarily White: Whites accounted for [a staggering] 83.6 percent of active psychologists. Racial/ethnic minority groups, including Asian (4.3 percent), Black/African American (5.3 percent), Hispanic (5.0 percent) and other racial/ethnic groups (1.7 percent), accounted for approximately 16.4 percent of active psychologists."[105] With the total number of the active workforce about 158,000 psychologists, this means approximately 8,400 were Black, whereas approximately 132,000 were white. The mental health profession's racial demographic disparity among its practitioners enforces and *re*inforces Black male silence on a large scale, in more ways than one; the disparity also leads to the prioritization of white people and white others. Unfortunately, Black pain can only be a fiction when the right – understanding, culturally and racially sensitive – experts are not available to validate such pain through professional diagnoses. Since the majority of therapists are white and non-Black, 94.7 percent, and since anti-Black racism is a pervasive problem, it is asking a lot of Black male sexual abuse victims to trust those who resemble offenders of a different kind: racists.[106] And if the abuser was rich and white like Sandusky, or simply "honest" like Iago, then multiple traumas intersect for the Black male victim, whose recovery would require a very specific kind of practitioner.

In general, Black males report sexual assault and seek professional help at much lower rates than their white counterparts, in part because they "are not socialized to fear that they could [even] be victims of sexual violation, abuse, or forcible rape."[107] It goes without saying that, among other factors, inadequate human resources and insufficient racial and cultural sensitivity in the mental health profession compound the silence around sexual abuse and sexual violence for Black men and boys. And the silence magnifies when the deafening sound of gun shots leaves Black boys and men dying in the streets after white hegemony tells them don't:[108] don't play rap music too loudly; don't worship God; don't run; don't walk through this neighborhood; don't exist as you are. Just don't, and you'll be fine. And the silent treatment, so to speak, can contribute to the victim-to-perpetrator cycle:[109] Victims themselves have the potential to become sexual violence perpetrators, projecting their pain and anger onto others, as I might suggest Othello does, because their silence renders *their* histories unknowable, histories sometimes even denied by themselves. Undoubtedly, jail and prison are places these perpetrators end up, adding to the widespread misperception of Black male suspiciousness and criminality that white people seem to remember most.[110] Many people remember *Othello* as a play about a Black man who murders his white wife, as opposed to remembering it as a play in which a Black man is severely abused by a white man's intercourse discourse.

Without a proper outlet for their suffering, and without the protection of herd invisibility afforded to white people, Black male victims of sexual abuse are left in perpetual survival mode as they confront the psychological, emotional, and physical consequences of a complicated issue that is rendered even more complex by harmful racist stereotypes and baseless categorical assertions designed to sustain white domination – for even in terms of care, the needs of white boys and men are deemed paramount. Their needs are attended to more. Despite Black males not being heard as often, or perhaps because they are not heard, there are lasting consequences for them, short- and long-term effects that accompany their suffering, consequences that need to be addressed and mitigated. The consequences can include both general health and other issues such as borderline personality disorder, obsessive compulsive disorder, post-traumatic stress disorder, sex addiction, bipolar disorder, and anxiety, to name a few.[111] The dangers of not hearing the screams of Black male sexual assault victims, of requiring them to hold their breath for centuries, are many, especially because their actions are often criminalized and, for children, adultified.[112]

But what if people *heard* Black boys and men, especially across the color-line, so as to eliminate the "consistent invalidation [that] leads to confusion and poor self-esteem," among other things?[113] What if people looked deep into the eyes of Black boys and men and saw their emotional and psychological pain as relevant? Looked at their bodies – not to sexualize, objectify, villainize, or fetishize them – but to honor the signs of trauma, the unhealed psychological wounds and scars that are tattooed reminders of pasts that haunt Black boys and men daily? What if people looked at "sexual abuse [as] the ultimate invalidation," as Neil R. Bockian et al. claim it is for all victims?[114] The Aarons, Princes of Morocco, Othellos, and Calibans of the world deserve to breathe and be heard. And so, too, do the Black Cleopatras[115] of the world who have existed, unjustly so, at the bottom of the gender-racial hierarchy for centuries.

Notes

1 June Jordan, "Poem about My Rights," from *The Essential June Jordan*, eds. Jan Heller Levi and Christoph Keller, Copper Canyon Press 2021 © 2023 June M. Jordan Literary Estate Trust. Used by permission. www .junejordan.com.

2 Dyson, *Tears We Cannot Stop*, 70.

3 L. Taylor Phillips and Brian S. Lowery explain the concept of herd invisibility as follows: "When individuals work to maintain their own innocence, [as white people are wont to do,] they shape shared social experiences, letting that innocence ripple beyond the individual. In turn, Whites benefit from herd invisibility that emerges at the societal level. We conceptualize herd invisibility by following the herd-immunity model of vaccination: When enough individuals are vaccinated, the incidence of disease is reduced for the entire population, protecting those who are not vaccinated. Similarly, herd invisibility protects innocence and privileges for all Whites, even without every individual White person acting on individual innocence or maintenance motives." "Herd Invisibility: The Psychology of Racial Privilege," *Current Directions in Psychological Science*, 27.3 (2018), 156–162; 158.

4 I first asked these questions in a 2019 essay I published in *The Sundial* (Brown, "'The Sonic Color Line'"). I thank Ayanna Thompson for inviting me to be part of the first collection of essays published in that venue.

5 Stoever, *The Sonic Color Line*, 6. In addition to being the author of *The Sonic Color Line*, Stoever is Editor-in-Chief of *Sounding Out!*, a sound studies blog: https://soundstudiesblog.com.

6 For a definition of intimate partner violence, see www.cdc.gov/violencepreven tion/intimatepartnerviolence/index.html.

7 The Centers for Disease Control and Prevention define ACEs as "potentially traumatic events that occur in childhood." For more information, see www .cdc.gov/violenceprevention/childabuseandneglect/acestudy/index.html.

8 See Frances Dolan, *Dangerous Familiars: Representations of Domestic Crime in England, 1550–1700* (Ithaca, NY: Cornell University Press, 1994), 117. And see Dennis Britton, *Becoming Christian: Race, Reformation, and Early Modern English Romance* (New York: Fordham University Press, 2014), 33.

9 Timothy A. Turner asserts, "*Othello* examines the effectiveness of a different kind of coercion, described here as a psychological assault that enables the "torturer," Iago, to break his victim without using physical force. The play's signature accomplishment lies in its portrayal of Iago's ability to refashion Othello's mind and, by extension, the general's sense of himself as a person." "Othello on the Rack," *Journal for Early Modern Cultural Studies*, 15.3 (Summer 2015), 102–136; 103.

10 I borrow/modify this term from Iago's language: "Even now, now, very now, an old black ram / Is tupping your white ewe" (1.1.90–91).

11 Stanley Edgar Hyman makes a case for Iago being motivated by "latent homosexuality" in "Iago Psychoanalytically Motivated," *The Centennial Review*, 14.4 (Fall 1970), 369–384; 369. See Arthur L. Little, Jr., "'An Essence That's Not Seen': The Primal Scene of Racism in Othello," *Shakespeare Quarterly*, 44.3 (Autumn 1993), 304–324, esp. 306.

12 Hyman argues that "the homosexual dynamics here are as simple and clear as they are fascinating: Iago has turned himself into a Desdemona for Cassio's sexual enjoyment on the surface of the spurious dream, and for Othello's in the latent content" ("Iago Psychoanalytically Motivated," 376). As I noted previously, from a Christian marital perspective, it is possible to see Iago as an amalgamation of Othello and Desdemona if we shift the optic.

13 Smith, *Race and Rhetoric*, 132–133.

14 Ania Loomba explains that "sexual intercourse between members of different groups was the kind of crossover that generated the greatest anxiety. Since sperm was widely understood as man's purest blood, sexual activity was an exchange of blood, a crossing of boundaries more profound than conversion." "'Delicious Traffick,'" 213.

15 Kyle Grady discusses the play's racism in "Othello, Colin Powell and Post-Racial Anachronisms," *Shakespeare Quarterly*, 67.1 (2016), 68–83; 72.

16 Ariane M. Balizet, *Blood and Home in Early Modern Drama: Domestic Identity on the Renaissance Stage* (New York: Routledge, 2014), 90.

17 Wendy Wall observes that "representations of domestic disorder on the stage might thus simply be said to anatomize the wayward passions to be mastered or pathologies to be cured so as to ensure the proper ordering of home and polity." *Staging Domesticity: Household Work and English Identity in Early Modern Drama* (Cambridge: Cambridge University Press, 2002), 2.

18 See Balizet, *Blood and Home in Early Modern Drama*, 2; Akhimie, *Shakespeare and the Cultivation of Difference*, 20; Chapman, *Anti-Black Racism*, 2–3; and Feerick, *Strangers in Blood*, 4–5.

19 See Amussen, *An Ordered Society*, 1; Wall, *Staging Domesticity*, 159, 191.

20 Smith, *Race and Rhetoric*, 74, 138. Also see Nubia, *Blackamoors*, 61.

21 Benson, *Shakespeare, Othello and Domestic Tragedy*, 118.

22 In her discussion of feminism, Mikki Kendall makes a distinction between "allies" and "accomplices." *Hood Feminism*, 257.

23 Racial differences are apparent even in relation to traffic stops in America. To understand the implications of "driving while black," see: www.nytimes.com/2015/10/25/us/racial-disparity-traffic-stops-driving-black.html.

24 In 2014, an Arizona State University Professor, Ersula Ore, was stopped by a white police officer for jaywalking after finishing her day of teaching. She was charged with assaulting an officer in this incident that made national headlines: www.phoenixnewtimes.com/news/ersula-ore-sues-asu-for-2-million-but-asu-supports-her-with-move-to-fire-cop-6635482.

25 In 2018, a white Yale student called the police on a Black Yale graduate student for taking a nap in her dorm's common room: www.cnn.com/2018/05/09/us/yale-student-napping-black-trnd/index.html.

26 In 2015, a Black fifteen-year-old girl, who was wearing only a bathing suit, was tackled and assaulted by a white police officer at a Texas pool party: www.essence.com/news/black-teen-white-cop-texas-pool-party-wins-settlement/.

27 In 2018, a white woman dubbed "BBQ Becky" called the police on two Black men who were just trying to enjoy their day and have a BBQ: www.newsweek.com/bbq-becky-white-woman-who-called-cops-black-bbq-911-audio-released-im-really-1103057.

28 In 2012, seventeen-year-old Black Jordan Davis was shot at a gas station by a white man because he was playing his rap music too loud, according to the white man's standards: www.newsweek.com/bbq-becky-white-woman-who-called-cops-black-bbq-911-audio-released-im-really-1103057.

29 In 2018, a white woman dubbed "Permit Patty" called the police on a Black eight-year-old girl for selling water: www.bbc.com/news/newsbeat-44601668.

30 In 2018, a white male CVS manager dubbed "Coupon Carl" wrongfully accused a Black woman of forging a coupon and called the police on her: www.theroot.com/coupon-carl-calls-cops-on-black-woman-at-cvs-for-alle-1827610838.

31 In 2018, the police were called on a twelve-year-old Black boy and his brother because they were cutting grass: www.huffpost.com/entry/black-kid-has-police-called-on-him-for-mowing-a-lawn_n_5b37b791e4b0f3c221a15bf5.

32 In 2018, the police were called on Rep. Janelle Bynum, a Black woman, as she was canvasing: https://splinternews.com/someone-called-the-cops-on-a-black-state-representative-1827342959.

33 In 2019, a white IRS security guard pulled a gun on a Black sheriff's deputy who was in full uniform: www.newsweek.com/white-security-guard-pulls-gun-black-police-officer-uniform-because-he-had-gun-1449428.

34 In 2018, a Smith College employee called the police on a Black student who was eating her lunch on campus in a common area. The employee said the student "seemed to be out of place": www.huffpost.com/entry/smith-college-student-police_n_5b630b98e4b0fd5c73d6ee6d.

35 In 2018, two Black men were arrested at a Starbucks after a white employee called the police: https://apnews.com/45547c3ae5324b679e982c4847ee1378.

36 In 2018, a white man verbally assaulted an older Black woman on a Ryanair flight, going so far as to call her an "ugly Black bastard": www.theroot.com/white-man-verbally-assaults-older-black-woman-on-flight-1829905812.

37 After checking out of an Airbnb in 2018, three Black people had the police called on them because someone in the neighborhood assumed they were burglars: www.cnn.com/2018/05/07/us/airbnb-police-called-trnd/index.html.

38 In 2018 a group of Black voters had their voting process interrupted in what appeared to be an incident of voter suppression: https://thinkprogress.org/georgia-black-voters-matter-bus-blocked-from-taking-seniors-to-vote-a3c3e6580c5b/.

39 In 2019, a white man called the police on a Black man, Wesley Michel, because he assumed Michel (who was waiting for a friend) was a trespasser at an apartment building: www.cnn.com/2019/07/10/us/san-francisco-apartment-confrontation-wednesday/index.html.

40 In 2018, Black Oakland, CA firefighters – Kevin Moore and some colleagues – had the police called on them while they were out performing a routine inspection: www.cnn.com/2018/06/27/us/oakland-firefighter-racial-profiling/index.html.

41 In 2018, the police were called on five African-American women who were accused of playing too slowly at a Pennsylvania golf course: www.cnn.com/2018/04/25/us/black-women-golfers-pennsylvania-trnd/index.html.

42 In 2018, the police were called on two Black men at an LA Fitness gym in New Jersey; the three gym employees involved were fired: www.foxnews.com/us/3-la-fitness-employees-in-nj-fired-for-asking-black-men-to-leave-calling-cops-report-says.

43 In 2018, a former Obama White House staffer was moving into a New York City apartment and the police were called on him (the reason for the call was "active burglary"): https://abcnews.go.com/Politics/profiling-real-obama-staffer-mistaken-burglar-moving-york/story?id=54877597.

44 In 2019, a white contractor showed up at the Atlanta, GA home of Allison and Zeke Brown – a Black couple – and he had a confederate flag on his truck. The Browns rightly rejected the contractor's services: www.insideedition.com/woman-calmly-fires-contractor-flying-confederate-flag-truck-our-money-wont-go-such-hate-54169.

45 In 2015, a Charleston, SC mass shooting took the lives of nine Black worshippers, when a young white man opened fire at Mother Emanuel AME Church: https://apnews.com/6127102807d5433e8aec096517d79284.

46 White supremacy and white privilege are also the reasons a white man can enter a Black church, interrupt the service by killing nine people and live to still have his voice heard while awaiting the death penalty: https://en.wikipedia.org/wiki/Dylann_Roof#Death_sentence_appeal.

47 For a general definition of "family of origin" see: www.strongbonds.jss.org.au/workers/professional/origin.html.

48 Thomas A. Foster, "The Sexual Abuse of Black Men under Slavery," *Journal of the History of Sexuality*, 20.3 (September 2011), 445–46, 447.

49 Salter et al. posit, "Representations of race, ethnicity, and nationality have never been just reflections of neutral categories; rather, they are historically derived ideas about superiority and inferiority. Contemporary racial categories and understandings of those concepts have their cultural-psychological roots in colonization and the transatlantic slave trade (Guthrie, 2004). Europeans constructed their identity as 'White' and imagined themselves as more developed and more human in comparison with the darker-skinned 'others' (whether African or indigenous) whom they dominated (Feagin, 2010)." Phia S. Salter, Glenn Adams, and Michael J. Perez, "Racism in the Structure of Everyday Worlds: A Cultural-Psychological Perspective," *Current Directions in Psychological Science*, 27.3 (2018), 150–155; 151.

50 See: www.psychologytoday.com/us/blog/psychoanalysis-unplugged/201711/sexual-assault-is-about-power.

51 Foster, "The Sexual Abuse of Black Men," 447.

52 Ibid., 450.

53 Ibid., 454

54 Ibid., 452.

55 For slaves as property, see Harris, "Whiteness as Property," 279.

56 Toni Morrison's *Beloved* centers on the kinds of familial issues that affected Black families. The myth of Black people as not belonging to families or not being capable of having families is itself a systemically destructive form of anti-Blackness that, in different ways, continues to wreak havoc socially.

57 Sexual coercion is considered a form of sexual abuse. See Foster, "The Sexual Abuse of Black Men," 447.

58 See Harris, "Whiteness as Property," 276–291.

59 Tommy J. Curry and Ebony A. Utley, "She Touched Me: Five Snapshots of Adult Sexual Violations of Black Boys," *Kennedy Institute of Ethics Journal*, 28.2 (June 2018), 205–241, 213.

60 Ibid., 206.

61 Ibid., 205.

62 hooks, *Black Looks*, 2.

63 Sometimes, medical professionals do not believe Black pain, at least not as much as they are willing to accept white people's pain. Becoming accustomed to not having their pain heard, even today, Black people may develop reluctance to seeking medical care since it could amount to a waste of time while also being a demoralizing experience. See www.theatlantic.com/health/archive/2017/02/chronic-pain-stigma/517689/.

64 Curry and Utley, "She Touched Me," 213.

65 Ibid., 212.

66 Ibid., 213.

67 Brown, "'Is Black So Base a Hue?,'" 144–145.

68 Although not a new phenomenon, the policing and killing of unarmed Black men in particular has become quite common. D. L. Hughley and Doug Mode

offer an insightfully satirical examination of the issue (and possible solutions) in *How Not to Get Shot*. They begin their text by informing readers that: "In America, a black dude is three times more likely to be killed in encounters with police than a white guy. If you're black, you already know why #thisbookmatters" (1).

69 See "Shooting of Trayvon Martin," Wikipedia: https://en.wikipedia.org/wiki/Shooting_of_Trayvon_Martin.

70 See "Shooting of Michael Brown," Wikipedia: https://en.wikipedia.org/wiki/Shooting_of_Michael_Brown.

71 See "Death of Freddie Gray," Wikipedia: https://en.wikipedia.org/wiki/Death_of_Freddie_Gray.

72 See "Shooting of Tamir Rice," Wikipedia: https://en.wikipedia.org/wiki/Shooting_of_Tamir_Rice.

73 Anne N. Banducci, Elana M. Hoffman, C. W. Lejuez, and Karestan C. Koenen, "The Impact of Childhood Abuse on Inpatient Substance Users: Specific Links with Risky Sex, Aggression, and Emotion Dysregulation," *Child Abuse and Neglect*, 38.5 (May 2014), 928.

74 Curry and Utley, "She Touched Me," 213. This quotation recalls Little, Jr.'s argument about Black Aaron's implication in Lavinia's rape in *Shakespeare Jungle Fever*, 25.

75 Miedzian, *Boys Will Be Boys*, xxvi.

76 Due to a variety of factors (from religious beliefs to racism), mental health care has been negatively stigmatized in the African-American community. See www.mcleanhospital.org/news/how-can-we-break-mental-health-barriers-communities-color.

77 See "Jerry Sandusky," Wikipedia: https://en.wikipedia.org/wiki/Jerry_Sandusky.

78 LaTonya D. Mouzon, Alicia Battle, Kevin P. Clark, Stephanie Coleman, and Roberta J. Oglet, "African-American College Students' Perceptions of Sexual Coercion," *The Health Educator*, 37.1 (Spring 2005), 16–21; 16.

79 Ibid.

80 Ibid., 17–18.

81 Ibid., 18.

82 Tyson R. Reuter, Michael E. Newcomb, Sarah W. Whitton, and Brian Mustanski, "Intimate Partner Violence Victimization in LGBT Young Adults: Demographic Differences and Associations with Health Behaviors," *Psychology of Violence*, 7.1 (2017), 101–109; 101.

83 Ibid., 102.

84 Bessel A. van der Kolk argues that humans must face the "reality of trauma." *The Body Keeps the Score: Brain, Mind, and Body in the Healing of Trauma* (New York: Penguin Books, 2014), 4.

85 Miedzian proposes that "many of the values of the masculine mystique, such as toughness, dominance, repression of empathy, extreme competitiveness, play a major role in criminal and domestic violence." Miedzian continues: "The masculine mystique manifests itself differently in different environments

but the end result is the same. For a poor ghetto youth, [who can be of any race,] proving that he is a man might involve a willingness to rob, assault, or kill someone [. . .] For a group of middle- or upper-class boys, it might mean participating in a gang rape." *Boys Will Be Boys*, xxiii, xxiv.

86 Charles Amos, Ronald J. Peters, Jr., Lena Williams, Regina Jones Johnson, Queen Martin, and George S. Yacoubian, Jr., "The Link between Recent Sexual Abuse and Drug Use among African American Male College Students: It's Not Just a Female Problem in and Around Campus," *Journal of Psychoactive Drugs*, 40.2 (June 2008), 165.

87 Kimberly Anne Coles, Kim F. Hall and Ayanna Thompson, "BlacKKKShakespearean: A Call to Action for Medieval and Early Modern Studies," Modern Language Association *Profession*, Fall 2019, https://profession.mla.org/blackkkshakespearean-a-call-to-action-for-medieval-and-early-modern-studies/.

88 Stoever, *The Sonic Color Line*, 7.

89 See Brian Johns' narrative about his experience with sexual violence as an African-American male: www.rainn.org/survivor-stories/brian%27s-story.

90 Salter et al. cite "three key insights on the psychology of racism derived from utilizing a cultural-psychology framework," insights that reveal overlap between the concerns of (premodern) critical race studies scholars and social psychologists: "(a) Dynamic reproduction of racist action can be found embedded in the structure of everyday worlds, (b) people inhabit cultural worlds that afford or promote particular racialized ways of processing and seeing the world, and (c) people shape, produce, and maintain racialized contexts through their selected preferences, practices, and actions." "Racism in the Structure of Everyday Worlds," 151.

91 For a basic definition of "mental health," see: www.mentalhealth.gov/basics/what-is-mental-health. Also see Heine, *Cultural Psychology*, 559–591.

92 Brown, "Remixing the Family," 111–133.

93 For an understanding of how sterilization works as a means for population control, see Lisa Ko, "Unwanted Sterilization and Eugenics Programs in the United States" (January 29, 2016): www.pbs.org/independentlens/blog/unwanted-sterilization-and-eugenics-programs-in-the-united-states/.

94 Brown, "'Is Black So Base a Hue?,'" 146–147.

95 Jones, *Race, Sex and Suspicion*, 59.

96 Othello has a little over 100 more lines than Desdemona (274 lines versus 165, respectively). See: www.opensourceshakespeare.org/views/plays/characters/charlines.php?CharID=othello&WorkID=othello and see www.opensourceshakespeare.org/views/plays/characters/charlines.php?CharID=desdemona&WorkID=othello.

97 Keith Hamilton Cobb, *American Moor* (New York: Methuen Drama, 2020). I had the privilege of seeing this play performed twice for predominantly white audiences – in Massachusetts at Mt. Holyoke College's Rooke Theater in 2018 and at New York City's Cherry Lane Theatre in 2019. After each show, I stayed for the talkback session. White people's insecurities were

palpable as audience members addressed Cobb to ask questions or make comments. It was, not to my surprise, as if some white audience members had not seen or heard the same play as me; and *that* was a testament to Cobb's skill both as an actor and writer.

98 Cobb, *American Moor*, 42.

99 As Ayanna Thompson stresses, "While Othello continues to inspire artists, audience members and scholars to re-tell the story as a way to control the play's stories, frames and contexts, it really should inspire a new breed of listener, one who can discern the significance and validity of those stories, frames and contexts." The need to listen, the need to be heard, is real. "Introduction," in *Othello Revised Edition*, ed. E. A. J. Honigmann (London: The Arden Shakespeare, 2016), 1–116.

100 At this symposium, I also learned that there is at least one early modern scholar who teaches *Othello* at the college level without discussing race. I was aware scholars did this in the past, for quite some time, as Matthieu Chapman calls attention to in *Anti-Black Racism*, but I naively did not think this *still* occurs today. When asked by another scholar of color how it is possible to teach Othello without talking about race, the attendee said they deferred to what their students found most interesting, with gender being among their chief concerns. As such, race did not fit into the syllabus, so to speak. In the moment, I pressed this attendee's response with facts from the play that show Othello's Blackness is important; and I also cited pertinent premodern critical race studies scholarship, the latter territory seemingly out of the speaker's critical comfort zone. This perception of mine was supported when a white male audience member approached me later to tell me that the attendee in question, who was a white woman, seemed "hurt" by my comment – it was apparently his job to defend her. In his eyes, she was a victim of my intellect; and I was a villain for displaying my knowledge, something Black people have been discouraged from doing for centuries, as Du Bois highlights in *The Souls of Black Folk*. And so, my terse response to this white man was, "I was hurt, too" by experiencing the erasure of Blackness and the denial of its fundamental importance in and to *Othello*. Without missing a beat, he replied, "Point taken." Even so, it was evident to me that white supremacy and centrality had done their work and that, sadly, it was possible for some white audience members to perceive me as striking Desdemona with an innocent, intellectual comment.

101 For a thorough analysis of *Keene*, see Brown, "I Feel Most White When I Am . . . ."

102 Stoever, *The Sonic Color Line*, 22.

103 Brown, "(Early) Modern Literature: Crossing the 'Sonic Color Line,'" 59.

104 Ayanna Thompson and Laura Turchi, "Embodiment and the Classroom Performance," in *The Oxford Handbook of Shakespeare and Embodiment: Gender, Sexuality, and Race*, ed. Valerie Traub (Oxford: Oxford University Press, 2016), 724–737; 724, 726–727.

105 See: www.apa.org/workforce/publications/13-demographics/.

106 I am not arguing that Black therapists are necessarily better suited to work with Black clients, for internalized racism is an issue many Black people deal with; I am also not suggesting that a Black client might automatically be more comfortable with a Black therapist, for the former's abuser has potential to be Black (and, in general, race is not a sufficient substitute for adequate practitioner credentials). What I want to make clear, especially by way of the workforce statistics, is just how challenging securing adequate mental health help is for Black males who, in an ideal situation, would need to find a non-racist therapist who does not remind them of their rapist *or* of people who have made the client a victim of interracial or intraracial racism or race-based prejudice. The therapist cannot be a trigger.

107 Curry and Utley, "She Touched Me," 230.

108 Many of the Black male victims of violent racism and policing have found themselves lying in the street. This is a trend in their final moments. I cite additional tragic incidents in "(Early) Modern Literature: Crossing the Color-Line," 75.

109 See: www.inspq.qc.ca/en/sexual-assault/fact-sheets/sexual-abuse-childhood-perpetrators.

110 According to Entman and Rojecki, "Psychologists have found more generally that people remember negative information most readily." They add that "prototype theory" helps explain white expectations of Black people: "Whites expect the typical Black, if not a criminal, to be a member of the serving class" (*The Black Image in the White Mind*, 6, 19, 62). In short, white expectations of Black people are often low.

111 See www.mhanational.org/sexual-assault-and-mental-health.

112 See www.apa.org/news/press/releases/2014/03/black-boys-older.

113 Neil R. Bockian, Nora Elizabeth Villagran, Valerie Ma Porr, and Theodore Millon, *New Hope for People with Borderline Personality Disorder: Your Friendly, Authoritative Guide to the Latest in Traditional and Complementary Solutions* (New York: Three Rivers Press, 2002), 38.

114 Ibid.

115 Francesca Royster reinforces how African Americans often claim Cleopatra as a Black cultural icon; like many before me, I appropriate here the image of our Black queen. See *Becoming Cleopatra*, 206, 208–209.

Conclusion
Artifactually: The Comedy of (T)errors

> The power of racial profiling lies in its ability to produce the suspect
> communities it claims to seek. The power lies with the profiler.
> – Patricia Akhimie, *Shakespeare and the Cultivation of Difference*[1]

In the process of examining whiteness, it becomes evident to me every day
that the invalidating racist environment white people create for Black
people (and, consequently, for themselves when they face Black resistance
to said invalidation), makes it difficult for many aspects of the Black
experience to be believable and taken seriously. Unfortunately, "power is
still not used to empower, but to overpower," as Neal Hall argues.[2] This is
particularly true when some white people, through the application of their
white logic, do not believe in the existence of Black people as real or equal
or worthy human beings. Often, this reality induces self-doubt within
Black folk.[3] Furthermore, it is impossible to establish a cohesive sense of
national, or global,[4] community and equity when the dominant culture,
white people, and even complicit Black and non-Black people,[5] draws
decisive and divisive lines of sisterhood and brotherhood demarcated by
who is suspect and who is not, who is superior and who is not. These
boundaries are often marked by some version of the color-line: interracial,
sonic, and/or intraracial. And so, the often promoted, ideal possibilities for
living in harmony as human brothers and sisters ring hollow when it
becomes undeniably apparent that white brothers and sisters down the
street,[6] or even downstairs or right next door, do not see it as their moral
responsibility and ethical obligation to stop racism, to stop injustices, to
stop death-by-police, to stop terrorizing Black people, to just stop.
Although it should be, antiracism is not their goal.

This ceaselessness defines what I call in this Conclusion's title the
racialized comedy of (t)errors. In one sense, this phrase speaks to the
repeated "mistakes,"[7] contradictions, and violations, the *re*current abuses,
killings, and microaggressions that take away, and take away from, Black

life – that induce Black pain, trauma, and post-traumatic stress disorder (PTSD), among other psychological issues – and thus are hardly funny for the victimized. These repeated realities form the comedy of (t)errors in which Black people – the ill-fated subjects in this genre of Black racial misfortune – find themselves steadily on the defensive, battling whiteness all because the sadomasochistic, ontologically insecure white self cannot seem to cease hurting Black people. Such behavior in turn counterproductively hurts the white self. And to reiterate: White people should avoid hurting themselves, for white self-harm is not only destructive but it is also potentially indicative of a kind of *racism-related* borderline personality disorder (BPD).[8] White self-harm is, in general, bad for the mental health of both victims and perpetrators. However, the continued existence of anti-Black racism and the deliberate avoidance of large-scale institutionalized and systemic antiracism would suggest that most white people have yet to take serious action to mitigate the negative impact of racism on their lives and the lives of others. As I noted earlier in this book, anti-Black racism is a problem for white people, and it is a self-induced, self-sustained white people problem: therefore, their problem to solve. It comes from within. And so, I say, "Don't hurt yourself"[9] because the body, your body, my body, keeps score.[10]

In *The Essential Companion to the Diagnostic and Statistical Manual of Mental Disorders: DSM-5 Guidebook*, Donald Black and Jon Grant outline the BPD criteria, noting that a diagnosis must meet at least five of the following:

1. Frantic efforts to avoid real or imagined abandonment. (Note: Do not include suicidal or self-mutilating behavior covered in Criterion 5.)
2. A pattern of unstable and intense interpersonal relationships characterized by alternating between extremes of idealization and devaluation.
3. Identity disturbance: markedly and persistently unstable self-image or sense of self.
4. Impulsivity in at least two areas that are potentially self-damaging (e.g., spending, sex, substance abuse, reckless driving, binge eating). (Note: Do not include suicidal or self-mutilating behavior covered in Criterion 5.)
5. Recurrent suicidal behavior, gestures, or threats, or self-mutilating behavior.
6. Affective instability due to a marked reactivity of mood (e.g., intense episodic dysphoria, irritability, or anxiety usually lasting a few hours and only rarely more than a few days).

7. Chronic feelings of emptiness.
8. Inappropriate, intense anger or difficulty controlling anger (e.g., frequent displays of temper, constant anger, recurrent physical fights).
9. Transient, stress-related paranoid ideation or severe dissociative symptoms.[11]

Here, I engage in a brief thought experiment: In a racist society, most of these criteria outlined by Black and Grant are applicable to the responses from and/or behaviors observed in white people. *Criterion 1* regarding abandonment recalls how necessary it is for white people to belong to whiteness, the ultimate social and racial ingroup, to retain white privilege, dominance, and innocence. Being in this ingroup means always being able to dip their hands in the invisible knapsack. Those who jeopardize their racial whiteness by not upholding its tenets are sometimes deemed "race traitors"; they risk being abandoned by their white counterparts, who see them as defectors.[12] Abandonment by the white majority is something many white people, particularly those who are racist, those who support racism, want to avoid, for it is better to have access to the herd (invisibility) than not.

Additionally, the attention to "self-damage" in *criteria 4 and 5* recall my earlier discussion of how racist behavior is a form of self-harm that creates psychological problems for white people as well as their victims. *Criterion 6*, which focuses on anxiety, implies how fragile racial whiteness is an internal and external manifestation of the self-induced stress experienced by white people in a racist society. And one can see the substance of *criterion 8* embodied in white people who harbor anger, resentment, fear, and racial animosity toward Black people for innumerable irrational reasons, and sometimes for no reason at all. If simultaneously present in one white person, the abovementioned five criteria – numbers 1, 4, 5, 6, and 8 – would, in theory, be enough for that individual to meet the diagnosis for what might be considered racism-related borderline personality disorder: a race-crafted, self-created mental illness that does not give the white victimizer the right to be viewed as white victim, especially when such BPD goes untreated at will. Antiracism, its acceptance and implementation, is the only remedy. And while Black people can certainly help, as was my intention with writing this book and trying to shed some light on the oppressors' complexities,[13] the onus will remain on white people to pull themselves up by their bootstraps. Only then can they reach out for help: once their hands are free and they themselves are stable enough to grasp what antiracist activists have put within reach.

Dying for Laughter

The comedic aspect of the racial and racist comedy of (t)errors comes into play partly because some white people find Black suffering pleasure-inducing and amusing, particularly visible forms of physical, psychological, and emotional Black suffering that remain the spectacle[14] and "spectacular secret"[15] of a perverse, dark, white sense of humor that serves as both terror and error. I say "remain" because white people being entertained, nour-ished, and amused by Black suffering is nothing new; even Shakespeare touches on the matter in the final Act of *Titus*, as I write about else-where.[16] For more recent, concrete examples, however, one need only think back to images of lynchings in America, as Amy Louis Wood does in *Lynching and Spectacle*, to see that Black suffering as entertainment is a pastime with a long history,[17] one that unarguably continues today through the mass circulation, by bystanders, spectators, and (social) media outlets, of images of police brutality and other forms of anti-Black violence.

In May 2020, as much as I tried avoiding it, to protect my own psychological well-being and to avoid triggering my own anti-Black rac-ism-related PTSD, it was impossible not to see both video footage and still shots of a racist white police officer heinously overwriting what it means to take a knee[18] in the post-postracial era: A white officer kneeled on the throat of George Floyd, a Black man, a Black father of two, for nearly ten minutes.[19] Ten long minutes. This excessive act of terror, one of a few 2020 incidents that sparked massive protests and other forms of socio-political resistance,[20] caused the death of yet another unarmed twenty-first-century American Black man. And it generated much fear and frus-tration at a time when Black Americans were already on edge due to the Covid-19 pandemic that disproportionately affected Black lives – medi-cally, economically, emotionally, psychologically, and physically.[21] For some white folks, namely those who value white supremacy in ways big and small, the disparities were satisfaction. *This* is the comedy of (t)errors.

For some white people, such as those who laugh at, take secret pleasure in, or are apathetic to the Black plight and Black striving,[22] the comedy of (t)errors is both a literal and figurative space where they get to perform the error or mistake that racism becomes only when they finally get caught in the metaphorical racist theater: laughing, mocking,[23] having a smile on their faces, making impromptu 911 calls that apply racist theatrical impro-visation skills[24] or, worse, placing a knee on a Black man's neck until he dies in a paradoxically adultified-infantilized position, calling out for his mother[25] while making it abundantly clear he is taking his last breaths, like Eric Garner,[26] a Black man who met a similar fate in 2014. They could not breathe. I cannot breathe.

The comedy of (t)errors is like the funnyhouse where we find Adrienne Kennedy's Negro-Sarah, a character who is psychologically tormented by her biracialism, a character specifically tormented by white people like her Landlady and Jewish boyfriend Raymond, who laugh at her. They never laugh with her. Living in a racist world and instilled with racism, instillment that ensures racism is internalized and insures its own sustainment, the Othellos, Aarons, Cleopatras, Negro-Sarahs, and Patrice Lumumbas[27] of the world do not get to revel in the joys of laughter when they are drowning in struggle, drowning in *the* struggle.[28] Their Blackness does not allow for recreational joy when their focus must be survival. My Blackness does not allow for recreational joy when the focus must be on survival and negotiating whiteness. This is true, too, for my sister April and for all Black women.

Instead, laughter, the sadistic kind witnessed in Kennedy's *Funnyhouse of a Negro*, is an act experienced on one side of the interracial color-line. This kind of racist laughter is reserved for whites only, much like the perceived racialized freedom purchased with the privilege of whiteness. To be clear: The deindividualizing effects and costs of sustaining white dominance and maintaining herd invisibility far outweigh the benefits, but the socio-political symbolic goodness of the white identity and white solidarity warps that unfortunate reality. This is evident in Figure 5.1, the "iconic" 1930 lynch mob photo of Thomas Shipp and Abram Smith taken by Lawrence Beitler (Marion, Indiana, August 7).[29] In the photo are white people betraying the human race to preserve their interdependent white race through barbarous anti-Black violence. These white people were traitors of the *inter*racial human race, a fact that makes them morally reprehensible white people. Yet, in this context, these white people were not *intra*racial race traitors. This fact likely made them believe they were actually very fine people dressed in their fine clothes for the public[30] lynching show,[31] a show that rendered these Black men unprotected by the racist legal policies sanctioning their murders.[32]

In terms of what is on display, there are many striking aspects of the black-and-white Thomas Shipp and Abram Smith lynching photograph, aspects whose relevance depends on the context in which one assesses the image. In the comedy of (t)errors, I am struck by the sea of inter-generational white faces, particularly those on the image's left side, where we find one white man with a disturbing smile on his face and another

Figure 5.1   The lynching of Tom Shipp and Abram Smith at Marion, Indiana, August 7,
1930. Image: Popperfoto/Contributor/Getty Images.

white man who looks directly into the camera with a chilling smirk of
satisfaction. I am struck by the spectators' stolid eyes, through which I see
the reflection of the two lynched Black bodies silently screaming "Black
lives don't matter." And they are right to scream, to shout beyond the
photo at the white men and women who (re)produce the white boys and
girls who, in essence, become racists-in-training. For the children present,
this moment was educational in the worst way, a moment that epitomized
the failure of adults to model what is ethically, morally, and humanly right.
Moreover, I am struck by the raised white hand that has a pointed finger,
gesturing toward the lifeless Black male body on the right. The pointing
itself is gratuitous, unnecessarily excessive, since the brutalized Black men
are impossible for anyone to miss. Nevertheless, whiteness directs our
attention upward as it somehow still manages to center itself when all eyes
should be on the lost lives.

But then, again, the white lives are lost here, too, at least in the sense of their being lost souls; the emotional and spiritual deadness of these white lives matters for my argument.[33] I am also struck by how staring at and reflecting deeply on this picture enables one to feel the palpable patholog- ical racist hatred that persists today. And even more so, I am struck by what is not in the frame: the physical, emotional, and psychological damage done to Black people (and as a result, the entirety of America) and the loved ones of Thomas Shipp and Abram Smith. I am struck by the absence of the redness of their Black blood that was shed, for it would be incontrovertible proof of the effects of white anti-Black racism. These bodies are not black dolls strung up to a tree, despite what the mind might want to believe; peculiarly, the Black blood would somehow keep alive the humanness of this artifactual reflection of the treatment of Black folk. Yet, in this photo, we pay attention to whiteness. White history is most alive.

Psychologically "Bruised with Adversity"

Staring at and analyzing the Thomas Shipp and Abram Smith lynching photo can make one feel the overbearing weight of pervasive racist hatred, as was the case for me when I took the time to scrutinize the image over several months. Studying the photo affirmed how racist violence, anti-Black racism in particular – in its various forms, even the non-physical – has psychological impact, especially for the oppressed. Patricia Akhimie suggests as much in her essay "Bruised with Adversity: Reading Race in *The Comedy of Errors*," an extended version of which appears in her field-advancing monograph *Shakespeare and the Cultivation of Difference: Race and Conduct in the Early Modern World*.[34] While critiquing Shakespeare's *Comedy of Errors*, Akhimie uses an/*other* race play to think about identity as well as actions, like racial profiling, that can occur when people are stigmatized and organized by superficial but still significant somatic markers such as bruises and skin color.[35]

The Comedy of Errors tracks the narrative of two sets of identical twins who are separated at birth: Antipholus of Syracuse and Antipholus of Ephesus, and Dromio of Syracuse and Dromio of Ephesus. The Syracusan twins end up in Ephesus and this leads to confusion among those who know Antipholus and Dromio of Ephesus because they mistake the Syracusan men for the two that they know. Beyond generating confusion for everyone involved because of mistaken identity, more serious incidents occur such as beatings, false accusations, and even arrest.

Ultimately, in the spirit of Shakespearean comedy, the play's central issues are resolved and there are even happy reunions. However, the process that leads to joy is an arduous one. The process that leads to joy in the play rarely plays out in the modern-day real world when the global causes of mistaken identity for Black people are racist stereotypes that have deindividualized us for centuries, as Du Bois articulates in *The Souls of Black Folk*.

When reading Shakespeare's *Comedy of Errors*, I am hit hard by the play's (threats of) violence and the fact that such acts are a frontloaded and constant comedic component of the play (see 1.2.79, 92; 2.2.51–53, 80; and 2.2.23, for example). I am struck by how miscommunication – or what can also be read as the listener's deliberate denial of hearing the truth – contributes to the play's violence. Such moments resonate with me on a visceral level because I have, in racist incidents with authorities, been accused of lying because my Black truth, the truth, registers as impossible to receive. For me, and for Antipholus of Syracuse, the result is confusion. Toward the end of Act 2, Syracuse asks questions that I cannot help but find triggering. They are questions I have asked myself many times, albeit in different words: "Am I in earth, in heaven, or in hell? / Sleeping or waking, mad or well-advised? / Known unto these, and to myself disguised?" (2.2.211–213). For Antipholus of Syracuse, self-doubt is reinforced when he is repeatedly told he is not who he thinks he is. On a more literal level, the characters he interacts with from Ephesus represent the dominant anti-Black racist culture that has tried all my life to tell me I am not who I am, I cannot be who I want to be. Dare I say, fuck that, for sometimes I cannot find any better, more accurate words to articulate how frustrating it is to have to reject the imposition of an identity on me. I cannot find more accurate words to articulate how frustrating it is to watch those in the world around me "shuck and jive" and internalize the dominant white culture's racist expectations.[36] Something else I read in Shakespeare's play is how the confusion between the two Dromios leads to accusations of stolen identity. On a more literal level, this dynamic reminds me of cultural appropriation and how this phenomenon leads to the commodification of Blackness that, in the end, never truly benefits Black people. Somehow, "everyone knows us [Black folk] and we know none," to borrow a line from Antipholus of Syracuse (3.2.151). The system knows us better than we know ourselves.

Astutely, Akhimie prompts readers through her insightful reading of the twin Antipholus brothers' collective plight, for example, to recognize how "the play makes visible the suffering the system causes to anyone for whom meaning has attached to their body without their consent or knowledge, especially to anybody that is indistinct in some way, vulnerable to gener-alizations."[37] In a racist world that strips people of their individuality, the white supremacist system, its socio-political institutions, and cultural apparatuses that help create and disseminate meaning, is also the problem. The intraracial color-line is the problem, too, since it defines the battle in whiteness that doubles as the war on whiteness. My overt identification of whiteness' self-conflict and self-policing, which contribute to the produc-tion of violent anti-Blackness, enables my departure from Akhimie's reading of profiling-as-conduct to a phenomenon that is also directly linked to racism and anti-Blackness.

To exist without full ownership over one's identity, and not be able to influence how that identity is perceived, renders that particular individual a victim of a kind of identity theft: deindividualization and/or mistaken identity. *This* is the comedy of (t)errors, which produces confusion that oscillates between the comical and potentially tragic in Shakespeare's play, and between life and death with respect to modern anti-Blackness and racial profiling. To exist without full ownership of one's identity can have destabilizing effects, including psychological ones, because of the unfreedom to control identity, body,[38] and mind, because of the inability to be seen as an individual rather than a substitute for the abject aggregate. In such circumstances, as *The Comedy of Errors* shows, identity is predetermined and prescribed. More often than not, this truth about identity leads to Black people being vilified in society simply because we are Black.

This truth is one of the fundamental dangers of racial profiling,[39] which has certainly contributed to the more recent hypervisibility of anti-Black state violence – at least since the 2012 shooting of Trayvon Martin, the 2013 shooting of Miriam Carey,[40] and the 2014 shooting of Akai Gurley,[41] to name a few instances, though the 1992 LA riots[42] would suggest anti-Black state violence has remained a part of the contemporary Black existence for some time. The main difference now is that people get to witness the spectacle of this kind of violence more frequently because of advanced technology, and likely still not as frequently as it actually occurs, especially for Black women whose "relationship [with] the state was birthed in violence, through the establishment of slavery in the colonial world," as Black law professor Michelle S. Jacobs observes.[43] *This* is the comedy of (t)errors: a figurative and literal space where the dominant culture, by creating self-fulfilling prophesies, simultaneously validates and invalidates the Black self and sometimes even who the Black self has the potential to become.

The deindividualization of supposed inferior and marginalized people, especially Black people, is troubling and demoralizing. Assuming control of another's individuality, akin to a kind of psychological rape, is often enacted by the privileged, the wielders of some kind of power, those with the power to profile, as noted in this chapter's epigraph. In *Titus Andronicus*, one of the more traditional race plays that pairs nicely with *The Comedy of Errors*, we witness this kind of tension play out as Aaron's character develops, and as characters within the text, and the outside audience, respond to his character development. For the early modern white audience, Aaron stands in for the Black man and even Black people. Shakespeare depicts him, albeit not so simply, as violent, hypersexual, savage, barbaric, murderous, uncivilized, and largely unsympathetic.

Yet, Aaron is a misguided representation of Blackness, a hyperbolic generalization of what Blackness would have represented for white people in the period and even what it represents now among those who are prejudiced, racist, and anti-Black. Fortunately, Aaron's character is not one- or even two-dimensional. The overt complexity of his character – the three-dimensionality, which would otherwise be a missing piece of his character profile if not especially for Act 4, Scene 2 and the arrival of his infant Black son – reflects something significant that was clearly transpiring in Shakespeare's white imagination with respect to domesticity: the idea that a Black man, while portrayed as "large, threatening, powerful, uncontrollable, ubiquitous, and supernatural,"[44] could also be a protective father or proud of his Black humanity, or even subvert the dominant culture's ideas about family and brotherhood.[45] However, in the white minds of the play, Blackness does not get to define its meaning; and something similar occurs in *The Comedy of Errors*, a play that centers whiteness and allows us, as Patricia J. Williams remarks of Shakespeare's work, "to evaluate a range of still valid human dilemmas."[46] The identity of Aaron's baby, and by extension Aaron's adult Black male identity, is defined by and summarized in the white Nurse's response to the child. Son and father are "loathsome, joyless, dismal, black sorrowful devil[s]" (4.2.65–68). Why the simplistic reading of Blackness by the white figures in this play before, during, and after Act 4, Scene 2?

Something sounds off in the Nurse's description. Something is missing. And that something is Aaron's suffering. That something is the suffering of his Black child, who is unwanted by his white mother and white brothers. Perhaps adequately capturing and centering Black suffering was an artistic challenge for Shakespeare. I say this because Act 4, Scene 2 includes Black suffering, but stresses white suffering (for example, Chiron, Demetrius, the Nurse, and eventually Titus). The result is the amplification of white suffering; and this white suffering is multiplied to ensure the plays center whiteness. As such, the centrality of whiteness positions white people as always available to be victims of not only the interracial "Other" but also the white other, a dynamic that speaks to how white people can harm themselves. Given this, racial asymmetry is even more pronounced than is typically thought, because of the white other's existence.

In this *Titus* scene I am revisiting, the prescriptive abilities of whiteness equalize the Black adult father and his newborn son: they are Black and bad according to white culture, and both do not get to define their individual Black identities in this moment or in Act 5, Scene 1, where Lucius declares the child "too like the sire for ever being good" and threatens to hang the baby and Aaron from a tree to visually torture Aaron (line 50).[47] Like the Dromios, they are amalgamated bodies, but Black ones. Aaron and his baby are Thomas Shipp and Abram Smith, too; and their Black skin is a death sentence. It is the somatic marker that automatically absorbs the baby into Aaron's racialized suffering. Father and son need not trade places like the Dromios. Black skin is what makes the baby destined to suffer, at the very least psychologically, if he is to live in a world dictated by white supremacy, white logic, and white methods. With the baby physically absent from the play's final action, there is nothing conclusive that indicates his future will be devoid of racism. Being optimistic, one can only hope Lucius will fulfill his promise to Aaron and see that the child survives and is nourished. However, the baby is placed in white hands. And as *Antony and Cleopatra* prompts us to ask seriously, whose white hands can be trusted? In whose white hands does a Black life matter unconditionally?

Missing the Piece: Missing Peace

A commonality between those marked as "Other" and thus somehow deemed inferior, whether they are Black or non-Black, is rather simple: There is no peace for the individual who does not get to own the rights to their identity, for there is perhaps nothing more precious and personal than self-actualization and defining who one is on one's own terms.

As I neared the completion of this book, it dawned on me that I am not simply just like Othello[48] or Aaron or Caliban or the Prince of Morocco, that I am not just Cleopatra, a Black woman figure who is wary and weary of whiteness.[49] I am not just Shakespeare's Black characters in the sense that they are the ones with whom I, or any Black person, identifies most – or so I thought, at least for a moment, until I realized I was not wholly at peace with this idea, an idea that left me unsettled.

While writing this book, I discovered I am a lot like Hamlet, too, and that he – the famous Prince of Denmark – is, indeed, not just for white people, as many theater companies imply he is through their homogenous, color *un*conscious casting choices that I noted previously. I am like Hamlet, rejected because of blackness and sometimes deemed effeminate, rejected because I am a gay Black man.[50] I am like Hamlet, someone whose blackness leads him into an existential crisis, contemplating "to be, or not to be" (3.1.57), asking as rapper Tupac Shakur does in his 1998 song "Changes": "Is life worth livin'? Should I blast myself?"[51] Peace to Blackness, the world surrenders not. I am also like Dromio, who is not somatically Black but who is bruised with adversity. And I am even sort of like Hero. I say sort of because she only "fall[s]" figuratively into the "pit of ink," as her father Leonato laments (4.1.139–140). I, on the other hand, emerged from the pit of ink, my mother Audreta's Black womb, with the permanence of Blackness that I don as proudly as Shakespeare's Aaron does his (4.2.100–101), for this Ethiop, so to speak, cares not to be washed white.

But that is where the Black alignment with such white figures ends and where racism begins, for racism is like a two-way mirror that separates a racially privileged figure like white Hamlet from Othello – and me. Because I, like many, have been socialized to understand whiteness, I can see Hamlet, but he cannot see me. I can understand him, but he cannot understand me. And if he cannot see me or hear me, then he certainly cannot teach me anything about being Black, or about my Black self, especially anything I do not already know. To suggest Hamlet can do such a thing is to imbue a fictional figure with supreme white power, as white scholar Gary Taylor has done with respect to *Hamlet* and Black Lives Matter (BLM) – a move that centers silently white male superiority by placing three white "wise men," Hamlet, Shakespeare, and Taylor, in the role of white teacher/scholar.[52] Linking *Hamlet* to BLM in this way exemplifies how racial awareness and sensitivity can be limited; forcing this kind of link between *Hamlet* and BLM contradicts, in harmful ways, my reading of Hamlet as a figure who "acts black," a figure whose white otherness does not allow him to be a purveyor of the BLM mission at all, a mission that is explicit in its aims to "eradicate white supremacy."[53]

Playing the role of Wulf Sachs, in a sense, Taylor consolidates "three black men" – his son,[54] Michael, Adrian Lester, and Killer Mike[55] – into the role of *Black Hamlet*'s John Chavafambira, learning from them so he can exploit his new knowledge in a write-up that elides important premodern critical race studies work. In so doing, Taylor misses a critical opportunity to amplify actively the voices of his Black Shakespeare colleagues whose lives and scholarship matter. Taylor's piece in question reproduces white logic even as it makes use of scholarly authority. *That* is the power and privilege of whiteness. Often, racism can cause people to miss the point; this is part of the privilege that comes with whiteness and maleness, for instance. People *get it* faster when they must. So, here is a point I want white people to mind: *Hamlet* is best suited for helping us understand why "White Lives Matter" need not be a thing because white lives have always mattered, as my white other concept stresses. If *Hamlet* is touted as a, or the, go-to play for thinking about Black lives, Black struggle, Black liberation, and BLM, then it is evident Hamlet's life, his fictional white life, matters way too much. Racial asymmetry reigns.

Because of racism, there is an inherent limit to how much a Black person can embody and identify with Hamlet.[56] There is a limit to how much the Black woman can embody and identify with Hero. White figures can wear, fall into, cloak themselves in, and internalize blackness; for them, it is never the target or the death sentence that is having Black skin. Being Black while actually being non-Black, or white, won't get you killed so easily (think racial/cultural appropriation, blackfishing,[57] and co-option, for example). Rachel Dolezal and Jessica Krug are fine. They can *breathe*.[58] In that respect, the limits become clear: Black identification with and embodiment of whiteness does not work in the same way that white identification with and embodiment of Blackness works. As noted in Chapter 2, Hamlet is a murderous white man who, according to him, feigns madness; his character profile, his identity, is a privilege of his whiteness (and class status). Hamlet essentially kills five times as many people as Black Aaron (five white men and one white woman, respectively), but critics do not speak of Hamlet in terms that would make us think Aaron and Hamlet have anything nefarious in common.[59] And yet, they do.

The clear distinction in critical treatment of these racially different characters is troubling because it mirrors the real-world privileges that white people benefit from today: the ability to be shielded by their whiteness and to have reprehensible actions justified because said actions contradict the assumed inherent goodness of whiteness and thus create confusion. It is much easier to condemn Aaron because he is Black and because he, like Othello, kills a white woman, the same white woman who tells him to kill his own child. The assumed goodness of whiteness makes it hard for the mind to reconcile *bad whiteness*. After murdering Polonius, Hamlet floats around Elsinore, unrestrained, free to kill again. Like a serial killer, he does commit more murders. Conversely, Aaron is captured and essentially imprisoned by Lucius after he kills. Without trivializing murderous violence, or Aaron's role in the play's other acts of violence where he is complicit, I home in on the Black father's defensive killing of the Nurse because I only want to make the following point: All of Shakespeare's Black male figures must pay in these plays when they violate white womanhood or get too close. This is true for Aaron, Othello, the Prince of Morocco, and Caliban. On the other hand, Hamlet's verbal and physical aggression toward Ophelia and his mother is tolerated. Moreover, his murder of Polonius is swept behind the arras. Regardless of the motivation, killing people does not have the same outcome for Hamlet as it does for Aaron; and one cannot take race and racial difference, whiteness and Blackness, out of the equation as we calculate the reasons why the treatment is vastly different. The message is clear when we pay close attention and compare: In Shakespearean drama, a Black man cannot kill and still have his freedom, or his life, but a white man can. It is this kind of policing of Black people, this kind of racial double standard that kills me, even today. The racial double standard further reveals *Hamlet*'s and Hamlet's sheer inadequacy with respect to providing education about Black Lives Matter. Without access to equal pieces of justice, and power, there is no peace for the collateral souls of Black folk caught in the crossfires of warring whiteness.[60]

D. W. B.: "Sincerely, A Frustrated Citizen"

As I conclude this book, I think of James Baldwin, who asserts in "Why I Stopped Hating Shakespeare" that his "relationship, then, to the language of Shakespeare revealed itself as nothing less than [his] relationship to [himself] and [his] past."[61] The same is true for me. While growing up in late twentieth-century, predominantly low-income South Norwalk, Connecticut, which was deeply affected by the police magnets that were the crack epidemic of the 1980s and the gang activity perpetrated by the

Latin Kings and other organized groups in the 1990s,[62] I learned about violent death by age four or five, definitely by 1989,[63] well before I knew anything about Shakespeare and how his early modern tragedies would teach me about senseless murder and centuries-old anti-Black violence. Even though I did not have the sophisticated technical language to articulate my perceptions of the world as a child, I learned empirically that bullets and guns, and the people who use them, do irreparable physical, emotional, and psychological harm as they inflict damage on the human body. Growing up within the Du Boisian Veil[64] – in my Connecticut hood, prior to its faux-posh capitalistic rebranding as "SoNo" and its subsequent twenty-first century gentrification that made it more palatable and "safe" for white people – I learned contrary to Michael Jackson's 1991 racial equality anthem that it does, indeed, matter if you're Black or white. I learned that the notion of bullets not having names on them is utterly false, as it never seemed, it never seems, that way for people with Black skin, Black boys and girls, Black women and men. This was *hood* pedagogy.[65] Thus, I grew up, and sometimes still live, wrapped tightly in anxiety, with the fear that the bullets will find me because of whatever I am *doing while Black*. It don't matter what. Even now, now, very now, I could simply be reading, teaching, or writing about Shakespeare when the bullet suddenly becomes the trigger.[66] Imagine that.

For that reason alone, I was acutely aware, and need you to be acutely aware, of how much was at stake in producing this book – the stakes for me, my parents, my family, my culture, my race, my field, my students, my colleagues, and you. Even in times when I allowed life to get in the way, I had to be careful, remaining aware of the not-so-simple fact that there is always a bullet ready to have my name on it.[67] All I have to do is make that one wrong move, the one move that becomes the right move for the trigger to be pulled so I then bleed out like my Black brethren David McAtee,[68] Alton Sterling,[69] Michael Brown. Whatever I am doing while Black, it rarely ceases to feel like I am dodging bullets in this comedy of (t)errors that does not keep the law from breaking Black people like me even when we do not break the law. If at times this book reads as though it was written like my life depended on it, make no mistake about your assumption. Truthfully, I sometimes feel like I am on the dramatic trajectory of one of Shakespeare's tragic protagonists: Act 5 is inevitable and I am running out of time. We are running out of time.

For me, one of the most distressing things about being a Black adult, if I am to be frank, is living daily with a traumatic infantilizing childhood fear that the bullets will find me – no matter what I am doing while Black, hence the sense of urgency around getting these ideas out of my body. I could not let them die, not with me; I must die without them. Thus, with the presentation of one last artifact, I explicitly want to drive this conversation back to the comedy of (t)errors, what I see as a genre of racial misfortune: for Black people, and for white people (and those with internalized whiteness) whose racist delusions, or "systematic suppression of the truth," keep reality at a distance.[70] I feel inclined to conclude this book by sharing a poignant story, as it touches on many of the topics I converge in this study. I use this final chapter as the vehicle to publish and share this story – *my* story – because in many ways it inspired and informed the critical-personal-experiential nature of this book. Moreover, I share this story to situate it in conversation with the intersecting critical-personal-experiential antiracist discourses within (premodern) critical race studies, Shakespeare studies, genre studies, critical whiteness studies, social psychology, Black male studies, Black feminist studies, sound studies, and other fields and spaces devoted to undoing white supremacy while exploring racial formation.

In 2001, as a seventeen-year-old Black kid from South Norwalk on the verge of adulthood, I found myself in a position all too familiar for people who share the somatic mark of Blackness, especially in America: that is, driving – my very first car, mind you – while Black. Repeatedly stopped, four times by three different police officers over the course of six months between December 2001 to June 2002 during my senior year of high school, I, a Black adolescent, responded to antagonistic police the safest way I felt I could: I wrote. I penned a letter for my future, and the futures of people in my neighborhood who looked like me. With stories of anti-Black police violence sealed "within the book and volume of my brain" then (*Hamlet*, 1.5.104), I penned a letter, quite literally to save my life, or at least buy me more time, in hopes that I would not one day find myself in the terrifyingly tragic position of Amadou Diallo,[71] Sean Bell,[72] or Philando Castile.[73] Black body, Black person, riddled with police bullets. While the "what if's" I anxiously allude to in the letter's conclusion have yet to become my reality, the same is not true for so many Black people mentioned in this book, and not mentioned in this book. With the permission of my vulnerable teenage self, to whom I dedicate this book, I end *Shakespeare's White Others* here by sharing with you an early twenty-first-century letter I wrote to the Police Commissioner, Mayor, and Police Chief of my hometown, South Norwalk, Connecticut – a place that, after 2002, has not fully felt quite like home, safe.

6/29/02

To: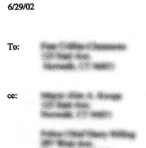

cc:

Subject: Larsen Street Internal Two-Way Conflict

I, David S. Brown, am an eighteen-year-old African American who lives on Larsen Street in Norwalk. I have been stopped by three different police officers on four separate occasions for committing an "alleged" traffic offense. I say "alleged" because there seems to be a misunderstanding in regard to definition.

On December 29th, 2001 I was stopped by a police officer as I was on my way out of the street towards the intersection of Larsen and South Main Street. The police officer stopped next to my car and told me that Larsen was a "ONE-WAY". I attempted to tell him that it was not, but he insisted that he was correct... I didn't argue. He let me go and gave me a warning. I later told my father who went down to the police station on December 31st and gave a copy of the attached diagram from the Norwalk Traffic Authority to Officer Yolanda who was at the front desk. Having never had this problem before my father assumed that would be enough.

Three months later I was stopped on March 22nd, 2002 around 9 p.m. This officer was the same one who stopped me in December. Having given me a warning in December he took action this time. He told me that I must back up my car and turn around. Annoyed at the situation, I backed my car into my driveway and sat there. His vehement tone troubled my nerves, and as I backed my car up I hit my passenger's side rear view mirror on my gate... my car was slightly damaged because of an incident that should have never occurred.

Approximately six hours later, the day now being March 23rd, Officer Evans stopped me for a third time. She stopped me for committing this "alleged" traffic violation, going the wrong way out of a "ONE-WAY". This time I was prepared... so I thought. I had the attached paper from the Norwalk Traffic Authority that clearly explains, with coherent words and a simple diagram, the legal way for traffic to flow in and out of Larsen Street. When she finally came to my car she asked me, " Whose car is this?" She also asked me, "Why is she(my girlfriend) in the back seat?"(a question that I feel in no way related to the reason I was stopped). I hesitantly answered her anyway. Once again my nerves were shaken... I had just been stopped for the same "alleged" infraction hours before. This was also mentioned to Officer Evans, who had an obvious lack of interest in any of my comments. When I showed her the paper from the Norwalk Traffic Authority she said, "Okay, this paper is dated from 1998." She claimed that the paper was not valid because it was from 1998. This I did not understand because it was still the same street. The Constitution was created in 1789 so does this mean that it too is not valid? She ultimately issued me a ticket for committing this "alleged" traffic violation. Later that morning my father had a telephone conversation with Officer Lisoby in regard to the incident. He also spoke to Officer Evans' supervisor, Sergeant Catore, in the afternoon around 4:15 p.m. Sgt. Catore assured my father and I that the situation would be taken care of.

Three months later, on June 23rd , 2002, another male officer stopped me again at about twelve in the afternoon. He pulled up next to my car and said, "Do you know that this is a "ONE-WAY"?" I answered him by confidently saying, " No... it is not". He said, "Yes it is... so I think you need to turn around before someone comes by and messes up your ride." Tired of playing the "yes it is" "no it's not" game I complied with the officer's request because this situation, quite frankly, has made my nerves weary. He waited at the end of Larsen and Woodward until he saw me turn my car around and then he left. I must add that I did not feel as though I were being spoken to as if I were the intelligent individual that I am. I guess he assumed that by me being a teenager from South Norwalk I would comprehend those words better... words that I feel were demeaning.

Larsen is not a "ONE-WAY"... it never has been. In 1998, four years ago, the Norwalk Traffic Authority placed "DO NOT ENTER" signs at the intersection of Larsen and Woodward Ave. I do not understand why it has not been a problem until now. By the straightforward laws of definition Larsen Street was no longer a "TWO-WAY" street because of the "DO NOT ENTER" signs. Thus it became an "INTERNAL TWO-WAY" street in 1998. There are no "ONE-WAY" signs on any of the four corners of Larsen... there never have been. In order for any street to be a "ONE-WAY" it must fit the definition of that type of street.... Larsen Street does not.

The fact that I have been stopped four times is indicative of the failure of some individual's ability to observe the definition of a simple term, respect common citizens, and reason logically and socially. I appear to be a typical male from "the hood" frequently wearing a "du-rag" to cover my braids… I am not. It seems to be too much of a coincidence that I am the only individual on my street that has ever been stopped by the police for this "alleged" traffic offense. I am the only one who looks like me… I hope I am not being profiled. I look forward to my complaint being dealt with. I want my words to be read, not looked at. I want this situation to be mollified, not ignored. I want the irritation and aggravation to end before any hypothetical situation that is fathomable occurs. So please, let's take care of this before the "what if's" become reality.

A frustrated citizen,

David S. Brown

Notes

1 *Shakespeare and the Cultivation of Difference: Race and Conduct in the Early Modern World* (p. 189), Patricia Akhimie © 2023 Taylor & Francis Group LLC (Books) US. Reproduced by permission of Taylor & Francis Group. Reproduced with permission of the Licensor through PLSclear.

2 Neal Hall, *The Trembling Tiber: A Black Poet's Musings on Shakespeare's Julius Caesar* (Stockholm: l'Aleph, 2020), viii.

3 Howard, "'Is Black So Base a Hue?,'" 113.

4 Akhimie asserts, "Globalization has enabled the profiling of whole regions of the world. Globally, vast numbers of people identified as threats come under scrutiny, and locally whole neighborhoods, whole communities, even whole cities predominantly populated by marked people are considered suspect and vulnerable to aggressive policing or continuous surveillance." *Shakespeare and the Cultivation of Difference*, 190.

5 I cannot stress enough that anti-Black racists are not just white. People of color perpetuate anti-Blackness as well. And Black people are not immune to internalized racism, which can lead to their exhibiting conflicted anti-Black sentiments as well.

6 Commenting on the importance of community, Gloria Anzaldúa writes: "We are our sisters' and brothers' keepers; no one is an island or has ever been . . . We are each responsible for what is happening down the street . . . ." "Acts of Healing," in *This Bridge Called My Back: Writing By Radical Women of Color*, ed. Cherríe Moraga and Gloria Anzaldúa (Albany, NY: State University Press of New York, 2015), xxviii.

7 Prejudice and racism are not "mistakes," particularly since such behavior is learned. I put "mistakes" in quotation marks because it is a cliché go-to expression for non-Black people who get their hands caught in the racist cookie jar.

8 Donald Black and Jon Grant explain general personality disorder diagnostic criteria and, from those points, I believe it is possible to see how white people in a racist society can display behavior that suggests racism makes them susceptible to racism-related borderline personality disorder. See "Personality Disorders," in *The Essential Companion to the Diagnostic and Statistical Manual of Mental Disorders: DSM-5 Guidebook*, Inline Edition (Washington, DC: American Psychiatric Publishing, 2014), chapter 18, 301.83 (F60.3).

9 See Brown, "'Don't Hurt Yourself.'"

10 Here, I invoke the title of an invaluable mental health and trauma resource that was recommended to me by an Untitled Othello Project ensemble member and colleague, Welland Scripps, who noted succinctly and powerfully that this book is relevant "for anyone who has a body": van der Kolk, *The Body Keeps the Score*.

11 Black and Grant, "Personality Disorders," in *DSM-5 Guidebook*, Chapter 18, 301.83 (F60.3).

12 Noel Ignatiev explains that white race traitors seek to disrupt the "normal functioning" of whiteness and "violate the rules of whiteness in ways that can have social impact." See "How to Be a Race Traitor: Six Ways to Fight Being White," in *Critical White Studies: Looking behind the Mirror*, eds. Richard Delgado and Jean Stefancic (Philadelphia, PA: Temple University Press, 1997), 613.

13 Lori Hale has suggested that "without a dominant group exerting power, there are no marginalized groups to oppress." "Globalization: Cultural Transmission of Racism," *Race, Gender & Class*, 21.1/2 (2014), 112–125; 119. As such, it seems that more effort should be put into understanding the oppressor, the source of racism's unyielding energy, as opposed to the oppressed.

14 Amy Louise Wood asserts, "It was the spectacle of lynching, rather than the violence itself, that wrought psychological damage, that enforced black acquiescence to white domination." *Lynching and Spectacle: Witnessing Racial Violence in America, 1890–1940* (Chapel Hill: University of North Carolina Press, 2009), 2, 8–9.

15 Jacqueline Goldsby offers a thorough study of white America's past (and still relevant) obsession with lynching and anti-Black violence in *A Spectacular Secret: Lynching and American Life and Literature* (Chicago: University of Chicago Press, 2006).

16 In previous scholarship, I have read *Titus Andronicus*, a tragedy that contains much (sometimes racialized) comic relief, as a kind of comedy of (t)errors in that racist horrors are presented for the onstage and offstage audiences as sources of entertainment. For example, when Lucius threatens to hang Aaron's newborn Black baby and let the Black father watch, Shakespeare touches on the spectacle of anti-Black violence. See "'Is Black So Base a Hue?,'" 146–147.

17 Wood explains, "The pleasure that white spectators experienced from an execution thus required a certain disidentification from the condemned and stemmed from a notion that the hanging not only established legal justice but also reaffirmed a larger social and racial justice. Seeing the pain and suffering of the condemned only intensified the crowd's enjoyment and sense of gratification." *Lynching and Spectacle*, 29.

18 As a silent but powerful form of social protest in 2016, former 49ers NFL player Colin Kaepernick began taking a knee during the singing of "The Star-Spangled Banner" (a song whose original full version includes controversial lyrics that register as anti-Black in the third verse that mentions the word "slave"). Kaepernick was eventually blacklisted by the NFL over his choice to peacefully protest and show support for Black lives, which were and continue to be targets of anti-Black state violence.

19 See "Death of George Floyd." https://en.wikipedia.org/wiki/Death_of_George_Floyd.

20 Ibid.

21 Keeanga-Yamahtta Taylor, "The Black Plague," *The New Yorker*, April 16, 2020. www.newyorker.com/news/our-columnists/the-black-plague.

22 W. E. B. Du Bois acknowledges Black striving throughout his treatise *The Souls of Black Folk*, beginning with his first chapter titled "Of Our Spiritual Strivings," where he notes how the Black man "simply wishes to make it possible to be both a Negro and an American, without being cursed and spit upon by his fellows, without having the doors of Opportunity closed roughly in his face" (3–4).

23 In the aftermath of George Floyd's death in 2020, white people could be seen mocking Floyd's tragic end online in what I might deem racist online bullying. For example, as reported in the *New York Post*, three British teens used the social media app Snapchat to display a photo in which two of the teens imitate Floyd, who died prostrate on the ground with a white police officer's knee on his throat. https://nypost.com/2020/06/01/george-floyds-death-mocked-by-laughing-british-teens-in-sick-photo/.

24 In May 2020, a white woman, Amy Cooper, was recorded making false accusations to the New York police about a Black man, Christian Cooper (no relation between them), all because Christian politely requested that Amy follow the law in New York's Central Park and leash her dog. www.forbes.com/sites/terinaallen/2020/05/29/3-things-amy-cooper-did-in-central-park-that-destroyed-her-life/#4796e41a6198.

25 Lonnae O'Neal writes about George Floyd's invocation of his absent mother in his dying moments. See "George Floyd's mother was not there, but he used her as a sacred invocation." https://theundefeated.com/features/george-floyds-death-mother-was-not-there-but-he-used-her-as-a-sacred-invocation/.

26 See "Death of Eric Garner." https://en.wikipedia.org/wiki/Death_of_Eric_Garner.

27 In Kennedy's *Funnyhouse of a Negro*, Patrice Lumumba is an official character that exists as one of Negro-Sarah's four selves, the others being the Duchess of Hapsburg, Queen Victoria, and Jesus.

28 One of the key subjects this Obie Award-winning play makes us think about is the Black person's perpetual psychological trauma. See Adrienne Kennedy, *Funnyhouse of a Negro* (New York: Samuel French, Inc., 2011).

29 The 1930 Marion, Indiana lynching drew thousands of white people whose racism was on full display as they actively and passively took part in celebrating anti-Black violence against Thomas Shipp and Abram Smith. www.blackpast.org/african-american-history/marion-indiana-lynching-1930/.
Berry offers important historical facts that reveal how the 1920s, 1930s, and 1940s were fraught with racial tension in other places like Detroit, Michigan, tension that has persisted into the twenty-first century in similar ways. Writing about a 1943 Detroit riot and the clear racial disparities, Berry notes: "In black neighborhoods, blacks destroyed and looted stores owned by whites and attacked whites whenever they encountered them. The police were apparently more lenient with white violators than black ones, as depicted in one photograph which shows a white man beating a black man who is being held by police. Thirty-four persons were killed in the violence, twenty-five blacks and nine whites. Fifteen of the blacks, and none of the whites, were killed by policemen. Of the nineteen-hundred persons arrested, three-fourths were black." *Black Resistance/White Law*, 165.

30 "Lynching was a very public drama," as D. Marvin Jones makes clear in *Race, Sex and Suspicion*, 25.

31 In August 2017, Donald Trump, then U.S. president, asserted that there were "very fine people" (a phrase meant to include white nationalists) at a violent

Unite the Right rally that ended tragically for Heather Heyer, a civil rights activist who was killed. See "Unit the Right rally": https://en.wikipedia.org/wiki/Unite_the_Right_rally.

32 Berry, *Black Resistance/White Law*, ix.

33 Mab Segrest asserts, "The pain of dominance is always qualitatively different from the pain of subordination. But there is a pain, a psychic wound, to inhabiting and maintaining domination." Segrest considers and seeks to answer the following question, which is one my book addresses as well: "What happens, in white supremacist culture, to the souls of white folks?" "The Souls of White Folks," in *The Making and Unmaking of Whiteness*, eds. Birgit Brander Rasmussen, Eric Klinenberg, Irene J. Nexica, and Matt Wray (Durham, NC: Duke University Press, 2001), 43–71; 45, 51.

34 In *The Comedy of Errors*, Adriana says to Luciana: "A wretched soul, bruised with adversity, / We bid be quiet when we hear it cry" (2.1.34–35).

35 Patricia Akhimie, "Bruised with Adversity: Reading Race in *The Comedy of Errors*," in Traub, *The Oxford Handbook of Shakespeare and Embodiment*, 186–196; 187. Part of the impetus for the style and candor of my conclusion here was the coda in Akhimie's *Shakespeare and the Cultivation of Difference*, titled "Pedestrian Check." I recommend all read her book, especially that part. There, Akhimie makes clear that she is part of a Black family as she discusses concern and expresses love for her brother, a Black man who is vulnerable to American society's anti-Black racism. In her brother, I saw myself and other Black men that I love, such as my father. And I saw the need to tell my own story, as the final words of my Conclusion reveal.

36 See the *Urban Dictionary* entry on "shuck and jive." www.urbandictionary.com/define.php?term=shuck%20and%20jive.

37 Akhimie, "Bruised with Adversity," 190.

38 Ibid., 192.

39 Davis, *Freedom Is a Constant Struggle*, 33–34.

40 Michelle S. Jacobs recounts the full details of Miriam Carey's death and struggle in a way that situates her unfortunate end within the larger context of state violence and Black women's invisibility in "The Violent State: Black Women's Invisible Struggle against Police Violence," *William and Mary Journal of Women and the Law*, 24.1 (2017) 39–100; 55–58. Also see Davis, *Freedom, Is a Constant Struggle*, 84–85.

41 See "Shooting of Akai Gurley": https://en.wikipedia.org/wiki/Shooting_of_Akai_Gurley.

42 See "1992 Los Angeles Riots": https://en.wikipedia.org/wiki/1992_Los_Angeles_riots.

43 Jacobs, "The Violent State," 41. Davis, *Freedom Is a Constant Struggle*, 86–87.

44 Williams, *The Alchemy*, 72.

45 Brown, "Remixing the Family," 112–114.

46 Williams, *The Alchemy*, 82.

47 Emily Detmer-Goebel claims the following: "After Aaron is captured and expresses concern for the child, Lucius seeks to abuse him through this

affection for the child. Lucius orders the Goth soldiers to 'hang the child, that [Aaron] may see it sprawl / a sight to vex a father's soul withal' (5.1.51–52). Hurting an enemy through his or her family depends on and exploits family bonds." "'Then Let No Man but I/Do Execution on My Flesh and Blood': Filicide and Family Bonds in *Titus Andronicus*," *Medieval and Renaissance Drama in England: An Annual Gathering of Research, Criticism and Reviews*, 28 (2015), 110–122, 115.

48 See Cobb, *American Moor*, 17–21. Ian Smith writes, "I would suggest that we approach Othello's request for a responsible, explanatory narrator as an invitation to make legible the 'continued dominance' of the forms of racial discourse that misread Othello's social location as a black man. Through the heuristic construct of the critic's divided self – racially white but having to tell a black man's story – the play positions its audience to have its racial knowledge and intelligence tested." "We Are Othello: Speaking of Race in Early Modern Studies," *Shakespeare Quarterly*, 67.1 (Spring 2016), 104–124; 123.

49 Elsewhere, I argue that in the racist white imagination the Black man has potential to be the Black woman and vice versa, because Black people are thought of by white people as simply amalgamated bodies. See "'Is Black So Base a Hue?'" 147–148.

50 Returning to Michael Jackson, whom I mentioned in this book's Introduction, I must note that he, too, was rejected and his masculinity was questioned. In *Are We Not Men?*, Phillip Brian Harper comments on one of Jackson's public statements, "I am proud to be a black American": "What is the meaning of this statement by the self-proclaimed 'King of Pop', made to Oprah Winfrey during a live television interview in February 1993? [...] For while Jackson's profession of racial pride was not most obviously meant to counter judgments that his physical appearance is unacceptably 'white', it also spoke to a widespread suspicion that his feminized demeanor signals a lack of self-respect, the 'feminine' still strongly connoting degradation even at this late historical moment. Jackson's assertion carried this dual significance because the abiding worry over his sexual and gender identities is itself also a manifestation of concern about the status of his blackness." *Are We Not Men?*, ix.

51 See the lyrics to Tupac Shakur's posthumously Grammy-nominated "Changes," second line. https://genius.com/2pac-changes-lyrics.

52 Gary Taylor, "What *Hamlet* Can Teach Us about Black Lives Matter," *Tampa Bay Times*, June 14, 2020: www.tampabay.com/opinion/2020/06/14/what-hamlet-can-teach-us-about-black-lives-matter-column.

53 See "About" on the Black Lives Matter website. https://blacklivesmatter.com/about/

54 The son, as an extension of Taylor's paternalism, is an extension of the white father, and so a reinforcement and reflection of Taylor's white power and influence.

55 See Taylor, "What *Hamlet* Can Teach Us."

56 As Ruben Espinosa reminds us, "Some lives, we know, are rendered more vulnerable than others." *Shakespeare on the Shades of Racism* (New York: Routledge, 2021), 1.

57 See the *Urban Dictionary* definition of "Blackfishing": www.urbandictionary .com/define.php?term=Blackfishing

58 See "Rachel Dolezal." https://en.wikipedia.org/wiki/Rachel_Dolezal; "Jessica Krug": https://en.wikipedia.org/wiki/Jessica_Krug.

59 Among the body count I attribute to Hamlet, I am including Rosencrantz and Guildenstern, since his white hands are directly responsible for their deaths even though he does not literally kill them with his own hands.

60 Here, I allude to the slogan, "No justice, no peace," which is often cited at protests devoted to addressing racism in America and beyond. In the days following George Floyd's death, protesters could be heard all around America shouting: "No justice, no peace," a chant that "has been around since the 1970s." Dot Wordsworth, "Where Did 'No Justice, No Peace' Come From?" *The Spectator*, January 18, 2004. www.spectator.co.uk/article/where-did-no- justice-no-peace-come-from-.

61 James Baldwin, "Why I Stopped Hating Shakespeare," from his *The Cross of Redemption*, www.folger.edu/sites/default/files/Why%20I%20Stopped%20 Hating%20Shakespeare_JamesBaldwin.pdf.

62 Avi Slazman, "Sifting the Evidence for Gang Activity," *The New York Times*, May 15, 2005, 3.

63 In 1989, I attended the funeral of a paternal uncle who was gunned down in Chicago, Illinois. I was five years old.

64 Du Bois, *Souls*, 1.

65 *Hood Pedagogy* is the title of my second book, under contract with Cambridge University Press.

66 Here, I interlace part of Iago's racist language, quoted in Chapter 4, with my own language in an attempt to reframe the phrasing.

67 Producing a book is hard work – I know that now. During the production of *Shakespeare's White Others*, I lost several Black family members, some of whom died too soon and are named in the dedication; and I experienced other personal racism-related challenges. I read all of those memories between the lines of this book, which is itself a trigger, paradoxically so.

68 See "Shooting of David McAtee." https://en.wikipedia.org/wiki/Shooting_of_ David_McAtee.

69 See "Shooting of Alton Sterling." https://en.wikipedia.org/wiki/Shooting_of_ Alton_Sterling.

70 George Lipsitz, *The Possessive Investment in Whiteness: How White People Profit from Identity Politics* (Philadelphia, PA: Temple University Press, 2018), 278.

71 See "Amadou Diallo killed by police." www.history.com/this-day-in-history/ amadou-diallo-killed-by-police-new-york-city.

72 See "Shooting of Sean Bell." https://en.wikipedia.org/wiki/Shooting_of_ Sean_Bell.

73 See "Shooting of Philando Castile." https://en.wikipedia.org/wiki/Shooting_ of_Philando_Castile.

DEPARTMENT OF PUBLIC WORKS

TO: Norwalk Traffic Authority

FROM: F. William Grumman, P.E.L.S.
Director of Public Works

DATE: November 12, 1998

SUBJECT: Request for "Do Not Enter"
Larsen Street from Woodward Ave.

      The Department has received a petition from the residents of Larsen Street (copy attached) requesting that Larsen Street be a one way street with traffic entering from So. Main Street. We have met with several of the residents and the owner of the commercial property on the north side of Larsen Street in order to resolve issues of access to the commercial property which has driveways from both Woodward Avenue and Larsen Street.

      The Department recommends that "Do Not Enter" signs be installed at the intersection of Larsen Street and Woodward Avenue, making Larsen Street a two-way internal street, with entrance and exit onto So. Main Street and exit only onto Woodward Avenue. See sign location and traffic plan attached.

CC:

g:\TRAFFIC\LARSEN.DOC

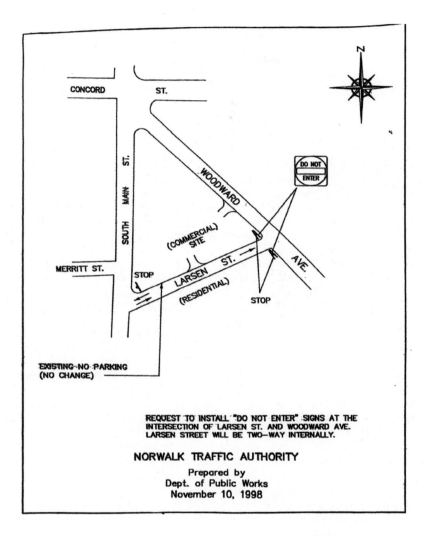

REQUEST TO INSTALL "DO NOT ENTER" SIGNS AT THE
INTERSECTION OF LARSEN ST. AND WOODWARD AVE.
LARSEN STREET WILL BE TWO—WAY INTERNALLY.

NORWALK TRAFFIC AUTHORITY

Prepared by
Dept. of Public Works
November 10, 1998

Select Bibliography

Adams, Brandi K. "The King, and Not I: Refusing Neutrality—." *The Sundial*, ACMRS Press, June 2020. https://medium.com/the-sundial-acmrs/the-king-and-not-i-refusing-neutrality-dbab4239e8a9.

Adelman, Janet. *Suffocating Mothers: Fantasies of Maternal Origin in Shakespeare's Plays, Hamlet to the Tempest* (Routledge, 1992).

Ahmed, Sara. "A Phenomenology of Whiteness." *Feminist Theory*, 8.2 (2007), 149–168.

Akhimie, Patricia. "'Fair' Bianca and 'Brown' Kate: Shakespeare and the Mixed-Race Family in José Esquea's The Taming of the Shrew." *Journal of American Studies*, 54.1 (2020), 89–96.

    Shakespeare and the Cultivation of Difference: Race and Conduct in the Early Modern World (Routledge, 2020).

Amos, Charles, Ronald J. Peters, Jr., Lena Williams, Regina Jones Johnson, Queen Martin, and George S. Yacoubian. "The Link between Recent Sexual Abuse and Drug Use among African American Male College Students: It's Not Just a Female Problem in and Around Campus." *Journal of Psychoactive Drugs*, 40.2 (2008), 161–166.

Amussen, Susan Dwyer. *An Ordered Society* (Columbia University Press, 1988).

Anderson, Lisa M. "When Race Matters: Reading Race in Richard III and Macbeth." In *Colorblind Shakespeare: New Perspectives on Race and Performance*, ed. Ayanna Thompson (Routledge, 2006), 89–102.

Andrea, Bernadette. "Black Skin, The Queen's Masques: Africanist Ambivalence and Feminine Author(ity) in the Masques of Blackness and Beauty." *English Literary Renaissance*, 29.3 (1999), 246–281.

Anzaldúa, Gloria. "Acts of Healing." In *This Bridge Called My Back: Writing By Radical Women of Color*, eds. Cherríe Moraga and Gloria Anzaldúa (State University of New York Press, 2015), xxvii–xxviii.

Archer, John Michael. "Antiquity and Degeneration in Antony and Cleopatra." In *Race, Ethnicity, and Power in the Renaissance*, ed. Joyce Green MacDonald (Associated University Presses, 1997), 145–164.

    Citizen Shakespeare: Freemen and Aliens in the Language of the Plays (Palgrave Macmillan, 2005).

Bach, Rebecca Ann. "Manliness Before Individualism: Masculinity, Effeminacy, and Homoerotics in Shakespeare's History Plays." In *A Companion to*

Shakespeare's Works, Volume II: The Histories, eds. Richard Dutton and Jean E. Howard (Blackwell Publishing, 2003), 220–245.

Bahr, Stephanie M. "Titus Andronicus and the Interpretive Violence of the Reformation." *Shakespeare Quarterly*, 68.3 (2017), 241–270.

Baldwin, James. "Why I Stopped Hating Shakespeare." In *The Cross of Redemption: Uncollected Writings*, ed. Randall Kenan (Pantheon, Kindle Edition, 2010), 65–69.

Balizet, Ariane M. *Blood and Home in Early Modern Drama: Domestic Identity on the Renaissance Stage* (Routledge, 2014).

Banducci, Anne N., Elana M. Hoffman, C. W. Lejuez, and Karestan C. Koenen. "The Impact of Childhood Abuse on Inpatient Substance Users: Specific Links with Risky Sex, Aggression, and Emotion Dysregulation." *Child Abuse and Neglect*, 38.5 (2014), 928–938.

Barthelemy, Anthony Gerard. *Black Face, Maligned Race: The Representation of Blacks in English Drama from Shakespeare to Southerne* (Louisiana State University Press, 1987).

Bautista, Richard. "Survey of Biological Factors Affecting the Determination of the Postmortem Interval." Scientia et *Humanitas*, 2 (2012), 13–22.

Benson, Sean. *Shakespeare, "Othello" and Domestic Tragedy* (Bloomsbury, 2011).

Bernasconi, Robert. "Waking Up White and in Memphis." In *White on White / Black on Black*, ed. George Yancy (Rowman & Littlefield Publishers, Inc., 2005), 17–26.

Bernstein, Robin. *Racial Innocence: Performing American Childhood from Slavery to Civil Rights* (New York University Press, 2011).

Berry, Helen and Elizabeth Foyster. *The Family in Early Modern England* (Cambridge University Press, 2007).

Berry, Mary Frances. *Black Resistance/White Law: A History of Constitutional Racism in America* (Meredith Corporation, 1971).

Black, Donald and Jon Grant. *The Essential Companion to the Diagnostic and Statistical Manual of Mental Disorders: DSM-5 Guidebook* (American Psychiatric Publishing, 2014).

Blits, Jan. *New Heaven, New Earth: Shakespeare's Antony and Cleopatra* (Lexington Books, 2009).

Bloom, Gina. *Voice in Motion: Staging Gender, Shaping Sound in Early Modern England* (University of Pennsylvania Press, 2007).

Blow, Charles M. "The Lowest White Man Thinks He's Better." *Miami Times*, January 11, 2018.

Bonilla-Silva, Eduardo. "The Invisible Weight of Whiteness: The Racial Grammar of Everyday Life in America." *Michigan Sociological Review*, 26 (2012), 1–15.

"Toward a Definition of White Logic and White Methods." In *White Logic, White Methods: Racism and Methodology*, eds. Tukufu Zuberi and Eduardo Bonilla-Silva (Rowman & Littlefield Publishers, Inc., 2008), 3–30.

Boose, Lynda E. "'The Getting of a Lawful Race': Racial Discourse in Early Modern England and the Unpresentable Black Woman." In *Women, Race, and Writing*, eds. Margo Hendricks and Patricia Parker (Routledge, 1994), 35–54.

Botelho, K. *Renaissance Earwitnesses* (Springer, 2009).

Bottoms, Greg. *Lowest White Boy* (West Virginia University Press, 2019).

Bozio, Andrew. "'Whiteness as Property' in As You Like It." *Shakespeare Studies*, 50 (2022), 24–32.

Bray, Alan. *Homosexuality in Renaissance England* (Gay Men's Press, 1982).

Breitenberg, Mark. *Anxious Masculinity in Early Modern England* (Cambridge University Press, 1996).

Briante, Susan. "Seeing White: The Painful Ways the World Teaches Race and Color." *Guernica/A Magazine of Global Arts & Politics*, October 2017. www .guernicamag.com/seeing-white/.

Britton, Dennis Austin. "Ain't She a Shakespearean: Truth, Giovanni, and Shakespeare." In *Early Modern Black Diaspora Studies: A Critical Anthology*, eds. Cassander Smith, Nicholas Jones, and Miles P. Grier (Palgrave Macmillan, 2018), 223–228.

Becoming Christian: Race, Reformation, and Early Modern English Romance (Fordham University Press, 2014).

Brown, David Sterling. "Code Black: Whiteness and Unmanliness in *Hamlet*." In *Hamlet: The State of Play*, eds. Sonia Massai and Lucy Munro (Arden Shakespeare, 2021), 101–127.

"'Don't Hurt Yourself': (Anti)Racism and White Self-Harm." *Los Angeles Review of Books*, July 6, 2021. https://lareviewofbooks.org/article/antira cism-in-the-contemporary-university/#_ftn2

"(Early) Modern Literature: Crossing the Color-Line." *Radical Teacher*, 105 (2016), 69–77.

"(Early) Modern Literature: Crossing the 'Sonic Color Line.'" In *Shakespeare and Digital Pedagogy*, eds. Diana Henderson and Kyle Vitale (Arden Shakespeare, 2021), 51–62.

"'Hood Feminism': Whiteness and Segregated (Premodern) Scholarly Discourse in the Post-Postracial Era." *Literature Compass* 18.10 (2020), 1–15.

"I Feel Most White When I Am … : Foregrounding the 'Sharp White Background' of Anchuli Felicia King's *Keene*." *Shakespeare Bulletin*, 39.4 (2021), 577–593.

"'Is Black So Base a Hue?': Black Life Matters in Shakespeare's *Titus Andronicus*." In *Early Modern Black Diaspora Studies, A Critical Anthology*, eds. Cassander Smith, Nicholas Jones, and Miles P. Grier (Palgrave Macmillan, 2018), 137–155.

"Remixing the Family: Blackness and Domesticity in Shakespeare's *Titus Andronicus*." In *Titus Andronicus: The State of Play*, ed. Farah Karim-Cooper (Arden Shakespeare, 2019), 111–133.

"'Shake Thou to Look on't': Shakespearean White Hands." In *White People in Shakespeare*, ed. Arthur L. Little, Jr. (Arden Shakespeare, 2023), 105–199.

"'The Sonic Color Line': Shakespeare and the Canonization of Sexual Violence Against Black Men." *The Sundial*, AMCRS Press (August 2019). https://medium.com/the-sundial-acmrs/the-sonic-color-line-shakespeare-and-the-canonization-of-sexual-violence-against-black-men-cb166dca9af8.

"Things of Darkness: 'The Blueprint of a Methodology.'" *The Hare*, 5.1 (September 2020). https://thehareonline.com/article/things-darkness-%E2%80%9C-blueprint-methodology%E2%80%9D.

Brown, David Sterling, Patricia Akhimie, and Arthur L. Little, Jr. "Seeking the (In)Visible: Whiteness and Shakespeare Studies." *Shakespeare Studies*, 50 (2022), 17–23.

Brown, David Sterling and Jennifer Lynn Stoever. "'Blanched with Fear': Reading the Racialized Soundscape in Macbeth." *Shakespeare Studies*, 50 (2022), 33–43.

Burton, Jonathan. "Race." In *A Cultural History of Western Empires in the Renaissance (1450–1650)*, ed. Ania Loomba (Bloomsbury, 2018), 203–224.

Burton, Robert. *The Anatomy of Melancholy: The First Partition* (J. M. Dent & Sons Ltd., 1932).

Callaghan, Dympna. *Shakespeare without Women* (Routledge, 2000).

Cardon, Lauren. *The "White Other" in American Intermarriage Stories, 1945–2008* (Springer, 2012).

Carr, Morwenna. "Material/Blackness: Race and Its Material Reconstructions on the Seventeenth-Century English Stage." *Early Theatre*, 20.1 (2017), 77–95.

Cassidy, Kevin D., Kimberly A. Quinn, and Glyn W. Humphreys. "The Influence of Ingroup/Outgroup Categorization on Same- and Other-Race Face Processing: The Moderating Role of Inter- versus Intra-Racial Context." *Journal of Experimental Social Psychology*, 47 (2011), 811–817.

Chakravarty, Urvashi. *Fictions of Consent: Slavery, Servitude, and Free Service in Early Modern England* (University of Pennsylvania Press, 2022).

"More Than Kin, Less Than Kind: Similitude, Strangeness, and Early Modern English Homonationalisms." *Shakespeare Quarterly*, 67.1 (2016), 14–29.

Chapman, Matthieu. *Anti-Black Racism in Early Modern English Drama: The Other "Other"* (Routledge, 2017).

"The Appearance of Blacks on the Early Modern Stage: *Love's Labour's Lost*'s African Connections to Court." *Early Theatre*, 17.2 (2014), 77–94.

Coates, Ta-Nehisi. "Foreword." In *The Origin of Others*, by Toni Morrison (Harvard University Press, 2017), vii–xvii.

Cobb, Keith Hamilton. *American Moor* (Methuen Drama, 2020).

Coles, Kimberly Anne, Kim F. Hall, and Ayanna Thompson. "BlacKKKShakespearean: A Call to Action for Medieval and Early Modern Studies." *Modern Language Association Profession* (Fall 2019). https://profession.mla.org/blackkkshakespearean-a-call-to-action-for-medieval-and-early-modern-studies/.

Collins, Patricia Hill and Sirma Bilge. *Intersectionality* (Polity Press, 2016).

Corredera, Vanessa. "Get Out and the Remediation of Othello's Sunken Place: Beholding White Supremacy's Coagula." *Borrowers and Lenders*, 13.1 (2020), n.p.

"Not a Moor Exactly: Shakespeare, *Serial*, and Modern Constructions of Race." *Shakespeare Quarterly*, 67.1 (2016), 30–50.

Craven, Alice Mikal. *Visible and Invisible Whiteness* (Springer, 2018).

Crenshaw, Kimberlé, Neil Gotanda, Gary Peller, and Kendall Thomas. *Critical Race Theory* (The New Press, 1995).

Cressy, David. *Birth, Marriage, and Death: Ritual, Religion, and the Life-Cycle in Tudor and Stuart England* (Oxford University Press, 1997).

Curry, Tommy J. and Ebony A. Utley. "She Touched Me: Five Snapshots of Adult Sexual Violations of Black Boys." *Kennedy Institute of Ethics Journal*, 28.2 (2018), 205–241.

Dadabhoy, Ambereen. "The Unbearable Whiteness of Being (in) Shakespeare." *Postmedieval* 11.2–3 (2020), 228–235.

Daileader, Celia R. "The Cleopatra Complex: White Actresses on the Interracial 'Classical' Stage." In *Colorblind Shakespeare: New Perspectives on Race and Performance*, ed. Ayanna Thompson (Routledge, 2006), 205–220.

D'Amico, Jack. *The Moor in English Renaissance Drama* (University of South Florida Press, 1991).

Davis, Angela. *Freedom Is a Constant Struggle* (Haymarket Books, 2016).

De Barros, Eric L. "'My Fleece of Woolly Hair That Now Uncurls': Shakespeare's *Titus Andronicus*, 'Black' Hair, and the Revenge of Postcolonial Education." *College Literature*, 49.4 (2022), 628–651.

de Grazia, Margreta. *"Hamlet" without Hamlet* (Cambridge University Press, 2007).

Delgado, Richard, and Jean Stefancic, eds. "An Interview with Noel Ignatiev of Race Traitor Magazine, 'Treason to Whiteness Is Loyalty to Humanity.'" In *Critical White Studies: Looking behind the Mirror* (Temple University Press, 1997), 607–612.

Critical Race Theory: An Introduction (New York University Press, 2001).

Critical White Studies (Temple University Press, 1997).

Detmer-Goebel, Emily. "'Then Let No Man but I/Do Execution on My Flesh and Blood': Filicide and Family Bonds in *Titus Andronicus*." *Medieval and Renaissance Drama in England: An Annual Gathering of Research, Criticism and Reviews* 28 (2015), 110–122.

De-yan, Guo. "Hamlet's Femininity." *Canadian Social Science*, 5.5 (2009), 89–95.

DiGangi, Mario. *The Homoerotics of Early Modern Drama* (Cambridge University Press, 1997).

Dolan, Frances E. *Dangerous Familiars: Representations of Domestic Crime in England, 1550–1700* (Cornell University Press, 1994).

Du Bois, W. E. B. *The Souls of Black Folk* (Tribeca Books, 2011).

Dyson, Michael Eric. *Tears We Cannot Stop* (St. Martin's Press, 2017).

Entman, Robert M. and Andrew Rojecki. *The Black Image in the White Mind* (University of Chicago Press, 2001).

Erickson, Peter. "Can We Talk about Race in Hamlet?" In *Hamlet: Critical Essays*, ed. Arthur Kinney (Routledge, 2002) 207–213.

"'God for Harry, England, and Saint George': British National Identity and the Emergence of White Self-Fashioning." In *Early Modern Visual Culture: Representation, Race, Empire in Renaissance England*, eds. Peter Erickson and Clark Hulse (University of Pennsylvania Press, 2000).

Erickson, Peter and Kim F. Hall. "'A New Scholarly Song': Rereading Early Modern Race." *Shakespeare Quarterly*, 67.1 (2016), 1–13.

Fanon, Frantz. *Black Skin, White Masks* (Grove Press, 2008).

The Wretched of the Earth (Grove Press, 1963).

Feather, Jennifer. "Shakespeare and Masculinity." *Literature Compass*, 12.4 (2015), 134–145.

Feather, Jennifer and Catherine E. Thomas. *Violent Masculinities* (Palgrave Macmillan, 2013).

Field, Corinne T. *The Struggle for Equal Adulthood* (University of North Carolina Press, 2014).

Fields, Karen E. and Barbara J. Fields. *Racecraft* (Verso Books, 2014).

Fleming, Crystal Marie. *How to Be Less Stupid about Race* (Beacon Press, 2018).

Fletcher, Anthony. *Gender, Sex, and Subordination in England 1500–1800* (Yale University Press, 1996).

Foster, Thomas A. "The Sexual Abuse of Black Men under Slavery." *Journal of the History of Sexuality*, 20.3 (2011), 445–464.

Foucault, Michel. *The History of Sexuality* (Pantheon Books, 1978).

Foyster, Elizabeth A. *Manhood in Early Modern England* (Longman Publishing Group, 1999).

Frank, Bernhard. "'The Rest Is Silence': Hamlet, A Closet Case." *Hamlet Studies*, 20.1–2 (1998).

Fryer, Peter. *Black People in the British Empire: An Introduction* (Pluto Press, 1988).

Fudge, Erica. *Brutal Reasoning: Animals, Rationality, and Humanity in Early Modern England* (Cornell University Press, 2006).

Gaines, Kevin K. *Uplifting the Race: Black Leadership, Politics, and Culture in the Twentieth Century* (University of North Carolina Press, 1996).

Gerzina, Gretchen. *Black England* (John Murray Publishers Ltd., 1995).

Gilbert, Sky. "A Sparrow Falls: Olivier's Feminine Hamlet." *Brief Chronicles*, 1, (2009), 193–204.

Gilroy, Paul. *Against Race: Imagining Political Culture beyond the Color Line* (Belknap Press, An Imprint of Harvard University Press, 2001).

Goldsby, Jacqueline. *A Spectacular Secret: Lynching and American Life and Literature* (University of Chicago Press, 2006).

Gordon-Chipembere, Natasha. *Representation and Black Womanhood: The Legacy of Sarah Baartman* (Palgrave Macmillan, 2011).

Gosson, Stephen. *Plays Confuted in Five Actions in Markets of Bawdrie: The Dramatic Criticism of Stephen Gosson* (Institut für Englische Sprache und Literatur, Universität Salzburg, 1974).

Gotanda, Neil. "A Critique of 'Our Constitution Is Color-Blind.'" In *Critical Race Theory: The Key Writings That Formed the Movement*, eds. Kimberlé

Crenshaw, Neil Gotanda, Gary Peller, and Kendall Thomas (The New Press, 1995), 257–275.

Grady, Kyle. "Othello, Colin Powell and Post-Racial Anachronisms." *Shakespeare Quarterly*, 67.1 (2016), 68–83.

Grier, Miles P. "Inkface: The Slave Stigma in England's Early Imperial Imagination." In *Scripturing the Human: The Written as Political*, ed. Vincent L. Wimbush (Routledge, 2015), 193–220.

"The Color of Professionalism: A Response to Dennis Britton." In *Early Modern Black Diaspora Studies: A Critical Anthology*, eds. Cassander Smith, Nicholas Jones, and Miles P. Grier (Palgrave Macmillan, 2018), 229–238.

Grossman, Marshall. "Hamlet and the Genders of Grief." In *Grief and Gender*, eds. Jennifer C. Vaught and Lynne Dickson Bruckner (Palgrave Macmillan, 2003), 177–196.

Habib, Imtiaz. *Black Lives in the English Archives, 1500–1677* (Routledge, 2008).

"Othello, Sir Peter Negro, and Blacks of Early Modern England: Colonial Inscription and Postcolonial Excavation." *Literature Interpretation Theory*, 9.1 (2008), 15–30.

Shakespeare and Race: Postcolonial Praxis in the Early Modern Period (University Press of America, Inc., 2000).

Hale, Lori. "Globalization: Cultural Transmission of Racism." *Race, Gender & Class*, 21.1/2 (2014), 112–125.

Hall, Kim F. "Beauty and the Beast of Whiteness: Teaching Race and Shakespeare." *Shakespeare Quarterly*, 47.4 (1996), 461–475.

"Object into Object: Some Thoughts on the Presence of Black Women in Early Modern Culture." In *Early Modern Visual Culture: Representation, Race, Empire in Renaissance England*, eds. Peter Erickson and Clark Hulse (University of Pennsylvania Press, 2000), 315–345.

Things of Darkness (Cornell University Press, 1995).

"'Troubling Doubles': Apes, Africans, and Blackface in Mr. Moore's Revels." In *Race, Ethnicity and Power in the Renaissance*, ed. Joyce Green MacDonald (Associated University Presses, 1997), 120–144.

Hall, Neal. *The Trembling Tiber* (L'Aleph, 2020).

Hannah-Jones, Nikole. "Preface." In *The 1619 Project: A New Origin Story*, ed. Nikole Hannah-Jones (OneWorld, 2021), xvii–xxxiii.

Harper, Phillip Brian. *Are We Not Men?: Masculine Anxiety and the Problem of African-American Identity* (Oxford University Press, 1996).

Harris, Cheryl I. "Whiteness as Property." In *Critical Race Theory: The Key Writings That Formed the Movement*, eds. Kimberlé Crenshaw, Neil Gotanda, Gary Peller, and Kendall Thomas (The New Press, 1995), 276–291.

Harris, Jonathan Gil. "Shakespeare's Hair: Staging the Object of Material Culture." *Shakespeare Quarterly*, 52.5 (2001), 479–491.

Harris-Perry, Melissa V. *Sister Citizen: Shame, Stereotypes and Black Women in America* (Yale University Press, 2011).

Hartman, Saidiya. "The Time of Slavery." *The South Atlantic Quarterly*, 101.4 (2002), 757–777.

Heine, Steven J. *Cultural Psychology*. 3rd ed. (W. W. Norton & Company, 2016).

Hendricks, Margo. "Gestures of Performance: Rethinking Race in Contemporary Shakespeare." In *Colorblind Shakespeare: New Perspectives on Race and Performance*, ed. Ayanna Thompson (Routledge, 2006), 187–203.

"Surveying 'Race' in Shakespeare." In *Shakespeare and Race*, eds. Catherine M. S. Alexander and Stanley Wells (Cambridge University Press, 2000), 1–22.

Hendricks, Margo, and Patricia Parker, eds. *Women, "Race" and Writing in the Early Modern Period* (Routledge, 1994).

Heng, Geraldine. *The Invention of Race in the European Middle Ages* (Cambridge University Press, 2018).

Holmberg, Eva Johanna. *Jews in the Early Modern English Imagination* (Routledge, 2016).

hooks, bell. *Black Looks* (Routledge, 2014).

Howard, Jean E. "Is Black So Base a Hue?" In *Shakespeare in Our Time: A Shakespeare Association of America Collection*, eds. Dympna Callaghan and Suzanne Gossett (Bloomsbury, 2016), 107–114.

Hübinette, Tobias, and Catrin Lundström. "The Phases of Hegemonic Whiteness: Understanding Racial Temporalities in Sweden." *Social Identities*, 20.6 (2014), 423–437.

Hughey, Matthew W. "Black Guys and White Guise: The Discursive Construction of White Masculinity." *Journal of Contemporary Ethnography*, 20.10 (2012), 1–30.

"The (Dis)Similarities of White Racial Identities: The Conceptual Framework of 'Hegemonic Whiteness.'" *Ethnic and Racial Studies*, 33.8 (September 2010), 1289–1309.

White Bound (Stanford University Press, 2012).

Hughley, D. L. and Doug Moe. *How Not to Get Shot: And Other Advice from White People* (HarperCollins, 2018).

Hyman, Stanley Edgar. "Iago Psychoanalytically Motivated." *The Centennial Review*, 14.4 (1970), 369–384.

Ignatiev, Noel. *How the Irish Became White* (Routledge, 1995).

"How to Be a Race Traitor: Six Ways to Fight Being White." In *Critical White Studies: Looking behind the Mirror*, eds. Richard Delgado and Jean Stefancic (Temple University Press, 1997), 613.

Itzigsohn, José and Karida L. Brown. *The Sociology of W. E. B. Du Bois* (New York University Press, 2020).

Iyengar, Sujata. *Shades of Difference: Mythologies of Skin Color in Early Modern England* (University of Pennsylvania Press, 2004).

Iyengar, Sujata and Lesley Feracho. "Hamlet (RSC, 2016) and Representations of Diasporic Blackness." *Cahiers Élisabéthains*, 99.1 (2019), 147–160.

Jacobs, Michelle S. "The Violent State: Black Women's Invisible Struggle against Police Violence." *William and Mary Journal of Women and the Law*, 24.1 (2017), 39–100.

Jones, D. Marvin. *Race, Sex, and Suspicion: The Myth of the Black Male* (Greenwood Publishing Group, 2005).

Jones, Eldred. "Aaron and Melancholy in Titus Andronicus." *Shakespeare Quarterly*, 14.2 (1963), 178–179.

Jordan, June. *Directed by Desire: The Collected Poems of June Jordan* (Copper Canyon Press, 2005).

Jordan, Winthrop D. *White Over Black: American Attitudes toward the Negro 1550–1812* (University of North Carolina Press, 1968).

Kaeuper, Richard W. *Medieval Chivalry* (Cambridge University Press, 2016).

Kafantaris, Mira Assaf. "Meghan Markle, Good English Housewife." *The Rambling*, 3 (January 2019). https://the-rambling.com/2019/01/26/issue3-kafantaris/.

Karim-Cooper, Farah. *Cosmetics in Shakespearean and Renaissance Drama* (Edinburgh University Press, 2019).

  The Hand on the Shakespearean Stage: Gesture, Touch and the Spectacle of Dismemberment (Arden Shakespeare, 2016).

Katz, Judy H. *White Awareness: Handbook for Anti-Racism Training* (University of Oklahoma Press, 1978).

Kendall, Mikki. *Hood Feminism: Notes from the Women That a Movement Forgot* (Viking, 2020).

Kennedy, Adrienne. *Funnyhouse of a Negro* (Samuel French, Inc., 2011).

Knecht, Ross. "'Shapes of Grief': Hamlet's Grammar School Passions." *ELH*, 82.1 (2015), 35–58.

Kolk, Bessel A. van der. *The Body Keeps the Score: Brain, Mind, and Body in the Healing of Trauma* (Penguin Books, 2014).

Korda, Natasha. *Shakespeare's Domestic Economies* (University of Pennsylvania Press, 2012).

Korpiola, Mia, and Anu Lahtinen. "Cultures of Death and Dying in Medieval and Early Modern Europe: An Introduction." *COLLeGIUM*, no. 18 (2015), 1–31.

Laing, R. D. *The Divided Self: An Existential Study in Sanity and Madness* (Penguin Books, 1965).

Larner, Christina. *Witchcraft and Religion: The Politics of Popular Belief* (Basil Blackwell, 1984).

Laroque, François. "Italy vs. Africa: Shakespeare's Topographies of Desire in Othello, Antony and Cleopatra and the Tempest." *Shakespeare Studies*, 47 (2009), 1–16.

Lehmann, Courtney. "Faux Show: Falling into History in Kenneth Branagh's *Love's Labour's Lost*." In *Colorblind Shakespeare: New Perspectives on Race and Shakespeare*, ed. Ayanna Thompson (Routledge, 2006), 69–88.

Leonardo, Zeus. "Tropics of Whiteness: Metaphor and the Literary Turn in White Studies." *Whiteness and Education*, 1.1 (2016), 3–14.

Levine, Laura. *Men in Women's Clothing: Anti-Theatricality and Effeminization* (Cambridge University Press, 1994).

Lipsitz, George. *The Possessive Investment in Whiteness: Profit from Identity Politics* (Temple University Press, 2018).

Little, Jr., Arthur L. "'An Essence That's Not Seen': The Primal Scene of Racism in *Othello*." *Shakespeare Quarterly*, 44.3 (1993), 304–324.

"'Is It Possible to Read Shakespeare through Critical White Studies?'" *The Cambridge Companion to Shakespeare and Race*, ed. Ayanna Thompson (Cambridge University Press, 2021), 268–280.

"Re-Historicizing Race, White Melancholia, and the Shakespearean Property." *Shakespeare Quarterly*, 67.1 (2016), 84–103.

Shakespeare Jungle Fever: National-Imperial Re-Visions of Race, Rape, and Sacrifice (Stanford University Press, 2000).

Loomba, Ania. "'Delicious Traffick': Racial and Religious Difference on Early Modern Stages." In *Shakespeare and Race*, eds. Catherine M. S. Alexander and Stanley Wells (Cambridge University Press, 2000), 203–224.

"Early Modern or Early Colonial?" *Journal for Early Modern Cultural Studies*, 14.1 (2014), 143–148.

"Periodization, Race and Global Contact." *Journal of Medieval and Early Modern Studies*, 37.3 (2007), 595–620.

Low, Jennifer. *Manhood and the Duel* (Palgrave Macmillan, 2003).

"Manhood and the Duel: Enacting Masculinity in 'Hamlet.'" *The Centennial Review*, 43.3 (1999), 501–512.

MacDonald, Joyce Green. *Race, Ethnicity, and Power in the Renaissance* (Fairleigh Dickinson University Press, 1997).

Women and Race in Early Modern Texts (Cambridge University Press, 2004).

MacFarlane, Alan. *Witchcraft in Tudor and Stuart England* (Routledge & Kegan Paul, 1970).

Mahoney, Martha R. "Racial Construction and Women as Differentiated Actors." In *Critical White Studies: Looking behind the Mirror*, eds. Richard Delgado and Jean Stefancic (Temple University Press, 1997), 305–309.

"The Social Construction of Whiteness." In *Critical White Studies: Looking behind the Mirror*, eds. Richard Delgado and Jean Stefancic (Temple University Press, 1997), 330–333.

Mannoni, Octave. *Prospero and Caliban* (University of Michigan Press, 1990).

Massai, Sonia, and Lucy Munro, eds. "Introduction." *Hamlet: The State of Play* (Arden Shakespeare, 2021), 1–26.

Mazzocco, Philip J. *The Psychology of Racial Colorblindness* (Springer, 2017).

McBride, Kari Boyd. *Domestic Arrangements in Early Modern England* (Duquesne University Press, 2002).

McCarthy, Andrew D. "King Lear's Violent Grief." In *Violent Masculinities*, eds. Jennifer Feather and Catherine E. Thomas (Palgrave Macmillan, 2013), 151–168.

McDonnell, Myles. *Roman Manliness: Virtus and the Roman Republic* (Cambridge University Press, 2006).

Miedzian, Myriam. *Boys Will Be Boys* (Doubleday, 1991).

Miller, Shannon. *Engendering the Fall: John Milton and Seventeenth-Century Women Writers* (University of Pennsylvania Press, 2008).

Mitchell, Robin. *Vénus Noire* (University of Georgia Press, 2020).

Moncrief, Kathryn M. "Remembering Ophelia." In *Hamlet: The State of Play*, eds. Sonia Massai and Lucy Munro (Arden Shakespeare, 2021), 51–80.

Morrison, Toni. *Playing in the Dark: Whiteness and the Literary Imagination* (Harvard University Press, 1992).

The Origin of Others (Harvard University Press, 2017).

Mouzon, LaTonya D., Alicia Battle, Kevin P. Clark, Stephanie Coleman, and Roberta J. Ogletree. "African-American College Students' Perceptions of Sexual Coercion." *The Health Educator*, 37.1 (2005), 16–21.

Nakayama, Thomas K., and Robert L. Krizek. "Whiteness: A Strategic Rhetoric." *Quarterly Journal of Speech*, 81.3 (1995), 291–309.

Ndiaye, Noémie. "Aaron's Roots: Spaniards, Englishmen, and Blackamoors in *Titus Andronicus*." *Early Theatre*, 19.2 (2016), 59–80.

Scripts of Blackness: Early Modern Performance Culture and the Making of Race (University of Pennsylvania Press, 2022).

Neely, Carol Thomas. *Distracted Subjects* (Cornell University Press, 2004).

Newell, Bridget M. "Being a White Problem and Feeling It." In *White Self-Criticality beyond Anti-Racism: How Does It Feel to Be a White Problem?*, ed. George Yancy (Lexington Books, 2015), 121–140.

Novy, Marianne. *Shakespeare and Outsiders* (Oxford University Press, 2013).

Nubia, Onyeka. *Blackamoores: Africans in Tudor England, Their Presence, Status and Origins* (Narrative Eye Ltd., 2013).

England's Other Countrymen (Zed Books, 2019).

Oluo, Ijeoma. *Mediocre: The Dangerous Legacy of White Male America* (Seal Press, 2020).

Painter, Nell Irvin. *The History of White People* (W. W. Norton & Company, 2010).

Park, Jennifer. "Discandying Cleopatra: Preserving Cleopatra's Infinite Variety in Shakespeare's Antony and Cleopatra." *Studies in Philology*, 11.3 (2016), 595–633.

Parker, Patricia. "Black Hamlet: Battening on the Moor." *Shakespeare Studies*, 31 (2003), 127–164.

Patterson, Orlando. *Slavery and Social Death* (Harvard University Press, 2018).

Peterson, Kaara L. "Hamlet's Touch of Picture." In *Hamlet: The State of Play*, eds. Sonia Massai and Lucy Munro (Arden Shakespeare, 2021), 27–50.

Phillips, L. Taylor and Brian S. Lowery. "Herd Invisibility: The Psychology of Racial Privilege." *Current Directions in Psychological Science*, 27.3 (2018), 156–162.

Poitevin, Kimberly. "Inventing Whiteness: Cosmetics, Race, and Women in Early Modern England." *Journal for Early Modern Cultural Studies*, 11.1 (2001), 59–89.

Pollard, Tanya. "What's Hecuba to Shakespeare?" *Renaissance Quarterly*, 65.4 (2012), 1060–1093.

Prynne, William. *Histrio-Mastix: The Player's Scourge or Actor's Tragedy* (Johnson Reprint Corp., 1972).

Rankine, Claudia and The Racial Imaginary Institute. *On Whiteness: The Racial Imaginary Institute* (SPBH Editions/The Racial Imaginary Institute, 2022).

Ramsey, Jarold. "The Perversion of Manliness in *Macbeth*." *Studies in English Literature*, 13.2 (1973), 285–300.

Rankine, Claudia. "I Wanted to Know What White Men Thought about Their Privilege. So I Asked." *The New York Times Magazine*, July 17, 2019. www .nytimes.com/2019/07/17/magazine/white-men-privilege.html.

Just Us (Graywolf Press, 2020).

Rankine, Claudia, Beth Loffreda, and Max King Cap, *The Racial Imaginary: Writers on Race in the Life of the Mind* (Fence Books, 2016).

Rasmussen, Birgit Brander, Irene J. Nexica, Eric Klinenberg, and Matt Wray. *The Making and Unmaking of Whiteness* (Duke University Press, 2001).

Reuter, Tyson R., Michael Newcomb, Sarah W. Whitton, and Brian Mustanski. "Intimate Partner Violence Victimization in LGBT Young Adults: Demographic Differences and Associations with Health Behaviors." *Psychology of Violence*, 7.1 (2017), 101–109.

Roach, Joseph. *Cities of the Dead* (Columbia University Press, 1996).

Roberts, Dorothy. "Race." In *The 1619 Project: A New Origin Story*, ed. Nikole Hannah-Jones (OneWorld, 2021), 45–61.

Roelofs, Monique. "Racialization as an Aesthetic Production: What Does the Aesthetic Do for Whiteness and Blackness and Vice Versa?" In *White on White / Black on Black*, ed. George Yancy (Rowman & Littlefield Publishers, Inc., 2005), 83–124.

Ron, Nathan. *Erasmus and the "Other"* (Springer, 2019).

Rose, Jacqueline. "Wulf Sachs's Black Hamlet." In *The Psychoanalysis of Race*, ed. Christopher Lane (Columbia University Press, 1998), 333–352.

Ross, Thomas. "White Innocence, Black Abstraction." In *Critical White Studies: Looking behind the Mirror*, eds. Richard Delgado and Jean Stefancic (Temple University Press, 1997), 263–266.

Rowe, Katherine. *Dead Hands: Fictions of Agency, Renaissance to Modern* (Stanford University Press, 1999).

Royster, Francesca T. *Becoming Cleopatra: The Shifting Image of an Icon* (Palgrave Macmillan, 2003).

"Cleopatra as Diva: African-American Women and Shakespearean Tactics." In *Transforming Shakespeare: Contemporary Women's Re-Visions in Literature and Performance*, ed. Marianne Novy (St. Martin's Press, 1999), 103–126.

"White-Limed Walls: Whiteness and Gothic Extremism in Shakespeare's *Titus Andronicus*." *Shakespeare Quarterly*, 51.4 (2000), 432–455.

Sacks, Karen Brodkin. "How Did the Jews Become White Folks?" *Critical White Studies: Looking behind the Mirror*, eds. Richard Delgado and Jean Stefancic (Temple University Press, 1997), 395–401.

Salter, Phia S., Glenn Adams, and Michael J. Perez. "Racism in the Structure of Everyday Worlds: A Cultural-Psychological Perspective." *Current Directions in Psychological Science*, 27.3 (2018), 150–155.

Sanchez, Melissa E. *Erotic Subjects: The Sexuality of Politics in Early Modern English Literature* (Oxford University Press, 2011).

Schiesari, Juliana. *The Gendering of Melancholia* (Cornell University Press, 1992).

Scott-Douglass, Amy. "Shades of Shakespeare: Colorblind Casting and Interracial Couples in Macbeth in Manhattan, Grey's Anatomy, and Prison Macbeth." In *Wayward Macbeth: Intersections of Race and Performance*, eds. Scott Newstok and Ayanna Thompson (Palgrave Macmillan, 2010), 193–202.

Segrest, Mab. "The Souls of White Folks." In *The Making and Unmaking of Whiteness*, eds. Birgit Brander Rasmussen, Eric Klinenberg, Irene J. Nexica, and Matt Wray (Duke University Press, 2001), 43–71.

Shakespeare, William. *The Complete Works of William Shakespeare*, ed. David Bevington, 7th ed. (Pearson Education, Inc., 2014).

Singh, Nikhil Pal. *Black Is a Country* (Harvard University Press, 2005).

Slazman, Avi. "Sifting the Evidence for Gang Activity." *The New York Times*, May 15, 2005.

Smith, Bruce R. *The Acoustic World of Early Modern England: Attending to the O-Factor* (University of Chicago Press, 1999).

Shakespeare and Masculinity. Oxford Shakespeare Topics (Oxford University Press, 2000).

Smith, Ian. *Black Shakespeare: Reading and Misreading Race* (Cambridge University Press, 2022).

Race and Rhetoric in the Renaissance: Barbarian Errors (Palgrave Macmillan, 2009).

"We Are Othello: Speaking of Race in Early Modern Studies." *Shakespeare Quarterly*, 67.1 (2016), 104–124.

Spillers, Hortense. "Mama's Baby, Papa's Maybe: An American Grammar Book." *Diacritics*, 17.2 (1987), 64–81.

Startwell, Crispin. "Wigger." In *White on White / Black on Black*, ed. George Yancy (Rowman & Littlefield Publishers, Inc., 2005), 35–48.

Stoever, Jennifer Lynn. *The Sonic Color Line* (New York University Press, 2016).

Stubbes, Phillip. *The Anatomie of Abuses* (Printed by Richard Jones, 1583).

Taylor, Keeanga-Yamahtta. *How We Get Free: Black Feminism and the Combahee River Collective* (Haymarket Books, 2017).

Terry, Reta A. "'Vows to the Blackest Devil': Hamlet and the Evolving Code of Honor in Early Modern England." *Renaissance Quarterly*, 52.4 (1999), 1070–1086.

Thandeka. *Learning to Be White* (Continuum, 1999).

Thompson, Ayanna, ed. *Colorblind Shakespeare: New Perspectives on Race and Performance* (Routledge, 2006).

"Did the Concept of Race Exist for Shakespeare and His Contemporaries?" In *The Cambridge Companion to Shakespeare and Race*, ed. Ayanna Thompson (Cambridge University Press, 2021), 1–16.

"Introduction." In *Othello*. Revised ed. E. A. J. Honigmann (Arden Shakespeare, 2016), 1–116.

"Practicing a Theory/Theorizing a Practice: An Introduction to Shakespearean Colorblind Casting." In *Colorblind Shakespeare: New Perspectives on Race and Shakespeare*, ed. Ayanna Thompson (Routledge, 2006).

"What Is a 'Weyward' Macbeth?" In *Weyward Macbeth: Intersections of Race and Performance*, eds. Scott Newstok and Ayanna Thompson (Palgrave Macmillan, 2010), 3–10.

Thompson, Ayanna and Laura Turchi. "Embodiment and the Classroom Performance." In *The Oxford Handbook of Shakespeare and Embodiment: Gender, Sexuality, and Race,* ed. Valerie Traub (Oxford University Press, 2016), 724–737.

Traub, Valerie. "Jewels, Statues, and Corpses: Containment of Female Erotic Power in Shakespeare's Plays." In *Shakespeare and Gender: A History*, eds. Deborah Barker and Ivo Kamps (Verso, 1995), 120–141.

The Oxford Handbook of Shakespeare and Embodiment (Oxford University Press, 2016).

Trepagnier, Barbara. *Silent Racism: How Well-Meaning White People Perpetuate the Racial Divide* (Routledge, 2010).

Trubowitz, Rachel. *Nation and Nurture in Seventeenth-Century English Literature* (Oxford University Press, 2012).

Turner, Patricia A. *Ceramic Uncles & Celluloid Mammies* (Anchor Books, 2000).

Turner, Timothy A. "Othello on the Rack." *Journal for Early Modern Cultural Studies*, 15.3 (2015), 102–136.

Ungerer, Gustav. "The Presence of Africans in Elizabethan England and the Performance of *Titus Andronicus* at Burley-on-the-Hill, 1595/96." *Medieval and Renaissance Drama in England*, 21 (2008), 19–55.

Vaughan, Virginia Mason. *Performing Blackness on English Stages, 1500–1800* (Cambridge University Press, 2005).

"The Construction of Barbarism in Titus Andronicus." In *Race, Ethnicity and Power in the Renaissance*, ed. Joyce Geeen MacDonald (Associated University Presses, 1997), 165–180.

Vaught, Jennifer C. "Introduction." In *Grief and Gender: 700–1700*, eds. Jennifer C. Vaught and Lynne Dickson Bruckner (Palgrave Macmillan, 2003), 1–14.

Vogel, Laura B. "Cleopatra: Antony's Transformational Object." *PsyArt*, 29 (2015), 23–20.

Wall, Wendy. *Staging Domesticity: Household Work and English Identity in Early Modern Drama* (Cambridge University Press, 2002).

Walvin, James. *Black and White: The Negro and English Society 1555–1945* (Allen Lane/The Penguin Press, 1973).

Watson, Veronica T. *The Souls of White Folk* (University Press of Mississippi, 2013).

Whipday, Emma. *Shakespeare's Domestic Tragedies: Violence in the Early Modern Home* (Cambridge University Press, 2019).

Williams, Patricia J. *The Alchemy of Race and Rights* (Harvard University Press, 1991).

Wood, Amy Louise. *Lynching and Spectacle: Witnessing Racial Violence in America, 1890–1940* (University of North Carolina Press, 2009).

Wordsworth, Dot. "Where Did 'No Justice, No Peace' Come From?" *The Spectator*, January 18, 2004. www.spectator.co.uk/article/where-did-no-jus tice-no-peace-come-from/

Wright, George Thaddeus. *Hearing the Measures* (University of Wisconsin Press, 2001).

Yancy, George. "Introduction: Un-Sutured." In *White Self-Criticality beyond Anti-Racism: How Does It Feel to Be a White Problem?*, ed. George Yancy (Lexington Books, 2015).

White on White/Black on Black (Rowman & Littlefield, 2005).

Yungblut, Laura Hunt. *Strangers Settled Here amongst Us* (Routledge, 1996).

Zuberi, Tukufu and Eduardo Bonilla-Silva, eds. *White Logic, White Methods* (Rowman & Littlefield, 2008).

Index